DARINA ALLEN'S
SIMPLY DELICIOUS
RECIPES

DARINA ALLEN'S
Simply Delicious
RECIPES

Gill and Macmillan

Published in Ireland by
Gill and Macmillan Ltd
Goldenbridge
Dublin 8
with associated companies in
Auckland, Budapest, Dublin, Gaborone, Harare, Hong Kong,
Kampala, Kuala Lumpur, Lagos, London, Madras,
Manzini, Melbourne, Mexico City, Nairobi,
New York, Singapore, Sydney, Tokyo and Windhoek

© Darina Allen

0 7171 1986 6

Published in hardback 1992 by Macmillan London Ltd

Print origination by Florencetype Ltd, Kewstoke, Avon

Printed by Macmillan London Limited

A catalogue record is available for this book from the British Library

FOR MY SIMPLY DELICIOUS HUSBAND TIM

CONTENTS

IMPORTANT NOTES ABOUT MEASUREMENTS

Three systems of measuring ingredients are given in this book: Imperial (by weight)/metric (by weight)/American (by volume). Whichever you use, stick to the same system throughout the recipe.

In some cases, where great accuracy is not essential, the ingredient is given in tablespoons only. Tablespoons are notoriously unstandard. An American tablespoon is usually 15 ml in capacity, whereas a British one is more often 20 ml. Use the same tablespoon to measure your ingredients throughout since the proportion of ingredients to each other may be the most important thing. If your tablespoons are large (20 ml), err on the side of the smaller quantity where a range is given (and vice versa), and do this consistently throughout the recipe.

In the American measurements, tablespoons are often given for butter. One cup holds 16 tablespoons. Half a cup, 8 tablespoons, is the same as one stick of butter. One stick of butter is the equivalent of 4 ounces, and 1 tablespoon $\frac{1}{2}$ an ounce.

Teaspoons are more standard: usually 5 ml. Spoon measures for dry ingredients are level unless stated otherwise.

ACKNOWLEGEMENTS

Once again, I must pay tribute to my mother-in-law Myrtle Allen, who never fails to inspire me by her encyclopaedic knowledge and generosity of spirit. It was she who really taught me, through example, the deep respect I now hold for good Irish ingredients. Many of the recipes in this book are hers and are favorites from the Ballymaloe restaurant menu which she has so generously given me permission to share with you. My father-in-law, Ivan Allen, has been there always, gently nudging me forward to accept new challenges as they have come along and I have always been tremendously grateful for his and Myrtle's unstinting support.

Many thanks, also, to my teachers and assistants at the Ballymaloe Cookery School, Florrie Cullinane, Claire Wenham, Fionnuala Ryan, Susie O'Connor, Rachel O'Neill and Dervilla O'Flynn for cheerful and unstinting support during the past few years when I was writing the original *Simply Delicious* books.

A special mention for my chef-brother Rory O'Connell, who not only gave me permission to use several of his delicious Ballymaloe recipes, but was also responsible for the inspired food styling both for the television series and for the photographs in the book.

I am very grateful for the guidance and help of my editors, Dee-Rennison Kunz, Mary Dowey and Judith Hannam in getting the books written and edited.

A very special mention, too, for my secretaries, Rosalie Dunne and Adrienne Morrisey, who typed the manuscripts for the *Simply Delicious* series.

Last, but not least, a big thank you to my husband Tim, who was the first person to cook me a delectable piece of really fresh fish and who has been a wonderful support through all the books.

FOREWORD

It is twenty years since I came to Ballymaloe House fresh from hotel school in Dublin. I was the first student to come into Myrtle Allen's kitchen and she taught me herself. Her approach to cooking and the kind of food she served in her restaurant instantly appealed to me – real food with true flavours and simple sauces.

No imported foie gras or truffles here; we cooked the wonderful food produced around us. Fresh vegetables, fruit and herbs from the garden, fish from Ballycotton and superb beef and lamb from local pastures. When rosy-cheeked children came to the door with blackberries, damsons or field mushrooms these were included in the menu which was, and still is, written each day.

Myrtle recognised, nurtured and encouraged my enthusiasm, and I settled in; in fact I became one of the family by the simple expedient of marrying her eldest son! Now her philosophy is also mine. Through the years both she and my father-in-law, Ivan, encouraged me to start giving classes and eventually, in 1983, to open the Ballymaloe Cookery School. Here I teach people not only from Ireland but from all over the world how to cook on the principles that Myrtle taught me. I teach them how to find the very best raw ingredients, because they are the essential basis of good cooking, and I encourage them to cook food when it is in season, since it is at its best and cheapest then.

Much to my surprise, the Ballymaloe Cookery School has grown, from humble beginnings in a converted barn, into an internationally acclaimed school. We have gradually expanded our range of short and long courses and have enhanced our repertoire by bringing in, from time to time, guest chefs from all over the world – people of vast experience and often of different cultures. Jane Grigson, who was such an inspiration, taught here, and we have been introduced to the magical flavours of the East and Far

East by Deh Ta Hsuing, Claudia Roden, Sri Owen and Madhur Jaffrey.

I now find that I am a TV presenter and writer, as well as a teacher and cook. My TV series, *Simply Delicious*, which was shown first in Ireland, and the books that accompany them, generated a tremendous response. In fact, after the first *Simply Delicious* series was shown on Irish television, a woman stopped me in the street in Cork one day and said: 'You're a great girl, do you know you've got people into the kitchen who never cooked a thing before in their lives!' It was one of the nicest compliments I've ever had, because I love cooking and my greatest ambition has always been to show people that it really isn't difficult to cook, all you need is to learn a few basic techniques and then you can put them together in an infinite number of combinations to make a variety of different dishes.

This book is a compilation of recipes from *Simply Delicious 1*, *Simply Delicious 2* and *Simply Delicious Fish*, which have been published in Ireland, but not elsewhere. Many of the recipes I've chosen to share with you are recipes that Myrtle Allen taught me years ago. I've picked them not only because they are simple to cook and taste delicious, but also because they illustrate many important basic techniques; so once you have mastered them you can do lots of variations on the theme.

Gardening is my other great love and fresh herbs are an indispensable part of our cooking. We grow our own herbs and edible flowers in the formal herb garden here at Kinoith and I encourage you to do the same, even if it's only possible in pots or in a window box. Fresh herbs, more than anything else, can add real magic to your cooking.

Apart from the fact that good cooking contributes greatly to health and energy, sitting down together to eat and talk is the best recipe I know for cementing relationships. The food doesn't need to be particularly fancy, and you certainly don't need to spend hours in the kitchen or use expensive ingredients. However, the realisation that good quality ingredients are the essential basis of good cooking is the first step. Easy for me to talk I suppose, I am thrice blessed; I live on a farm in the country in the midst of an apple orchard. We grow a great deal of our own ingredients: our vegetables and fruit come from the *potager*-style kitchen gardens beside the school and we are fortunate to have greenhouses to produce tender and exotic crops. We are also right beside the sea, so we can buy our fish directly from the boats in the nearby fishing village of Ballycotton. Local farmers' wives rear free-range chickens, ducks, geese and turkeys, and our own hens scratching in the orchard recycle the scraps from the Cookery School to produce fresh eggs for breakfast. How's that for being spoiled! However, I am only too well aware that very few people are in this favoured position. But even if you have only a little patch of soil, you can still produce a surprising quantity of vegetables, fruit and herbs.

If this is not possible it is even more vital to be a discriminating shopper; think *flavour* as you choose your ingredients. We have access to excellent produce in these islands, but you must search for it. You shouldn't just grab the first thing that you find on the supermarket shelf; if you do you put yourself at a tremendous disadvantage. The success of your dishes depends as much on your ability to select ingredients as on your ability to cook.

Being able to cook may seem an insignificant skill to some people but I really believe that tasty, wholesome food is one of the great anchors of family life – I always feel a little sad when people tell me they don't enjoy cooking because most of us need to cook every day, anyway, so we might as well enjoy it. Besides, with this one skill we can be creative right there in our own kitchens and give so much pleasure to our family and friends.

More than anything else I want to take the mystique out of cooking and show everyone just how easy it is to cook Simply Delicious food – I hope you will enjoy it.

SOUPS

I consider soup to be one of the greatest mainstays any cook can master. It's heartwarming and wholesome and absolutely central to my philosophy that even the simplest food to prepare can also taste delicious! Soup can adapt itself to every occasion. Obviously it can be the first course of a dinner or a quick and nourishing lunchtime or after-school snack, but there's no doubt that a good home-made soup served with crusty brown bread and a green salad is a meal fit for a king.

There is one point I'd like to make, however: I'm not at all sure that I agree with people who feel that soup is a handy way of using up old vegetables and other left-overs. That seems to me to be a slightly hit and miss approach which can sometimes have delicious results but more often than not can be responsible for turning your entire family off 'soup' altogether, so for best results I suggest you use good ingredients and tried-and-tested recipes.

Mushroom Soup, an all-time favourite, appeals to both the simple and the sophisticated palate. It is the fastest of all the soups to make: just about 20 minutes from start to finish. It is also the exception that proves the rule about using vegetables in their prime, because this recipe actually tastes better if you use mush-rooms which are a few days old – handy if you have a forgotten bag of them at the bottom of the fridge, or if you have access to flat or wild mushrooms they are even better. As I write, the fields around my house are white with wild mushrooms and there is even an occasional mushroom on the lawn! In a situation of surplus like this, the great advantage of this recipe is that you can simply make and freeze the mushroom base and then add stock when you want to serve it.

For something slightly more unusual but equally tasty, I hope you will try Watercress Soup. The main ingredient is another

I

wonderful free food for country-dwellers (just make sure you pick it in streams of clean and constantly moving water) – and luckily watercress is now becoming more widely available in shops, too. This soup should be a fresh green colour and is full of vitamins and minerals.

Two more substantial soups are Celery and Lovage Soup (in which lovage contributes to the strong celery flavour but is not essential) and Potato and Smoky Bacon Soup, a recipe using two quintessentially Irish ingredients which was actually given to me by a German friend, Else Schiller. It was a favourite recipe in the Schleswig-Holstein area, where Else comes from.

I used to have a major mental block about making fish soups. Every recipe I read seemed to have an endless list of ingredients and a dauntingly complicated method. I've since discovered that with a few simple techniques fish soups are no more difficult to master than any other kind – yet they always look exciting. When you bring a fragrant fish soup to the table with tempting little bits of shellfish peeping out, it certainly seems much more exotic than spud soup (not that spud soup isn't delicious too!). Almost any fish can be used to produce wonderful soups of all sorts, from substantial chowders to light Chinese broths. Be sure to use good home-made fish stock if you possibly can. It's surprisingly quick and easy to make using either of the recipes here.

Purée of Onion Soup with Thyme Leaves

Serves 6

1½ oz/45 g/3 tablespoons butter

1 lb/450 g/4 cups chopped onions

5 oz/140 g/1 cup chopped potatoes

1 teaspoon fresh thyme leaves

1½ pints/900 ml/3¾ cups home-made chicken stock (see page 137)

¼ pint/150 ml/generous ½ cup cream *or* cream and milk mixed, approx.

salt and freshly ground pepper

GARNISH

fresh thyme leaves and thyme *or* chive flowers

a little whipped cream (optional)

PEEL and chop the onions and potatoes into small dice. Measure. Melt the butter in a heavy saucepan. As soon as it foams, add the onions and potatoes; stir until they are well coated with butter. Add the thyme leaves, season with salt and freshly ground pepper, cover with a paper lid (to keep in the steam) and the saucepan lid, and sweat on a low heat for approximately 10 minutes. The potatoes and onions should be soft but not coloured. Add the chicken stock, bring it to the boil and simmer until the potatoes are cooked, about 5–8 minutes. Liquidise the soup and add a little cream or creamy milk. Taste and correct seasoning if necessary.

Serve in soup bowls or in a soup tureen garnished with a blob of whipped cream; sprinkle with thyme leaves and thyme or chive flowers.

POTATO AND FRESH HERB SOUP

Serves 6

Most people have potatoes and onions in the house even if their cupboards are otherwise bare, so this 'simply delicious' soup can be made at a moment's notice. While the vegetables are sweating, pop a few white soda scones (see page 233) into the oven and then you will have a nourishing meal.

2 oz/55 g/4 tablespoons butter
4 oz/110 g/1 cup diced onions
15 oz/425 g/3 cups peeled diced potatoes
2–3 teaspoons in total of the following: parsley, thyme, lemon balm and chives, chopped

1 teaspoon salt
freshly ground pepper
1½ pints/900 ml/3¾ cups home-made chicken stock (see page 137)
4 fl oz/130 ml/½ cup creamy milk

MELT the butter in a heavy saucepan. When it foams, add the potatoes and onions and toss them in the butter until well coated. Sprinkle with salt and pepper. Cover and sweat on a gentle heat for 10 minutes. Add the fresh herbs and stock and cook until the vegetables are soft. Purée the soup in a blender or food processor. Taste and adjust seasoning. Thin with creamy milk to the required consistency. Serve sprinkled with a few freshly chopped herbs.

POTATO AND SMOKY BACON SOUP

Serves 8–9

A wonderfully warming winter soup – almost a meal in itself.

5 oz/140 g smoked streaky bacon

10 oz/300 g/2¹/₂ cups finely chopped onions

1 oz/30 g/2 tablespoons butter

2–3 tablespoons oil

1 lb 2 oz/500 g potatoes

1 pint/600 ml/2¹/₂ cups home-made chicken stock (see page 137)

1 pint/600 ml/2¹/₂ cups milk

1 tablespoon chopped parsley

salt and freshly ground pepper

REMOVE the rind from the bacon and keep aside. Chop the smoky bacon and onions very finely. Melt the butter and oil in a sauce-pan, add the bacon and cook for a few minutes, then add the onions; cover and sweat on a gentle heat until soft but not coloured. Add the stock and leave to simmer while you prepare the potatoes. Add the bacon rind to the stock. Peel the potatoes and chop very finely, add to the saucepan and stir until it becomes quite thick and sticky. Season with freshly ground pepper and a little salt (watch the salt because of the bacon). Keep on stirring and add the milk slowly. Boil until the potatoes are soft – they will disintegrate into a purée. Remove the bacon rind, add the chopped parsley, taste and serve. Add a little more chicken stock or milk if the soup is too thick.

CELERY AND LOVAGE SOUP

Serves 6–8

Lovage is a perennial herb with a pronounced celery flavour. Use it sparingly to enhance the flavour of soups, stews and stocks.

1½ oz/45 g/3 tablespoons butter
4 oz/110 g/1 cup chopped onions
5 oz/140 g/1 cup chopped potatoes
1 lb/450 g/4 cups finely chopped celery

2–4 sprigs lovage (optional)
1½ pints/900 ml/3¾ cups light home-made chicken stock (see page 137)
a little cream *or* creamy milk
salt and freshly ground pepper

MELT the butter in a heavy-bottomed saucepan. When it foams, add the potatoes, onions, celery and lovage; toss in the butter until evenly coated. Season with salt and freshly ground pepper. Cover with a paper lid (to keep in the steam) and the saucepan lid and sweat over a gentle heat for around 10 minutes, until the vegetables are soft but not cooked, approximately 10–12 minutes. Liquidise the soup; add a little more stock or creamy milk to thin to the required consistency. Taste and correct the seasoning.

MUSHROOM SOUP

Serves 8–9

Many people have forgotten how delicious a home-made mushroom soup can be; it's one of the fastest of all soups to make and surely everyone's favourite. Mushroom Soup is best made with flat mushrooms or button mushrooms a few days old, which have developed a slightly stronger flavour.

1½ oz/45 g/3 tablespoons butter
1 oz/30 g/scant ¼ cup flour
4 oz/110 g/1 cup very finely
chopped onion
1 lb/450 g/5 cups mushrooms,
very finely chopped

1 pint/600 ml/2½ cups milk
1 pint/600 ml/2½ cups
home-made chicken stock
(see page 137)
salt and freshly ground pepper

MELT the butter in a saucepan on a gentle heat. Toss the onions in it, cover and sweat until soft and completely cooked. Add the mushrooms to the saucepan and cook for a further 3 or 4 minutes. Now stir in the flour, cook on a low heat for 2–3 minutes, season with salt and freshly ground pepper, then add the stock and milk gradually, stirring all the time; increase the heat and bring to the boil. Taste and add a dash of cream if necessary.

WILD MUSHROOM SOUP

Every few years after a good warm summer, lots of wild mushrooms (*Agaricus campestris*) appear in the old meadows. Make them into a soup using the above recipe. If you have a surplus of wild mushrooms, just make the base of the soup, but don't add the stock or milk; this purée may be frozen and turned into a soup as you need it.

SPRING CABBAGE SOUP

Serves 6

Myrtle Allen puts this delicious soup on the menu at Ballymaloe several times during late spring.

2 oz/55 g/4 tablespoons butter

4 oz/110 g/1 cup chopped onions

5 oz/140 g/1 cup chopped potatoes

1 1/2 pts/900 ml/3 3/4 cups light chicken stock

9 oz/255 g/3 cups chopped spring cabbage leaves (stalks removed)

2–4 fl oz/55–130 ml/1/4–1/2 cup cream *or* creamy milk

salt and freshly ground pepper

MELT the butter in a heavy saucepan. When it foams, add the potatoes and onions and turn them in the butter until well coated. Sprinkle with salt and freshly ground pepper. Cover and sweat on a gentle heat for 10 minutes. Add the stock and boil until the potatoes are soft, then add the cabbage and cook *with the lid off* until the cabbage is cooked. Keep the lid off to retain the green colour. Do not overcook or the vegetables will lose both their fresh flavour and colour. Purée the soup in a liquidiser or blender, taste and adjust seasoning. Add the cream or creamy milk before serving.

If this soup is to be reheated, just bring it to the boil and serve. Prolonged boiling spoils the colour and flavour of green soups.

WATERCRESS SOUP

Serves 6–8

1½ oz/45 g/3 tablespoons butter
4 oz/110 g/1 cup chopped onions
5 oz/140 g/1 cup chopped potatoes
8 oz/225 g/1 cup chopped watercress

1 pint/600 ml/2½ cups water *or* light home-made chicken stock (see page 137)
1 pint/600 ml/2½ cups creamy milk
salt and freshly ground pepper

GARNISH

2–3 tablespoons/⅛ cup whipped cream (optional)

watercress leaves

MELT the butter in a heavy-bottomed saucepan. When it foams, add the potatoes and onions and toss them until well coated. Sprinkle with salt and freshly ground pepper. Cover and sweat on a gentle heat for 10 minutes. Add the stock and milk, bring to the boil and cook until the potatoes and onions are soft. Add the watercress and boil *with the lid off* for 4–5 minutes until the watercress is cooked. Do not overcook or the soup will lose its fresh green colour. Purée the soup in a liquidiser or food processor. Taste and correct seasoning.

Serve in warm bowls garnished with a blob of whipped cream and a watercress leaf.

LETTUCE, CUCUMBER AND MINT SOUP

Serves 6

1½–2 oz/45–55 g/3–4 tablespoons butter

4 oz/110 g/1 cup diced onions

5 oz/140 g/1 cup peeled diced potatoes

5 oz/140 g/1 cup unpeeled diced cucumber

6 oz/170 g/3 cups chopped lettuce leaves (without stalk)

1½ pints/900 ml/3¾ cups home-made chicken stock (see page 137)

2 teaspoons freshly chopped mint

2½ fl oz/60 ml/generous ¼ cup cream (optional)

salt and freshly ground pepper

MELT the butter in a heavy saucepan. When it foams, add the potatoes and onions and turn them until well coated. Sprinkle with salt and freshly ground pepper. Cover and sweat on a gentle heat for 10 minutes, until soft but not coloured. Add the cucumber and toss it in the butter. Add the stock, bring to the boil and cook until the potatoes, onions and cucumbers are completely cooked. Add the lettuce and boil *with the lid off* for about 4–5 minutes, until the lettuce is cooked. Do not overcook or the soup will lose its fresh green colour. Add the mint and cream if using, and liquidise. Taste and correct seasoning if necessary. Serve in warm bowls garnished with a blob of whipped cream and a little freshly chopped mint.

NOTE: A few tips:

1. We use the widely available butterhead lettuce; outside leaves are perfect.
2. Light chicken stock should be used.
3. Fresh mint is more fragrant in summer than in winter, so it may be necessary to use more mint towards the end of the season.
4. If this soup is to be reheated, just bring it to the boil and serve immediately. Prolonged boiling will spoil the colour and taste.

BASIC FISH STOCK

Makes approximately 3 pints/1.7 l/7½ cups.

Fish stock takes only 20 minutes to make. If you can get lots of fresh fish bones from your fishmonger it's well worth making 2 or 3 times this stock recipe, because it freezes perfectly and then you will have fish stock at the ready for any recipe that needs it.

½ oz/15 g/1 tablespoon butter
3½ oz/100 g/scant 1 cup finely sliced onion
2¼ lb/1 kg fish bones, preferably sole, turbot or brill
4–8 fl oz/130–250 ml/½–1 cup dry white wine

cold water to cover bones
4 peppercorns
bouquet garni containing a sprig of thyme, 4–5 parsley stalks, small piece of celery and a tiny scrap of bay leaf
no salt

CHOP the fish bones into pieces and wash thoroughly under cold running water until no trace of blood remains. In a large stainless steel saucepan melt the butter, add the onions and sweat them on a gentle heat until soft but not coloured. Add the bones to the saucepan, stir and cook very briefly with the onions. Add the dry white wine and boil until nearly all the wine has evaporated. Cover with cold water, add the peppercorns and a large bouquet garni. Bring to the boil and simmer for 20 minutes, skimming often. Strain. Allow to get cold and refrigerate.

Demi-glaze

Reduce the strained fish stock by half to intensify the flavour, chill and refrigerate or freeze.

Glace de poisson

Reduce the stock until it becomes thick and syrupy, then chill. It will set into a firm jelly which has a very concentrated fish flavour – excellent to add to fish sauces or soup to enhance the flavour.

HOUSEHOLD FISH STOCK

Makes approximately 4 pints/2.3 l/10 cups.

The fish stock will be slightly darker in colour and stronger in flavour but excellent for fish soups and most sauces.

4 lb/1.8 kg bones, head and skin (gills removed) of fresh fish (oily fish like mackerel and herring are not suitable)
1 large onion
1 carrot
1/2 oz/15 g/1 tablespoon butter
6–8 peppercorns

4–8 fl oz/130–250 ml/1/2–1 cup dry white wine
cold water to cover bones
bouquet garni containing a sprig of thyme, 4–5 parsley stalks, small piece of celery and a tiny scrap of bay leaf
no salt

CHOP the fish bones into pieces and wash thoroughly under cold running water until no trace of blood remains. Slice the onion and carrot finely. In a large stainless steel saucepan melt the butter, add the onion and carrot and sweat them on a gentle heat until soft but not coloured. Add the bones to the saucepan, stir and cook very briefly with the onions. Add the dry white wine and boil until nearly all the wine has evaporated. Cover with cold water, add the peppercorns and a large bouquet garni. Bring to the boil and simmer for 20 minutes, skimming often. Allow to get cold and refrigerate.

SEAFOOD CHOWDER

Serves 6

A chowder is a wonderfully substantial fish soup which could almost be classified as a stew. It is certainly a meal in itself and there are lots of variations on the theme.

1½ lb/675 g haddock, monkfish, winter cod *or* any other firm white fish (*or* a mixture), free of bones and skin

1 lb/450 g mixed, cooked shellfish e.g. mussels, clams, scallops, shrimps *or* prawns and the cooking liquor (see pages 111, 49, 45)

1–1½ tablespoons olive *or* sunflower oil

4 oz/110 g streaky bacon (rind removed), cut into ¼ in/7 mm dice (blanch if necessary)

6–8 oz/170–225 g/1½–2 cups onions, chopped

1 oz/30 g/scant ¼ cup flour

¾ pint/450 ml/scant 2 cups home-made fish stock (see page 11) *or* as a last resort water

¾ pint/450 ml/scant 2 cups milk

bouquet garni made up of 6 parsley stalks, 2 sprigs of thyme and a bay leaf

6 medium-sized 'floury' potatoes, cut into ¼ in/7 mm dice

pinch of mace

pinch of cayenne pepper

¼ pint/150 ml/generous ½ cup light cream

salt and freshly ground pepper

GARNISH

parsley and chives

HEAT the oil in a stainless steel saucepan and brown the bacon well until it is crisp and golden. Add the onion, cover and sweat for a few minutes over a low heat. Stir in the flour and cook for a couple of minutes more. Add the fish stock or water gradually, then the milk, bouquet garni and potatoes. Season well with salt, pepper, mace and cayenne. Cover and simmer until the potatoes are almost cooked (5–6 minutes).*

* May be prepared ahead to this point.

Meanwhile cut the fish into roughly 1 in/2.5 cm square pieces. Add the fish to the pot as soon as the tip of a knife will go through the potato. Simmer gently for 3 or 4 minutes, stir in the cream and add the shellfish and any liquor from opening the mussels or clams. When the soup returns to the boil remove from the heat. Remember that the fish will continue to cook in the heat of the chowder so it should not be overcooked. Taste, correct seasoning and sprinkle with freshly chopped parsley and chives. Crusty hot white bread or hot crackers are usually served with a chowder.

NOTE: You could use about 3 1/2 oz/100 g smoked haddock in this recipe. Poach it gently in some of the milk first and flake, then add to the chowder with the shellfish.

MEDITERRANEAN FISH SOUP WITH ROUILLE

Serves 6–8

Fish soups can be made with all sorts of combinations of fish. Don't be the least bit bothered if you haven't got exactly the fish I suggest, but use a combination of whole fish and shellfish. The crab adds almost essential richness in my opinion.

5 1/2 lb/2.5 kg mixed fish
– e.g. 1 whole plaice, 1/2 cod,
2 small whiting
3 swimming crab *or*
1 common crab, 6–8 mussels,
8–10 shrimps *or* prawns
1/4 pint/150 ml/generous 1/2 cup
olive oil
10 oz/300 g/2 1/2 cups finely
chopped onion
1 large clove garlic, crushed

5 large very ripe tomatoes *or*
1 × 14 oz/400 g tin tomatoes,
sliced
5 sprigs of fennel
2 sprigs of thyme
1 bay leaf
home-made fish stock or water
to cover (see page 11)
1/4 teaspoon saffron strands
pinch of cayenne
salt and freshly ground pepper

Rouille

Serves 8

1 × 2 in/5 cm piece of French
baguette bread
6–8 tablespoons hot fish soup
4 cloves garlic

1 egg yolk, preferably free-range
pinch of whole saffron stamens
6–8 tablespoons extra virgin
olive oil
salt and freshly ground pepper

GARNISH
chopped parsley

CROÛTONS

8 slices French bread

3–4 oz/85–110 g Gruyère cheese,
grated

CUT the fish into chunks, bones, head and all (remove gills first). Heat the olive oil until smoking, add garlic and onions, toss for a minute or two, add the sliced tomatoes, herbs and fish including shells, cook for 10 minutes, then add enough fish stock or water to cover. Bring to a fast boil and cook for a further 10 minutes. Add more liquid if it reduces too much.

Soak the saffron strands in a little fish stock. Pick out the mussel shells. Taste, add salt, freshly ground pepper, cayenne, saffron and soaking liquid. Push the soup through a mouli (this may seem like an impossible task but you'll be surprised how effective it will be – there will be just a mass of dry bones left which you discard).

Next make the rouille. Cut the bread into cubes and soak in some hot fish soup. Squeeze out the excess liquid and mix to a mush in a bowl. Crush the garlic to a fine paste in a pestle and mortar, add the egg yolk, the saffron and the soggy bread. Season with salt and freshly ground pepper. Mix well and add in the oil drip by drip as in making mayonnaise. If the mixture looks too thick or oily add 2 tablespoons of hot fish soup and continue to stir.

Make the croûtons. Toast slices of French bread slowly until they are dry and crisp. Spread croûtons with rouille and sprinkle with Gruyère cheese. Bring the soup back to the boil and float a croûton in each serving.

COCKLE AND MUSSEL SOUP

Serves 10–12

Molly Malone, after whom the song was named, was a famous Dublin fishmonger. Among other things she sold, 'cockles and mussels, alive, alive-o'.

4–5 lb/1.8–2.3 kg mussels	2 sprigs of fresh thyme
4–5 lb/1.8–2.3 kg cockles	2 sprigs of fresh fennel
3/4 pint/450 ml/scant 2 cups dry	1 clove garlic, mashed
white wine	1–2 pints/600 ml–1.1 l/2¹/₂–5
8–10 tablespoons shallots,	cups boiling milk
chopped	a little cream (optional)
10 sprigs of parsley	freshly ground pepper
1/2 fresh bay leaf	

ROUX

2 oz/55 g/4 tablespoons butter	2 oz/55 g/scant 1/2 cup flour

GARNISH

tiny crisp croûtons	finely chopped parsley

WASH the cockles and mussels in several changes of cold water checking that they are all tightly shut. Put the wine, shallots, parsley, bay leaf, thyme, fennel and garlic into a wide stainless steel saucepan and add the cockles and mussels. Cover and cook over a gentle heat for a few minutes, stir frequently and as soon as the shells start to open pick them out. Remove the cockles and mussels from their shells and keep in a bowl.

Strain the cooking liquid and reduce it over a high heat to concentrate the flavour; taste frequently while it boils to make sure it is not too salty. Thicken with roux (see glossary for method), then thin out to a light consistency with the boiling milk. (If the milk is not brought to boiling point the acid in the wine will cause it to curdle.)

Taste for seasoning. Just before serving, heat the soup, add a little cream and put some or all of the cockles and mussels back in.

16

Serve in old-fashioned soup plates with a sprinkling of chopped parsley on top. Serve tiny crisp croûtons separately (see below).

NOTE: If you have cockles and mussels left over, use for a salad or gratin. This soup is also very good made with mussels alone.

CROÛTONS FOR SOUP

Serves 8–12

2 slices slightly stale sliced bread, ¼ in/7 mm thick	1 oz/30 g/2 tablespoons butter
	2–2½ tablespoons olive oil

FIRST cut the crusts off the bread, then cut into ¼ in/7 mm strips and then into exact cubes.

Melt the butter in a clean frying pan with the olive oil. Turn up the heat and add the croûtons. The pan should be quite hot at first, then reduce the heat to medium and *keep tossing all the time* until the croûtons are golden brown all over. Drain on kitchen paper.

NOTE: Croûtons can be made several hours or even a day ahead.

CHINESE FISH SOUP WITH SPRING ONIONS

Serves 6

I adore light fish soups. Use this recipe as a formula and vary the fish and shellfish depending on what you have available – mussels and white crab meat are particularly delicious. You might even add some fresh chilli and lots of fresh coriander.

8 oz/225 g lemon sole *or* plaice fillets, skinned

18 prawns *or* shrimps, cooked and peeled

1 iceberg lettuce heart

2 pints/1.1 l/5 cups very well-flavoured Chinese stock (see below)

salt and lots of freshly ground white pepper

GARNISH

6 teaspoons spring onion (scallion), finely sliced at an angle

fresh coriander *or* flat-leaf parsley

prawn *or* shrimp roe if available

CUT the fish fillets into pieces about 1½ in/4 cm square. Shred the lettuce heart very finely. Bring the stock to the boil, add the salt and fish slices. Simmer for 1 minute. Add the prawns or shrimps and allow to heat through. Put about 2 tablespoons of the shredded lettuce into each Chinese soup bowl, add plenty of white pepper and immediately ladle the boiling soup over it. Garnish with spring onions, prawns or shrimp roe and lots of fresh coriander. Serve very hot.

BASIC CHINESE STOCK

Makes approximately 3½ pints/2 l/9 cups.

This delicious light but full flavoured stock is essential for Chinese fish or meat soups.

2 lb/900 g chicken pieces – wings, drumsticks, necks etc.

2 lb/900 g pork spare ribs (*or* total of 4 lb/1.8 kg either chicken pieces *or* ribs)

6 × ½ in/1 cm thick slices fresh ginger root, unpeeled

3–4 large spring onions (scallions)

cold water

4–5 tablespoons Shaoxing rice wine

TIE the spring onion in knots like a real Chinese chef! Put all the ingredients (except the rice wine) in a large saucepan and cover with cold water. Bring to the boil and skim off any scum. Reduce the heat, cover and simmer gently for approximately 4 hours, skimming regularly. Add the rice wine 5 minutes before the end of the cooking time. Strain the stock, cool, then refrigerate.

Remove the solidified fat from the top of the stock before use. The stock will keep in the refrigerator for at least a week; after that boil it every 2 or 3 days. It also freezes perfectly.

STARTERS

I feel that starters are a very important part of a meal because they can really set the mood, so aim to serve small portions of something that tastes delicious and looks tempting, such as the Crudités with Garlic Mayonnaise which begin this section.

The Pink Grapefruit Sorbet is tremendously versatile. It makes a deliciously refreshing starter but can also be served before the main course in a meal of several courses; it would then have the effect of cleansing the palate. In other words, you would feel less full and be able to tuck into several more courses quite happily – and have room for pudding as well!

I've included several lovely first courses for fish lovers. First among them is the best recipe I have ever tasted for Ceviche, given to me by my Peruvian friend, Susie Noriega. Until recently I think most people would have been appalled at the idea of being presented with what appears to be raw fish as the prelude to a dinner. However, fear not, the fish in Ceviche is actually slowly and splendidly 'cooked' by the action of the lime juice.

Oeufs Mimosa is a pretty variation of egg mayonnaise, in which a prawn is hidden as a surprise inside the shell of each hard-boiled egg half, covered with home-made mayonnaise and decorated with sieved egg yolk. Compare that with the hard-boiled egg and bottled salad cream that passes for egg mayonnaise in many places!

The Timbales of Smoked Salmon will steal the show. This is a very stylish starter but it only tastes as it should when made with really good smoked salmon. I mention this point particularly because there is a lot of smoked salmon of disgraceful quality on the market. Read your label carefully and make sure that you are actually buying smoked *Irish* salmon. *Irish smoked* salmon could and often does mean poor quality Canadian or Norwegian frozen salmon which is smoked in Ireland and sold at 'bargain prices'.

There is no such thing as a 'bargain' in smoked salmon; really good quality smoked salmon costs a lot to produce, so save your money for a special occasion and buy the best. Grated horseradish gives a delicious perk to the Timbales recipe, but if you can't find fresh horseradish, use a little extra lemon juice instead.

I decided to include Salmon Pâté and Salmon Rillettes because they are both excellent recipes which use left-overs of fresh or smoked salmon. In fact they are so good you could make them specially!

And so to prawns, the best loved seafood luxury of all. Wonderful fresh, fat Dublin Bay prawns are such a treat that they deserve special care. Buttery Bretonne Sauce with fresh herbs and green Maille mustard is one solution which can also transform many lesser fish into a feast.

A word of advice about the prawns you buy. Again, there is no such thing as a bargain: all the good ones are expensive, and the bigger they are, the better they will be to eat. If you find you have to use frozen prawns, the same rule applies. Beware the suspiciously cheap ones that look large and smooth. The trick that has been used here is to dip them in water and freeze them several times over, to add to their bulk. Don't fall for it! After defrosting, all that is left is a pool of salty water and miserable specimens in a mushy pile.

The fastest fish starter is Smoked Trout with Cucumber Salad and Horseradish Sauce, which takes only the few minutes required to grate fresh horseradish into a simple sauce and open a vacuum pack of tender, moist warm-smoked Irish trout, which is easy to find these days. Like the trout, fresh horseradish should be easy to track down. As it's useful in other ways and obligatory with roast beef, you may even decide to grow it if you have room in your garden for its expansion. In no time at all you'll have enough to supply your entire neighbourhood!

One of the great secrets is not to overdo things. If your first course is fairly substantial, serve small quantities and balance it with a lighter main course – and vice versa. People can just as easily feel hung over from having too much food as too much drink!

CRUDITÉS WITH GARLIC MAYONNAISE

Crudités with Garlic Mayonnaise is one of my favourite starters. It fulfils all my criteria for a first course: small helpings of very crisp vegetables with a good garlicky home-made mayonnaise. The plates of crudités look tempting, taste delicious and, provided you keep the helpings small, are not too filling. Better still, it's actually good for you – so you can feel very virtuous instead of feeling pangs of guilt!

Another great plus for this recipe I've discovered is that children love crudités. They even love garlic mayonnaise provided they don't hear some grown-up saying how much they dislike garlic, and you can feel happy to see your children polishing off plates of raw vegetables for their supper, really quick to prepare and full of wonderful vitamins and minerals.

Crudités are a perfect first course for winter or summer, but to be really delicious you must choose very crisp and fresh vegetables. Cut the vegetables into bite-sized bits so they can be picked up easily. You don't need knives and forks because they are usually eaten with the fingers.

Use as many of the following vegetables as are in season:

> very fresh button mushrooms, quartered
> tomatoes quartered, or left whole with the calyx on if they are freshly picked
> purple sprouting broccoli, broken (not cut) into florettes
> calabrese (green sprouting broccoli), broken into florettes
> cauliflower, broken into florettes
> French beans or mangetout
> baby carrots, or larger carrots cut into sticks about 2 in/5 cm long
> cucumber, cut into sticks approximately 2 in/5 cm long
> tiny spring onions (scallions), trimmed
> red cabbage, cut into strips
> celery, cut into sticks approximately 2 in/5 cm long

chicory, in leaves
red, green or yellow pepper, cut into strips about 2 in/5 cm long,
seeds removed
very fresh Brussels sprouts, cut into halves or quarters
whole radishes, with green tops left on
parsley, finely chopped
thyme, finely chopped
chives, finely chopped
sprigs of watercress

A typical plate of crudités might include the following: 4 sticks of
carrot, 2 or 3 sticks of red and green pepper, 2 or 3 sticks of celery,
2 or 3 sticks of cucumber, 1 mushroom cut in quarters, 1 whole
radish with a little green leaf left on, 1 tiny tomato or 2 quarters, 1
Brussels sprout cut in quarters, and a little pile of chopped fresh
herbs.

Wash and prepare the vegetables. Arrange in contrasting
colours on individual white side plates, with a little bowl of garlic
mayonnaise in the centre. Alternatively, do a large dish or basket
for the centre of the table. Arrange little heaps of each vegetable in
contrasting colours. Put a bowl of garlic mayonnaise in the centre
and then guests can help themselves.

Instead of serving the garlic mayonnaise in a bowl you could
make an edible container by cutting a slice off the top of a tomato
and hollowing out the seeds. Alternatively, cut a 1½ in/4 cm
round of cucumber and hollow out the centre with a melon baller
or a teaspoon. Then fill or pipe the garlic mayonnaise into the
tomato or cucumber. Arrange in the centre of the plate of crudités.

NOTE: All vegetables *must* be raw.

Mayonnaise

Mayonnaise is what we call a 'mother sauce' in culinary jargon. In
fact it is the 'mother' of all the cold emulsion sauces, so once you
can make mayonnaise you can make any of the daughter sauces
just by adding some extra ingredients.

I know it's very tempting to reach for the jar of 'well-known brand', but most people don't seem to be aware that mayonnaise can be made, even with a hand whisk, in under five minutes; and if you use a food processor the technique is still the same but it's made in just a couple of minutes. The great secret is to have all your ingredients at room temperature and to drip the oil very slowly into the egg yolks at the beginning. The quality of your mayonnaise will depend totally on the quality of your egg yolks, oil and vinegar and it's perfectly possible to make a bland mayonnaise if you use poor-quality ingredients.

2 egg yolks, free-range	1 tablespoon/15 ml white wine
1/4 teaspoon salt	vinegar
pinch of English mustard *or*	8 fl oz/250 ml/1 cup oil
1/4 teaspoon French mustard	(sunflower, arachide *or* olive oil,
	or a mixture)

PUT the egg yolks into a bowl with the salt, mustard and 1 dessertspoon of wine vinegar (keep the whites to make meringues). Put the oil into a measure. Take a whisk in one hand and the oil in the other and drip the oil on to the egg yolks, drop by drop, whisking at the same time. Within a minute you will notice that the mixture is beginning to thicken. When this happens you can add the oil a little faster, but don't get too cheeky or it will suddenly curdle because the egg yolks can absorb the oil only at a certain pace. When all the oil has been added, whisk in the remaining vinegar. Taste and add a little more seasoning if necessary.

If the mayonnaise curdles it will suddenly become quite thin, and, if left sitting, the oil will start to float to the top of the sauce. If this happens you can quite easily rectify it: another egg yolk or 1–2 tablespoons of boiling water into a clean bowl, then whisk in the curdled mayonnaise, a half teaspoon at a time until it emulsifies again.

Garlic Mayonnaise

ingredients as above *plus* 1–4
cloves garlic depending on size

2 teaspoons chopped parsley

CRUSH the garlic and add to the egg yolks just as you start to make the mayonnaise. Finally, add the chopped parsley and taste for seasoning.

NOTE: Here is a tip for crushing garlic. Put the whole clove of garlic on a board, preferably one that is reserved for garlic and onions. Tap the clove with the flat blade of a chopping knife, to break the skin. Remove the skin and discard. Then sprinkle a few grains of salt on to the clove. Again using the flat blade of the knife, keep pressing the tip of the knife down on to the garlic to form a paste. The salt provides friction and ensures the clove won't shoot off the board!

PINK GRAPEFRUIT SORBET

Serves 8

Sorbets are usually served at the end of a meal, but a grapefruit sorbet can be served at the beginning, in the middle, or at the end, so it is particularly versatile.

You may use ordinary yellow grapefruit, but this recipe is especially delicious if you can find pink grapefruit which are sweeter and have a pale pink juice. Pink grapefruit look very like ordinary ones although they sometimes have a pink blush and are always a bit more expensive. They are at their best between November and February when the flesh is very pink inside. If you are using ordinary grapefruit you will need to increase the sugar to about 10 oz/300 g.

1¾ pints/1 l
pink grapefruit juice
(10 grapefruit approx.)

8 oz/225 g/generous 1 cup caster
sugar approx.
1 egg white (optional)

GARNISH

4 grapefruit cut into segments   fresh mint leaves
  8 chilled white side plates

SQUEEZE the juice from the grapefruit into a bowl and dissolve the sugar by stirring it into the juice. Taste. The juice should taste rather too sweet to drink, because it will lose some of its sweetness in the freezing.

Make the sorbet in one of the following ways:

1. Pour into the drum of an ice-cream maker or sorbetière and freeze for 20–25 minutes. Scoop out and serve immediately or store in a covered bowl in the freezer until needed.

2. Pour the juice into a stainless steel or plastic container and put into the freezer or the freezing compartment of a refrigerator. After about 4 or 5 hours when the sorbet is semi-frozen, remove from the freezer and whisk until smooth; then return to the freezer. Whisk again when almost frozen and fold in one stiffly beaten egg white. Keep in the freezer until needed.

3. If you have a food processor freeze the sorbet completely in a stainless steel or plastic bowl, then break into large pieces and whizz up in the food processor for a few seconds. Add one slightly beaten egg white, whizz again for another few seconds, then return to the bowl and freeze again until needed.

TO SERVE: Chill the plates in a refrigerator or freezer. Carefully segment the grapefruit by first cutting off all the peel and pith. Then with a stainless steel knife remove each segment from the membrane. Put 1 or 2 scoops of sorbet on each chilled plate, garnish with a few segments of pink grapefruit, put a little grapefruit juice over the segments and decorate with fresh mint leaves.

ORANGE, MINT AND GRAPEFRUIT COCKTAIL

Serves 4

2 oranges
2 grapefruit

1 tablespoon sugar approx.
2 tablespoons freshly chopped mint

GARNISH
4 sprigs of fresh mint

PEEL and carefully segment the oranges and grapefruit into a bowl. Add the sugar and chopped mint; taste and add more sugar if necessary. Chill. Serve in pretty little bowls or, alternatively, arrange the segments of orange and grapefruit alternately on the plate in a circle; pour a little juice over the fruit. Garnish with a sprig of fresh mint.

FISH MOUSSE WITH SHRIMP BUTTER SAUCE

Serves 16–20

This recipe makes a large number of light fish mousses. It's a favourite on our menu and can be served with many sauces. Even though the mousse is light it is also very rich, so it's vital to cook it in small ramekins. They can be done in several batches as the raw mixture keeps perfectly overnight, covered in a cold fridge. Cooked crab meat, oysters, prawns, periwinkles or a tiny dice of cucumber could be added to a beurre blanc sauce to serve with them.

12 oz/340 g very fresh fillets of whiting *or* pollock, skinned and totally free of bone or membrane
1 teaspoon salt
pinch of freshly ground white pepper
1 egg, preferably free-range

1 egg white
generous 1 1/4 pints/750 ml/ generous 3 cups cream, chilled
beurre blanc sauce recipe × 2 (see below)
4–8 oz/110–225 g peeled cooked shrimps
1/4 oz/8 g/1/2 tablespoon butter

GARNISH

sprigs of chervil
whole cooked shrimps (optional)

small ramekins, 2 1/2 fl oz/60 ml capacity, 2 in/5 cm diameter, 1 in/2.5 cm deep

CUT the fish fillets into small dice, purée in the chilled bowl of a food processor, add the salt and freshly ground pepper and then add the egg and egg white and continue to purée until it is well incorporated. Rest and chill in the fridge for 30 minutes.

Meanwhile, line the ramekins with pure clingfilm or brush with melted butter. When the fish has rested for 30 minutes, blend in the cream and whizz again just until it is well incorporated. Check seasoning. Fill the mousse into the moulds and put them in a bain marie. Cover with a pricked sheet of tinfoil or greaseproof paper. Bring the water in the bain marie just to boiling point, put it in the oven at 200°C/400°F/gas 6 and bake for 20–30 minutes. The mousses should feel just firm in the centre and will keep perfectly for 20–30 minutes in a plate-warming oven.

Meanwhile, make the beurre blanc sauce (see below) and keep warm. When the mousses are cooked remove them to a warm place and leave to rest. Toss the shrimps in a very little foaming butter until hot through, add them to the sauce, taste and correct seasoning: the sauce should be very thin and light. Pour a little hot sauce on to each plate, unmould a mousse, place it in the centre and garnish with shrimps and sprigs of fresh chervil.

NOTE: It is vital to season the raw mixture well, otherwise the mousse will taste bland.

Beurre Blanc Sauce

2¹/₂ fl oz/60 ml/generous ¹/₄ cup white wine

2¹/₂ fl oz/60 ml/generous ¹/₄ cup white wine vinegar

1 generous tablespoon finely chopped shallots

1–1¹/₂ tablespoons cream

6 oz/170 g/³/₄ cup cold unsalted butter, cut into cubes

salt

pinch of ground white pepper

freshly squeezed lemon juice

PUT the wine, wine vinegar, shallots and pepper into a heavy-bottomed stainless steel saucepan and reduce down to about ¹/₂ tablespoon. Add the cream and boil again until it thickens. Whisk in the cold butter in little pieces, keeping the sauce just warm enough to absorb the butter. Strain out the shallots, season with salt, white pepper and lemon juice and keep warm in a bowl over hot but not simmering water.

FISH MOUSSE IN COURGETTE FLOWERS

This is a very grand way of serving the fish mousse described above – the perfect way to make use of all the flowers if you grow your own courgettes.

allow 1 male flower per person

fish mousse (see above)

PREPARE the flowers by removing the stamen and the tiny little thorns from the base. Drop the flowers into boiling salted water and immediately remove them and plunge them into a large bowl of iced water. Remove from the water and drain on kitchen paper. Fill the courgette flowers with the fish mousse (a piping bag with a plain nozzle is best for this fiddly operation).

Put them on a greased baking sheet which has been moistened with a little water, cover with tinfoil and bake in a preheated moderate oven, 180°C/350°F/gas 4, for 15–20 minutes or until firm to the touch. Serve on hot plates with beurre blanc sauce (see above).

Garnish with sprigs of chervil or fennel.

WARM SMOKED SALMON WITH CUCUMBER AND DILL

Serves 4

Rory O'Connell serves this warm smoked salmon recipe on his special menu at Ballymaloe. We use Bill Casey's salmon which is smoked on our farm.

6–8 oz/170–225 g smoked salmon

1/4 oz/8 g/1 tablespoon butter

6–8 tablespoons cucumber, peeled and cut into 1/4 inch/ 7 mm dice

salt, freshly ground pepper

squeeze of lemon juice

4 fl oz/120 ml/1/2 cup cream

2 teaspoons chopped fennel *or* 1 teaspoon chopped dill

SLICE the smoked salmon straight down on to the skin into 1/4 inch/5 mm thick slices. Melt the butter in a sauté pan and allow to foam. Place the smoked salmon slices carefully in the pan; after 30 seconds turn them carefully and add the cucumber dice. Season with salt, pepper and a squeeze of lemon juice. Add the cream and dill or fennel and allow the cream to bubble up and barely thicken. Check seasoning and serve immediately on hot plates.

TIMBALES OF SMOKED SALMON WITH CUCUMBER AND FENNEL SALAD

Serves 6
6 thin slices of smoked salmon

SMOKED SALMON AND TROUT PATÉ

4 oz/110 g smoked salmon
trimmings *or*
3 oz/85 g smoked trout and
1 oz/30 g smoked salmon
trimmings
5 fl oz/150 ml cream

1 oz/30 g/2 tablespoons unsalted
butter
1 tablespoon freshly grated
horseradish (optional)
lemon juice
salt and freshly ground pepper

CUCUMBER AND FENNEL SALAD
1/3 of a fresh cucumber

VINAIGRETTE

1 tablespoon wine vinegar
3 tablespoons sunflower oil

pinch each of mustard, salt,
freshly ground pepper and sugar

1/2 teaspoon finely chopped fennel (herb)

GARNISH

sprigs of chervil and fennel
little dice of fresh tomato flesh
(tomato concassé)

6 moulds, 2 in/5 cm in diameter,
1 in/2.5 cm deep, 2½ fl oz/
60 ml capacity

A FOOD processor is essential for this recipe, to achieve a really smooth filling.

Blend the smoked salmon and trout trimmings with the unsalted butter in a food processor, add cream and grated horse-radish, and lemon juice to taste. Check seasoning and do not over-process or the mixture will curdle.

Line the moulds with clingfilm. Put a slice of smoked salmon into each mould. Fill the moulds with the mousse, fold the ends of the smoked salmon over the mousse to cover. Cover with clingfilm and refrigerate for at least one hour.

Next make the vinaigrette by whisking the oil and vinegar together in a bowl for a few seconds. Season to taste with salt, freshly ground pepper, sugar and a pinch of mustard. Slice the cucumber very finely by hand or on a mandolin, toss the cucumber slices in 3 tablespoons of the vinaigrette and add the very finely chopped fennel.

To assemble: Arrange the cucumber slices in an overlapping circle on a large side plate. Place a timbale of salmon in the centre of the cucumber circle and glaze it with a little of the surplus vinaigrette. Garnish with sprigs of fresh chervil or fennel. Finally, a dessertspoon of tomato concassé or 2 cherry tomatoes peeled and halved can be used to make an attractive garnish on each plate.

Salmon Pâté with Fennel

Serves 6–8

This pâté is a delicious way of using up left-over cold salmon.

4 oz/110 g/1 cup cooked salmon, free of skin and bone
2–3 oz/55–85 g/4–6 tablespoons softened butter

¹/₄ teaspoon finely snipped fennel
¹/₂ teaspoon lemon juice
¹/₂ clove garlic, crushed to a paste

Blend all the ingredients in a food processor or just simply in a bowl, taste and add more lemon juice if necessary.

Fill into a bowl or little pots, put a sprig of fennel on top of each pot. Cover with a thin layer of clarified butter (see page 46). Chill in the refrigerator. Serve within 3 days.

This pâté can also be piped in rosettes on to ¹/₄ in/7 mm thick slices of cucumber and served as a starter or as part of an hors d'oeuvre or buffet.

RILLETTES OF FRESH AND SMOKED SALMON

Serves 8

The texture of this pâté should resemble that of pork rillettes, where the meat is torn into shreds rather than blended.

12 oz/340 g/2½ cups freshly cooked salmon

12 oz/340 g/2 cups smoked salmon

pinch of nutmeg

12 oz/340 g/1½ cups softened butter

lemon juice to taste

salt and freshly ground pepper

FOR COOKING THE SMOKED SALMON

1 oz/30 g/2 tablespoons butter   1–1½ tablespoons/30 ml water

MELT the 1 oz/30 g butter in a low saucepan, add the smoked salmon and the tablespoon of water. Cover and cook for 3–4 minutes or until it no longer looks opaque. Allow it to get quite cold.

Cream the butter in a bowl. With two forks, shred the fresh and smoked salmon and mix well together. Add to the soft butter still using a fork (do *not* use a food processor). Season with salt and freshly ground pepper and nutmeg. Taste and add lemon juice as necessary, and some freshly chopped fennel if you have it.

Serve in individual pots or in a pottery terrine. Cover with a layer of clarified butter (see page 46). Serve with hot toast or hot crusty white bread. Salmon Rillettes will keep perfectly in the refrigerator for 5 or 6 days provided they are sealed with clarified butter.

BALLYMALOE FISH TERRINE WITH TOMATO COULIS

Serves 10–12

Most fish terrines are based on sole, and though they are delicious when served hot, they can be very dull and bland when cold. This layered fish pâté is a great favourite. Its content varies depending on the fish available to us.

FIRST LAYER

4 oz/110 g cooked, shelled shrimps *or* 6 oz/170 g prawns (cut up if large, so that they will cover the base of the tin)
½ clove garlic
1 teaspoon thyme leaves

3½ oz/100 g/7 tablespoons clarified butter (see page 46)
2 teaspoons lemon juice
1–1½ tablespoons finely chopped parsley

5 × 8 in/13 × 20 cm bread tin

PREPARE the tin by lining it neatly with a double thickness of clingfilm. Crush the garlic into a paste with a little salt. Melt the butter in a saucepan with the thyme leaves and garlic and then bring to the boil. Add the shrimps or prawns and simmer gently for 3–5 minutes. Add lemon juice to taste. Allow to cool, pour into the tin in an even layer, sprinkle with a little chopped parsley and chill while you prepare the next layer.

SECOND LAYER

4 oz/110 g smoked salmon, mackerel *or* smoked herring flesh, free of bones and skin
3 oz/85 g/6 tablespoons softened butter

lemon juice to taste
1–1½ tablespoons finely chopped parsley *or* chives

BLEND the smoked salmon and butter together in a food processor. Taste and add lemon juice if necessary. When shrimps have

34

set hard spread this paste on top of them in an even layer. Sprinkle with a little more parsley or chopped chives. Refrigerate while you prepare the next layer.

THIRD LAYER

4 oz/110 g cooked salmon, free
of skin or bone
lemon juice to taste
3 oz/85 g/6 tablespoons softened
butter
1 small clove garlic

½ teaspoon finely chopped
fennel (optional)
1–1½ tablespoons chopped
parsley
salt and freshly ground pepper

CRUSH the garlic into a paste with a little salt. Blend it with the salmon and other ingredients in the food processor. Taste and correct seasoning. Smooth the mixture over the first two layers, sprinkle with a layer of parsley and keep chilled.

FOURTH LAYER

5 oz/140 g/1 cup mixed brown
and white crab meat, cooked
4 oz/110 g/½ cup softened
butter
1 medium clove garlic, crushed

2 teaspoons finely chopped
parsley
black pepper
2 teaspoons tomato chutney
(see page 189)

BLEND all the ingredients together in a food processor. Spread this final layer on to the fish terrine. Cover with clingfilm and press down well to compact the layers and chill until needed.

Tomato Coulis

1 lb/450 g tomatoes, as ripe
as possible
½ oz/15 g/⅛ cup chopped
onion
2 teaspoons white wine vinegar
2–3 tablespoons olive oil

1 level teaspoon salt
1 level teaspoon sugar
black pepper
2 basil leaves or 4 fresh mint
leaves

SKIN the tomatoes by scalding in boiling water for 10 seconds: pour off the water and the skin will peel off easily straightaway.

Halve and take out the pips. Blend the tomato flesh with the other ingredients and sieve if necessary. Taste and correct seasoning.

To serve: Turn the terrine out on to a chilled dish and remove the clingfilm. For a buffet, decorate with salad leaves and with any fresh herbs and herb flowers you can find. Serve in slices and offer a little tomato coulis with each helping. Alternatively, pour a little tomato coulis on to individual white plates, place a slice of the fish terrine on top and garnish with tiny sprigs of fennel or cress.

Roulade of Smoked Salmon with Cottage Cheese and Dill

Serves 4

This very stylish smoked salmon recipe also makes delicious canapés served on thick cucumber slices.

4 slices of smoked salmon, thinly sliced and about 6 in/ 15 cm long
4 oz/110 g/½ cup cream cheese
2–2½ tablespoons cream
salt and freshly ground pepper

1–1½ tablespoons finely chopped chives *or* 2 teaspoons finely chopped dill
¼ quantity sweet cucumber salad (see page 38)

GARNISH
sprigs of fennel *or* chervil

Mix the cream cheese, chives or dill and cream together and season to taste with salt and freshly ground pepper. Spread the cheese mixture on to each slice of salmon and roll them up carefully. Cover and refrigerate for at least 1 hour.

Next make the cucumber salad.

To assemble: Arrange 4 or 5 slices of cucumber salad on each plate. Cut the smoked salmon rolls into $^1/_2$–$^3/_4$ in/1–2 cm slices and place on top of the cucumber slices. Drizzle a little of the excess dressing from the cucumber salad on to the plate. Garnish with sprigs of fennel or chervil and serve immediately.

Gravlax with Mustard and Dill Mayonnaise

Serves 12–16

We are all addicted to this pickled salmon which keeps for up to a week. Fresh dill is essential.

1$^1/_2$–2 lb/675–900 g tail pieces of fresh wild Irish salmon
1 oz/30 g sea salt (e.g. Maldon)
1 oz/30 g sugar

1 teaspoon freshly ground black pepper
2–2$^1/_2$ tablespoons finely chopped fresh dill

Fillet the salmon and remove all the bones with tweezers. Mix the salt, sugar, pepper and dill together in a bowl. Place the fish on a piece of clingfilm and scatter the mixture over the surface of the fish. Wrap tightly with clingfilm and refrigerate for a minimum of 12 hours.

Mustard and Dill Mayonnaise

1 large egg yolk, preferably free-range
2–2$^1/_2$ tablespoons French mustard
1–1$^1/_2$ tablespoons white sugar
$^1/_4$ pint/150 ml/generous $^1/_2$ cup ground nut *or* sunflower oil

1–1$^1/_2$ tablespoons white wine vinegar
1–1$^1/_2$ tablespoons finely chopped dill
salt and freshly ground white pepper

Whisk the egg yolk with the mustard and sugar, drip in the oil drop by drop whisking all the time, then add the vinegar and fresh dill. Season.

To serve, wipe the dill mixture off the salmon and slice thinly. Arrange on a plate in a rosette shape. Fill the centre of the rosette with mustard and dill mayonnaise. Garnish with fresh dill. Serve with brown bread and butter.

SALMON TARTARE WITH A SWEET CUCUMBER SALAD

Serves 6–8

¹/₂ lb/225 g wild Irish salmon, pickled as for Gravlax (see above)

tiny dash of sweet mustard

squeeze of fresh lemon juice

1 teaspoon home-made mayonnaise (see page 23)

freshly ground pepper

¹/₄ pint/150 ml sour cream, lightly whipped

SWEET CUCUMBER SALAD

6 oz/170 g/1 cup approx. cucumber, thinly sliced

2 oz/55 g/¹/₂ cup approx. onion, thinly sliced

2 oz/55 g/generous ¹/₄ cup sugar

1¹/₄ level teaspoons salt

2–3 tablespoons white wine vinegar

GARNISH

small sprigs of dill

dill *or* chive flowers

WASH the Gravlax and dry well. Cut into tiny ¹/₈ in/3 mm dice and mix with the mayonnaise; add mustard and lemon juice. Season well with freshly ground pepper. Cover and leave in the fridge for 1 hour.

Meanwhile make the cucumber salad. Combine the sliced cucumber and onion in a large bowl. Mix sugar, salt and vinegar together and pour over the cucumber and onion. Place in a tightly covered container in the refrigerator and leave for at least 1 hour.

To serve the tartare, put a 2¹/₂ in/6.5 cm cutter on to each white plate, fill almost full with salmon mixture and smooth a little sour cream over the top with a palette knife. Lift off the cutter and put a ring of cucumber salad around the salmon tartare. Garnish the top with tiny sprigs of dill and perhaps some dill or chive flowers.

Serve with crusty white bread or hot toast.

CRAB PÂTÉ WITH CUCUMBER AND DILL SALAD

Serves 6–8

This pâté, which is made in a flash once you have the crab meat to hand, can be served in lots of different ways. We make it into a cylinder and roll it in chopped parsley when we want to be extra posh!

5 oz/140 g/1 cup mixed brown and white cooked crab meat (for method, see below)
4 oz/110 g/½ cup softened butter
1 medium clove garlic, crushed

1–2 teaspoons finely chopped parsley
few grinds of black pepper
fresh lemon juice to taste
tomato chutney (see page 189)

COATING

3–4 tablespoons finely chopped parsley

TO SERVE

cucumber salad (see below)

GARNISH

flat-leaf parsley, fennel *or* chervil
fennel *or* chive flowers, if available

Mix all ingredients (except the parsley for coating) together in a bowl or, better still, whizz them in a food processor. Taste carefully and continue to season until you are happy with the flavour: it may need a little more lemon juice or crushed garlic.

Form the pâté into a cylinder, roll up in greaseproof paper, twist the ends like a Christmas cracker and chill until almost firm.

Spread one-quarter sheet of greaseproof paper on the worktop, sprinkle the chopped parsley over the paper, unwrap the pâté and roll it in the parsley so that the surface is evenly coated. Wrap it up again and refrigerate until needed.

Make the cucumber salad.

TO SERVE: Arrange a circle of cucumber slices on individual white plates and put one or more slices of pâté (depending on the size of the roll) in the centre of each. Garnish with flat parsley, fennel or chervil and fennel or chive flowers if available. Serve with crusty white bread or hot toast.

Cucumber Salad

Serves 6

1 medium cucumber	1 teaspoon finely chopped fennel
2–4 teaspoons white wine	(herb)
vinegar	salt, freshly ground pepper and
	sugar

FINELY slice the cucumber (leave peel on if you like it). Sprinkle with wine vinegar and season with salt, freshly ground pepper and a good pinch of sugar. Stir in the snipped fennel and taste.

How to Cook Crab

Put the crab into a saucepan, cover with cold or barely lukewarm water (use 6 oz/170 g salt to every 4 pints/2.3 l water). This sounds like an incredible amount of salt but try it: the crab will taste deliciously sweet. Cover, bring to the boil and then simmer from there on, allowing 15 minutes for the first 1 lb/450 g, 10 minutes for the second and third (I've never come across a crab bigger than that!). We usually pour off two-thirds of the water half way through cooking, cover and steam the crab for the remainder of the time. As soon as it is cooked remove it from the saucepan and allow to get cold.

First remove the large claws. Hold the crab with the underside uppermost and lever out the centre portion – I do this by catching the little lip of the projecting centre shell against the edge of the table and pressing down firmly. The Dead Man's Fingers (lungs) usually come out with this central piece, but check in case some are left in the body and, if so, remove them.

Press your thumb down over the light shell just behind the eyes so that the shell cracks slightly, and then the sac which is underneath can be removed easily. Everything else inside the body of the crab is edible. The soft meat varies in colour from cream to coffee to dark tan, and towards the end of the season it can contain quite a bit of bright orange coral which is stronger in flavour. Scoop it all out and put it into a bowl. There will also be one or two teaspoonsful of soft meat in the centre portion – add that to the bowl also. Scrub the shell and keep it aside if you need it for dressed crab.

Crack the large claws with a hammer or weight and extract every little bit of white meat from them, and from the small claws also, using a lobster pick, skewer or even the handle of a teaspoon.

Mix the brown and white meat together or use separately, depending on the recipe.

TOMATOES STUFFED WITH CRAB MAYONNAISE

Serves 6

Crab mayonnaise is very versatile. It is delicious used as a filling for cucumber or tomato ring as well as a stuffing for tomatoes. It also marries very well with a simple tomato salad (see page 190) or as a first course for a dinner party.

5 oz/140 g/1 cup mixed white and brown fresh crab meat (1 medium-sized cooked crab should yield enough – for cooking method, see page 41)
6 large or 12 small very ripe firm tomatoes
salt and freshly ground pepper

6–8 fl oz/175–225 ml/3/4–1 cup home-made mayonnaise (see page 23) or a couple of tablespoons French dressing (see page 190) instead of some of the mayonnaise
1/2 teaspoon juice of finely grated onion

GARNISH

small lettuce leaves
garden cress *or* watercress

edible flowers e.g. chives

CUT the tops off the tomatoes, remove the seeds with a melon baller or a teaspoon, season with salt and turn upside down to drain while you prepare the filling.

Mix the crab meat with the mayonnaise, grate some peeled onion on the finest part of the stainless steel grater and add 1/2 teaspoon of the onion juice to the crab. Taste and season if necessary.

Fill the crab mixture into the tomatoes and replace the lids. Arrange a bed of lettuce and salad leaves on a white plate. Serve 1 large or 2 small tomatoes per person. Garnish with sprigs of fresh herbs and some edible flowers.

SUSIE NORIEGA'S PERUVIAN CEVICHE

Serves 10–12

2 lb/900 g very fresh fillets
of white fish, monkfish,
cod *or* plaice
4 limes
2 lemons
2 cloves garlic, finely
chopped

fresh coriander
3 oz/85 g/scant 1 cup finely
sliced onions
1–2 fresh chillies
1 green pepper and 1 red pepper,
finely diced
salt and freshly ground pepper

GARNISH

crisp lettuce leaves
5–6 spring onions

sweetcorn
2 avocados

SKIN the fish; slice or cube into ¹/₂ in/1 cm pieces and put into a deep stainless steel or china bowl. Squeeze the juice from the lemons and limes and pour over the fish. Sprinkle with salt, freshly ground pepper and chopped garlic. Cover and leave to marinade for 3 or 4 hours in a fridge. Next add the fresh coriander, sliced onions and chillies and half of the finely diced red and green peppers. Cover and leave for 2¹/₂ hours in the fridge. Then serve or keep covered until later.

TO SERVE: Arrange a few crisp lettuce leaves on a plate and place a tablespoon of Ceviche in the centre. Decorate with slices of avocado, remaining diced peppers, sweetcorn and spring onions. Serve with crusty white bread.

OEUFS MIMOSA

Serves 4

These may be served on a cold buffet, but be sure to garnish with prawns or shrimps to alert anyone who may be allergic to shellfish.

4 eggs, preferably free-range
16 shrimps *or* 8 cooked prawns
$^1/_4$ pint/150 ml/generous $^1/_2$ cup
home-made mayonnaise
(see page 23)

a few lettuce leaves
salt and freshly ground pepper

GARNISH

sprigs of watercress   a few whole shrimps or prawns

BRING a small saucepan of water to the boil; lower the eggs gradually into the water one by one, bring the water back to the boil and cook for 10 minutes; pour off the water and cover the eggs with cold water. When cold, shell and cut in half lengthways. Sieve the yolks, reserve a little for garnish, mix the remainder with 3–4 tablespoons of home-made mayonnaise and taste for seasoning.

Put 1 or 2 cooked shrimps or prawns into each egg white and spoon some egg mayonnaise mixture into each one; round off the top to look like whole eggs. Then thin the remaining mayonnaise with hot water to coating consistency and coat the eggs carefully. Sprinkle with the reserved egg yolk.

Serve on a bed of lettuce and garnish with sprigs of watercress and a few whole shrimps or prawns.

How to Cook Prawns

---

2 lb/900 g whole prawns (yields
6 oz/170 g approx. prawn tails)

4 pints/2.3 l/10 cups water
2–2½ tablespoons salt

BRING the water to the boil and add the salt. Remove the heads of the prawns and discard or use for making fish stock. With the underside of the prawn uppermost, tug the little fan-shaped tail at either side and carefully draw out the trail. (The trail is the intestine, so it is very important to remove it before cooking regardless of whether the prawns are to be shelled or not.)

Put the prawns into the boiling salted water and as soon as the water returns to the boil, test a prawn to see if it is cooked. It should be firm and white, not opaque or mushy. If cooked, remove prawns immediately. Very large ones may take ½ to 1 minute more. Allow to cool in a single layer and then remove the shells.

NOTE: Do not cook too many prawns together, otherwise they may overcook before the water even comes back to the boil.

Prawns on Brown Bread
with Mayonnaise

Serves 4

Don't dismiss this very simple starter. Prawns are wonderful served on good, fresh bread with a home-made mayonnaise.

6 oz/170 g freshly cooked
prawns *or* shrimps
4–8 leaves butterhead *or* oakleaf
or lollo rosso lettuce

3–4 tablespoons home-made
mayonnaise (see page 23)
4 slices of buttered Ballymaloe
brown yeast bread (see page 235)

GARNISH
sprigs of watercress, flat-leaf parsley, fennel *or* garden cress,
4 lemon segments

PUT a slice of buttered bread on a plate, arrange 1 or 2 leaves on top and place 5–6 fat, freshly cooked prawns on the lettuce. Pipe a coil of home-made mayonnaise on the prawns. Garnish with lemon segments and sprigs of watercress, flat parsley, fennel or garden cress.

NOTE: If using shrimps, use a little of the coral for garnish.

PRAWN AND BASIL PÂTÉ

Serves 6

This delicious pâté is particularly good for using up a few left-overs or soft prawns.

8 oz/225 g/1½ cups cooked, peeled prawns *or* shrimps
2 fl oz/50 ml/¼ cup olive oil
a dash of cayenne pepper

juice of 1 lime *or* ½ lemon
4 fresh basil leaves
salt if necessary
clarified butter to seal
(see below)

PUT all the ingredients into a food processor and whizz for a few seconds until they form a paste. Taste for seasoning; it may be necessary to add salt. Pack the mixture into little pots or a terrine. Seal with clarified butter. Serve chilled with hot, thin toast.

If you are using freshly boiled prawn tails in the shell, allow 1½ lb/675 g approximately gross measure, 3 lb/1.35 kg with heads on.

Clarified Butter

Melt 8 oz/225 g/1 cup butter gently in a saucepan or in the oven. Allow it to stand for a few minutes, then spoon the crusty white layer of salt particles off the top of the melted butter. Underneath this crust there is clear liquid – the clarified butter. The milky liquid at the bottom can be discarded or used in a béchamel sauce.

Clarified butter is excellent for cooking because it can withstand a higher temperature when the salt particles and milk are removed. It will keep covered in a refrigerator for several weeks.

BUTTERED PRAWNS WITH BRETONNE SAUCE

Serves 4

2 lb/900 g whole prawns (yields 6 oz/170 g prawn tails approx.)	4 pints/2.3 l/10 cups water
	2 tablespoons salt
	1 oz/30 g/2 tablespoons butter

BRETONNE SAUCE

1 egg yolk, preferably free-range	1 tablespoon mixed finely
1/2 teaspoon French mustard	chopped chives, fennel, parsley
(we use Maille mustard with	and thyme
green herbs)	3 oz/85 g/6 tablespoons butter

GARNISH
flat-leaf parsley *or* fresh fennel

BRING the water to the boil and add the salt. De-vein the prawns. Toss them into the boiling water and as soon as the water returns to the boil, test a prawn and then remove immediately. Very large prawns may take 1/2–1 minute more. Allow to cool and then remove the shells.

Next make the Bretonne sauce. Whisk the egg yolk with the mustard and herbs in a bowl. Bring the butter to the boil and pour it in a steady stream on to the egg yolk, whisking continuously until the sauce thickens to a light coating consistency as with a Hollandaise. Keep warm in a flask or place in a pottery or plastic bowl (*not* stainless steel) in a saucepan of hot but not boiling water.

Just before serving, toss the prawns in foaming butter until heated through. Heap them on to a hot serving dish. Coat with Bretonne sauce. Garnish with flat parsley or fresh fennel and serve immediately.

SMOKED TROUT WITH CUCUMBER SALAD AND HORSERADISH SAUCE

Serves 8

8 fillets of smoked trout	salt, freshly ground pepper and
(either smoked sea trout *or*	sugar
rainbow trout)	1 teaspoon chopped fresh fennel
1/2 cucumber	*or* 1/2 teaspoon chopped fresh dill
a sprinkle of wine vinegar	horseradish sauce (see below)

GARNISH

lemon segments	fresh dill *or* fennel

MAKE the horseradish sauce as directed below.

Thinly slice the unpeeled cucumber. Sprinkle with a few drops of vinegar and season with salt, sugar and a little freshly ground pepper. Stir in some finely chopped fennel or dill.

TO ASSEMBLE THE SALAD: Place a fillet of smoked trout on each individual serving plate. Arrange the cucumber salad along the side and pipe some fresh horseradish sauce on top of the trout. Garnish with a segment of lemon and some fresh herbs.

Horseradish Sauce

This makes a mild sauce; if you would like something that will really clear the sinuses, just increase the quantity of grated horseradish!

1 1/2 tablespoons grated	1 teaspoon lemon juice
horseradish	1/4 teaspoon mustard
4 fl oz/120 ml/1/2 cup cream,	1/4 teaspoon salt
softly whipped	a pinch of freshly ground pepper
2 teaspoons wine vinegar	1 teaspoon sugar

SCRUB the horseradish root well, peel and grate. Put the grated horseradish into a bowl with the vinegar, lemon juice, mustard, salt, freshly ground pepper and sugar. Fold in the softly whipped cream; do not over-mix or the sauce will curdle.

This sauce keeps for 2–3 days and may also be served with roast beef; cover so that it doesn't pick up flavours in the fridge.

CLAMS, PALOURDES OR ROGHANS GRATINÉE

Serves 6–8

Palourdes are a type of clam growing off the West Cork coast. This recipe may also be used for oysters but they will take longer under the grill.

48 clams, palourdes *or* roghans
1–1½ tablespoons olive oil
4 streaky bacon rashers (rindless)
4 oz/110 g/1¼ cups finely chopped mushrooms
salt and freshly ground pepper

1–1½ tablespoons chopped parsley
2–2½ tablespoons buttered crumbs (see page 103)
3–4 tablespoons finely grated Gruyère cheese

HEAT the olive oil in a frying pan, fry the rashers until crisp, remove and cut into tiny pieces. Toss the chopped mushrooms quickly over a high heat in the bacon fat, add the chopped parsley and season with salt and freshly ground pepper. Add the diced rashers and allow to cool. Mix the buttered crumbs with the cheese.

Put the clams in a covered pan over a low heat, remove as soon as the shells open, drain, remove the outer rind and the 'exhaust pipes' (siphons). Cover the clams first with the mushroom mixture and then sprinkle a little of the cheese and buttered crumb mixture on top.* Arrange in an ovenproof dish, brown under a hot grill for 3 or 4 minutes and serve immediately.

* May be prepared ahead to this point.

49

HOT BUTTERED OYSTERS

Serves 4

These wonderfully curvaceous oyster shells tend to topple over maddeningly on the plate allowing the delicious juices to escape. In the restaurant we solve this problem by piping a little blob of Duchesse potato on the plate to anchor each shell.

12 Pacific (Gigas) oysters
1 oz/30 g/2 tablespoons butter

$^1/_2$ teaspoon finely chopped parsley

TO SERVE

4 lemon segments

4 × hot buttered toast (optional)

OPEN the oysters and detach completely from their shells. You will need an oyster knife for this operation. Place the oyster on the worktop, deep shell down. Cover your hand with a folded tea-towel and hold the oyster firmly. Put the tip of the oyster knife into the crevice at the hinge of the oyster, push hard and then quickly twist the knife. You need to exert quite a bit of pressure, hence it is essential that the hand holding the oyster is protected, in case the knife slips. When you feel the oyster is opening, change the angle of the knife and, keeping the blade close to the shell, slice the oyster off the top shell in one movement. Then run the knife underneath the oyster in the deep shell and flip it over: be careful not to lose any of the delicious juices.

Discard the top shell but keep the deep shell and reserve the liquid. Put the shells into a low oven to heat through. Melt half the butter in a pan until it foams. Toss the oysters in the butter until hot through – 1 minute perhaps.

Put a hot oyster into each of the warm shells. Pour the reserved oyster liquid into the pan and boil up, whisking in the remaining butter and the parsley. Spoon the hot juices over the oysters and serve immediately on hot plates with a wedge of lemon.

Alternatively discard the shells and just serve the oysters on the hot buttered toast. The toast will soak up the juice – Simply Delicious!

SALADS

A simple green salad may be served either instead of or as well as vegetables. When it's eaten just after a main course it also has the magical effect of making you feel less full – which means you have room for pudding!

It is sometimes difficult to get a plain green salad in a restaurant. Often you will be given a mixed salad with peppers, tomatoes, cucumbers, etc. and, although there are many variations on the green salad theme, it should really only be made up of different kinds of lettuce and salad leaves. The variety of lettuces one can buy in the shops has improved enormously. Until recently, the only one that was widely available was the soft butterhead lettuce, but now it is possible to find Chinese leaves, iceberg and radicchio, as well as several 'frizzy' varieties, such as endive and the lovely, frilly, bronze-tinted lollo rosso.

However, the variety on offer is small in comparison with all the wonderful salad leaves that you can grow, given a little space. You might like to try some of the following: green or bronze oak-leaf lettuce, cos, radicchio trevisano, rocket or aruguala, lamb's lettuce, salad burnet, mizuna, sorrel, edible chrysanthemum leaves and golden marjoram. Depending on what the salad is to be served with, you can also add some edible flowers for extra excitement and pzazz. Our favourites are tiny pansies or violas, borage flowers, nasturtium flowers and tiny leaves, chive or wild garlic blossoms, and rocket flowers.

So gather up whatever you can for your salad bowl, wash and dry the leaves carefully and then make the dressing. The success of your dressing will depend on the quality of your oils and vinegars. Use a wine vinegar and extra virgin olive oil or a mixture of olive and a lighter oil, e.g. sunflower or arachide (see glossary) oil. A basic French dressing is usually one part vinegar to three parts oil, plus salt, freshly ground pepper and perhaps a spot of garlic and mustard. We make many different kinds of dressings, but Billy's French Dressing, named after a chef in the kitchen called Billy Motherway, seems to be a great favourite. We usually liquidise the ingredients, but this is not necessary if you make a paste of the garlic and chop the herbs finely.

Any dressing is best on the day it's made, but if you intend to keep it, add the herbs and garlic just before you serve it. I find the garlic becomes a little bitter if the dressing is kept for a few days and the herbs lose their green colour. Some people also like to add a pinch of sugar to the dressing: that's fine, though not at all 'French'. Be careful not to make it too sweet!

The greatest discovery I've made as far as salad is concerned in the last few years is the salad mix Mesculum, Saladisi or Mysticana, depending on what brand name you buy. Basically this is a mixture of seeds in a packet which you can scatter on to some peat moss in a seed tray, and leave on your window or greenhouse or garden. In a few weeks a great assortment of different lettuces and salad leaves both green and bronze will emerge and then you just cut them with a knife, wash and dry them and put them into your salad bowl. You can leave the seed tray to recover for another few weeks and cut again once or, if you are lucky, twice more. We plant Mesculum in succession and find it tremendously useful.

I've also included in this chapter several salads that can be served as a meal on their own, or as starters. Carrot and Apple Salad with Honey and Vinegar Dressing looks and tastes delicious, and has the added advantages that it only takes a few minutes to make, the ingredients are cheap and you would probably have them in the house anyway. We serve it as a starter but it is also delightful as an accompanying salad with cold meats, particularly ham or pork.

The Old-fashioned Salad is just the sort of thing you would get for tea, perhaps with a slice of ham, if you went to visit your granny in the country on a Sunday. It is delicious served with this dressing, which Myrtle Allen got from a Quaker lady called Lydia Strangman, who lived in our house years ago, hence the name Lydia's Dressing. Nowhere is the importance of having superb flavourful ingredients more evident than in this simple salad: it can be glorious or dull, depending on the quality of your ingredients.

For a light first course, I'm particularly fond of the *salades tièdes* – warm salads – which to my mind are one of the most valuable parts of the legacy of *nouvelle cuisine*, the French food fashion of the eighties. Apart from Salade Tiède with Chicken Livers, Bacon and Croûtons, I have included several mouthwatering examples to show how easy it is to invent your own combination of ingredients for these light little starter salads, in which an interesting variety of cold salad leaves is topped with something tasty, hot from the pan. Their success depends upon the contrast of flavour and texture – hot *v*. cold, soft *v*. crisp, sharp *v*. mild.

There is plenty of scope to experiment with dressings, too, using different oils and vinegars. For example, you can use walnut and hazelnut oil as well as virgin olive oil, and sherry, balsamic and champagne vinegars as well as the more ordinary red and white ones. All you need is plenty of imagination and a measure of restraint! Don't get carried away and forget to concentrate on the flavour: they should taste as stunning as they look.

GREEN SALAD WITH BILLY'S FRENCH DRESSING

2 fl oz/50 ml/¼ cup wine vinegar
6 fl oz/150 ml/¾ cup olive oil *or* a mixture of olive and other oils, e.g. sunflower and arachide
1 level teaspoon mustard (Dijon *or* English)

1 large clove garlic, crushed
1 small spring onion (scallion)
sprig of parsley
sprig of watercress
1 level teaspoon salt
few grinds of pepper

French Dressing

PUT all the ingredients into a blender and run at medium speed for 1 minute approximately, or mix oil and vinegar in a bowl, add mustard, salt, freshly ground pepper and mashed garlic. Chop the spring onion, parsley and watercress finely and add in. Whisk before serving.

Green Salad

You will need a mild lettuce (e.g. the common butterhead) as the basis of the salad and as many of the following as you care to or can put in:

> Finely chopped parsley, mint or any herbs of your fancy, tiny spring onions, dice of cucumber, mustard and cress, watercress, the white tips of cauliflower, tips of purple sprouting broccoli, iceberg lettuce, cos, radicchio, oakleaf, Chinese leaves, rocket, salad burnet, edible chrysanthemum leaves, purslane, sorrel and any other interesting lettuces available.

Wash and dry the lettuces and other leaves very carefully. Tear into bite-sized pieces and put into a deep salad bowl. Cover with clingfilm and refrigerate, if not to be served immediately. Just before serving toss with a little dressing – just enough to make the leaves glisten. Serve immediately.

NOTE: Green salad must not be dressed until just before serving, otherwise it will be tired and unappetising.

GREEN SALAD
WITH EDIBLE FLOWERS

Prepare a selection of salad leaves (see above) and add some edible flowers, e.g. marigold petals, nasturtium flowers, borage flowers, chive flowers, rocket blossoms etc.; one or all of these or some other herb flowers could be added. Toss with a well-flavoured dressing just before serving.

This salad could be served as a basis for a starter salad or as an accompanying salad to a main course. Remember to use a little restraint with the flowers!

GREEN SALAD
WITH HONEY DRESSING

For this salad, we use delicious Irish grainy mustard, such as the Lake Shore mustard flavoured with honey made by Hilary Henry on the shores of Lough Derg.

a selection of lettuces and salad leaves, e.g. butterhead, iceberg, cos, oakleaf (green *or* bronze), Chinese leaves, lollo rosso, radicchio trevisano, rocket, salad burnet, golden marjoram *or* edible chrysanthemum leaves and edible flowers

HONEY DRESSING

12 fl oz/ 350 ml/1¹/₂ cups approx. virgin olive oil	1 tablespoon whole grain mustard *or* moutarde de Meaux
4 fl oz/130 ml/¹/₂ cup cider vinegar	1 clove garlic, crushed
	1 teaspoon pure honey

WASH and dry very carefully the lettuces, salad leaves and flowers. Tear into bite-sized pieces and put into a deep salad bowl. Cover with clingfilm and refrigerate, if not to be served immediately.

Meanwhile, make the dressing. Mix all the ingredients together, whisking well before use. Just before serving, toss the leaves with a little dressing – just enough to make the leaves glisten. Serve immediately.

NOTE: Green salad must not be dressed until just before serving, otherwise it will look tired and unappetising.

Salad of Carrot and Apple with Honey and Vinegar Dressing

Serves 6

This delicious salad is very quick to make but shouldn't be prepared more than half an hour ahead, as the apple will discolour.

8 oz/225 g/2 cups grated carrot

10 oz/300 g/2 cups grated dessert apple, e.g. Cox's Orange Pippin if available

DRESSING

2 good teaspoons pure honey

4 teaspoons white wine vinegar

GARNISH

a few leaves of lettuce
sprigs of watercress *or* parsley

chive flowers if you have them

DISSOLVE the honey in the wine vinegar. Mix the grated carrot and apple together and toss in the sweet and sour dressing. Taste and add a bit more honey or vinegar as required, depending on the sweetness of the apples.

Take 6 white side plates. Arrange a few small lettuce leaves on each plate and divide the salad between the plates. Garnish with sprigs of watercress or flat parsley and sprinkle with chive flowers if you have some.

NOTE: This salad may also be served as an accompaniment and goes particularly well with cold ham, bacon or pork.

OLD-FASHIONED SALAD WITH LYDIA'S DRESSING

Serves 4

This simple old-fashioned salad is one of my absolute favourites. It can be quite delicious when it's made with a crisp lettuce, good home-grown tomatoes and cucumbers, free-range eggs and home-preserved beetroot. If on the other hand you make it with pale battery eggs, watery tomatoes, tired lettuce and cucumber and – worst of all – vinegary beetroot from a jar, you'll wonder why you bothered!

We serve this traditional salad in Ballymaloe as a starter, with an old-fashioned salad dressing which would have been popular before the days of mayonnaise.

1 butterhead lettuce (the ordinary lettuce that you can buy anywhere)
2 hard-boiled eggs, quartered
2–4 tomatoes, quartered
16 thin slices of cucumber

2–4 sliced radishes *or* 4 slices of home-preserved beetroot
4 tiny spring onions (scallions)
sprigs of watercress
chopped parsley

LYDIA'S DRESSING

2 hard-boiled eggs
1 teaspoon dry mustard
pinch of salt
1 tablespoon soft brown sugar

1 tablespoon brown malt vinegar
2–4 fl oz/55–130 ml/¹/₄–¹/₂ cup cream

HARD-BOIL the eggs for the salad and the dressing: bring a small saucepan of water to the boil, gently slide in the eggs, boil for 10 minutes (12 if they are very fresh), strain off the hot water and cover with cold water. Peel when cold.

Wash and dry the lettuce and scallions.

Next make the dressing. Cut 2 eggs in half, sieve the yolks into a bowl, add the mustard, salt and sugar. Blend in the vinegar and cream. Chop the egg whites and add some to the sauce. Keep the rest to scatter over the salad. Cover the dressing until needed.

To assemble the salads: Arrange a few lettuce leaves on each of 4 plates. Scatter a few quartered tomatoes and 2 hard-boiled egg quarters, a few slices of cucumber and 1 radish or 2 slices of beetroot on each plate. Garnish with spring onion and watercress, scatter the remaining chopped egg white (from the dressing) over the salad and some chopped parsley.

Put a tiny bowl of Lydia's dressing in the centre of each plate and serve immediately while the salad is crisp and before the beetroot starts to run. Alternatively, the dressing may be served from one large bowl.

SALAD OF PRAWNS AND COURGETTES

Serves 4 as a starter

This salad, devised by my brother Rory O'Connell, both looks and tastes stunning. The courgette (zucchini) flowers are of course edible.

4 small courgettes (zucchini) with flowers (choose shiny, firm courgettes)

24 freshly cooked and shelled prawns (for method see page 45)

a little extra virgin olive oil

sea salt and freshly ground pepper

2–2$\frac{1}{2}$ tablespoons home-made mayonnaise (see page 23)

GARNISH

chervil *or* fennel sprigs

courgette petals

Separate the flowers from the courgettes. Remove the stamens and the little thorns from the base of the flowers.

Plunge the courgettes into boiling salted water and poach until barely tender (about 4 minutes). Remove from the pot and allow to cool slightly: they will continue to cook. While still warm cut them into $\frac{1}{4}$ in/7 mm slices at an angle. Season immediately with sea salt and freshly ground pepper, sprinkle with olive oil and toss gently.

To assemble the salad, arrange 6 courgette slices on each plate and place a prawn on top of each courgette slice. Cut the long courgette flowers in two horizontally and brush them with a little oil from the courgettes. Put the base section of one flower, which is an edible container, in the centre of each plate and fill with ¹/₂ tablespoon of mayonnaise, using a piping bag if possible. Garnish the plates with the courgette petals and sprigs of chervil or fennel. Serve immediately.

NOTE: Mussels or shrimps may be used instead of prawns: allow 6–12 mussels or 12 shrimps per starter portion. If using lobster, allow 2 oz/55 g cooked lobster per portion.

MUSSEL SALAD WITH A JULIENNE OF VEGETABLES

Serves 4 as a starter

2¹/₄ lb/1 kg fresh mussels
1 small carrot cut into very fine julienne strips 2 in/5 cm long
¹/₄ cucumber peeled, seeded and cut into julienne strips 2in/5 cm long
1 avocado (optional)
1¹/₂–2¹/₂ tablespoons French dressing (see page 190)

¹/₄ pint/150 ml/generous ¹/₂ cup home-made mayonnaise (see page 23)
8 leaves lollo rosso *or* oakleaf lettuce *or* enough lamb's lettuce to make a ring on a plate
salt, sea salt and freshly ground pepper

GARNISH
very finely chopped chives and chive flowers

CHECK that all the mussels are tightly closed, wash under cold water and drain. Put into a wide saucepan and cover with a lid or a folded tea-towel. Steam open on a medium heat (this will only take 2–3 minutes). Remove the mussels from the pan just as soon as the shells open, allow to cool, remove the beards and discard the shells. Strain the mussel liquid and reserve.

Put the julienne of carrot and cucumber into a bowl of iced water and season with sea salt. Peel and dice the avocado (if using). Dilute the mayonnaise with the mussel cooking liquor to a light coating consistency.

To serve, arrange a circle of lettuce leaves on each of 4 white plates. Mix the avocado with the mussels. Arrange a little mound of this mixture in the centre of each plate and coat with the light mayonnaise. Drain the julienne of carrot and cucumber, toss in French dressing and season with salt and pepper if necessary. Place about 1 dessertspoon of this on top of the mussels. Sprinkle with finely chopped chives and chive flowers and serve.

AVOCADO MOUSSE WITH TOMATO AND BASIL SALAD

Serves 6

This is a good way of using up avocados which may be a little too soft to prepare in the usual way.

Avocado Mousse

2 ripe avocados	2 tablespoons French dressing
1/4 teaspoon grated onion	(see Billy's French Dressing,
2 fl oz/50 ml/1/4 cup home-made	page 53)
chicken stock (see page 137)	1/4 teaspoon salt
2 teaspoons lemon juice	2 rounded teaspoons gelatine

GARNISH

sprigs of fresh basil, chervil *or* lemon balm

6 round moulds (2 1/2 in/6.5 cm diameter, 1 1/2 in/4 cm deep,
2 1/2 fl oz/60 ml capacity), brushed with a light oil, e.g. arachide

PEEL and stone the avocados. Liquidise the first six ingredients together, taste and season. For every 3/4 pint/450 ml/scant 2 cups, use 2 rounded teaspoons of gelatine and 2 tablespoons of water. Sponge the gelatine in the cold water; place the bowl in a pan of simmering water until the gelatine has completely dissolved. Add a little of the avocado mixture to the gelatine, stir well and then combine with the remainder of the avocado purée. Stir well again. Pour into the prepared moulds and leave to set for 4 or 5 hours.

To serve: Turn out each mousse and place in the centre of a white plate and garnish with a ring of Tomato and Basil Salad and some sprigs of basil, chervil or lemon balm.

NOTE: If the avocado purée does not measure ¾ pint/450 ml/ scant 2 cups, make up with one tablespoon or more of whipped cream.

Tomato and Basil Salad

6 very ripe, firm tomatoes	French dressing (see Billy's
salt and freshly ground pepper	French Dressing, page 53)
and sugar	1 teaspoon chopped fresh basil *or*
	mint

SLICE the tomatoes into 3 or 4 rounds through the centre. Arrange in a single layer on a flat plate. Sprinkle with salt, sugar and several grinds of pepper. Toss immediately in just enough French dressing to coat, and sprinkle with chopped mint or basil. Taste for seasoning. Tomatoes must be dressed immediately they are cut to seal in their flavour.

SALADE TIÈDE WITH CHICKEN LIVERS, BACON AND CROÛTONS

Serves 4

a selection of lettuces and salad leaves, e.g butterhead, iceberg, lollo rosso, frisée and golden marjoram

8 nasturtium flowers (optional)

12 tiny croûtons of white bread

4 oz/110 g streaky bacon, in one piece

6 fresh chicken livers

salt and freshly ground pepper

DRESSING

1 tablespoon red wine vinegar

1 small clove garlic, mashed

2 teaspoons chopped parsley

3 tablespoons olive oil *or* 1½ tablespoons olive oil and 1½ tablespoons sunflower oil

FIRST make the croûtons. If you can find a very thin French stick, cut ¼ in/7 mm slices off that; alternatively, stamp out slices in rounds from a slice of white bread with a biscuit cutter 1½ in/4 cm wide. Then spread a little butter on each side and bake in a moderate oven, 180°C/350°F/gas 4 for approximately 20 minutes or until golden on both sides; it may be necessary to turn them halfway through cooking. Drain on kitchen paper and keep warm. (Croûtons can be prepared ahead and reheated later.)

Next make the dressing by whisking all the ingredients together. Remove the rind from the bacon and cut into ¼ in/7 mm lardons (see glossary); blanch, refresh in cold water, drain and dry on kitchen paper. Wash and dry the salad leaves and tear into bite-sized bits. Wash and dry the chicken livers and divide each liver into 2 pieces. Just before serving, heat a dash of oil in a frying pan and sauté the lardons of bacon until crisp and golden.

TO SERVE: Shake the dressing and toss the salad leaves in just enough dressing to make them glisten. Divide between 4 plates making sure that there is some height in the centre; it should look as though it has been dropped on to the plate, but if it doesn't drop reasonably attractively you could rearrange the leaves slightly.

Scatter the hot bacon over the salad, season the chicken livers and cook gently in the bacon fat for just a few minutes. I like them slightly pink in the centre, but if you want them better done, cook for a minute or two longer. Arrange 3 pieces around the top of each salad, put 3 croûtons on each plate, garnish with a few nasturtium flowers for the peppery taste and extra 'posh' appearance and serve immediately.

Salade Tiède with Avocado, Bacon and Walnut Oil Dressing

Serves 6

a selection of lettuces and salad leaves, e.g. butterhead, iceberg, endive, radicchio trevisano, watercress, salad burnet, tiny spring onions etc. – the larger the selection the more interesting the salad will be 6 oz/170 g streaky bacon, in one piece, green *or* lightly smoked 4 slices of white bread 1 large *or* 2 small avocados

WALNUT OIL DRESSING

4 tablespoons walnut oil *or* 2 tablespoons each walnut oil and sunflower *or* arachide oil mixed
1 generous tablespoon vinegar

1 teaspoon chopped chives
1 teaspoon chopped parsley
salt and freshly ground pepper

GARNISH

18 walnut halves

WASH and dry the salad leaves and tear them into bite-sized pieces. Put into a bowl, cover and refrigerate until needed. Cut the rind off the piece of bacon and discard. Cut the bacon into ¼ in/ 7 mm lardons (see glossary) and then blanch and refresh in cold water if necessary. Dry on kitchen paper. Cut the crusts off the bread and cut into exact $^1/_4$ in/7 mm cubes. Fry until golden in clarified butter (see page 46) or a mixture of butter and oil. Drain on kitchen paper. Make the dressing in the usual way by whisking the ingredients together; add the chopped herbs. Halve the avocado, remove the stone, peel and cut into $^1/_2$ in/1 cm dice.

TO SERVE: Toss the salad in just enough dressing to make the leaves glisten. Add the crisp, warm croûtons and the diced avocado. Toss gently and divide the salad between 6 plates. Fry the bacon in a little olive oil in a hot pan until crisp and golden, then scatter the *hot* bacon over the salad. Garnish with a few walnut halves. Serve immediately.

A WARM SALAD OF MUSSELS WITH TOMATO CONCASSÉ AND WATERCRESS

Serves 4

a selection of as many types of lettuces and salad leaves as are available, e.g. iceberg, endive, rocket, oakleaf and butterhead watercress for garnishing
2 spring onions (scallions)
24 mussels

1 tomato peeled, seeded and flesh cut into $^1/_4$ in/7 mm dice (concassé)
1 avocado
salt, freshly ground pepper and sugar

FRENCH DRESSING

1 tablespoon wine vinegar
2 tablespoons sunflower oil *or* arachide oil
1 tablespoon virgin olive oil
1 small clove garlic (made into a paste)

1 tiny spring onion (scallion) finely chopped
1 teaspoon of finely chopped parsley
a pinch of mustard
salt and freshly ground pepper

LIQUIDISE or whisk the above ingredients for the dressing.
Wash and dry the required amount of salad leaves and tear into

bite-sized pieces. Season the tomato concassé with salt, freshly ground pepper and sugar. Cut the scallions, both green and white parts, into slices at an angle. Wash the mussels well, put them into a heavy frying pan in a single layer, cover with a folded tea-towel and place on a low heat. As soon as the shells start to open, lift them from the pan, take the mussels from their shells and remove the beard as you do so.

Halve and peel the avocado, remove the stone, cut the flesh into $1/4$ in/7 mm dice and season with salt and freshly ground pepper. Just before serving, toss the salad leaves gently with French dressing – just enough to make the leaves glisten. Arrange the salad on 4 white plates, heaping it slightly in the centre. Arrange the warm mussels and avocado on the salad as appetisingly as possible. Sprinkle with tomato concassé and sliced scallions. Garnish with sprigs of watercress and serve immediately.

WARM SALAD OF SCALLOPS WITH TOASTED PINE KERNELS AND AVOCADO

Really fresh pine kernels are difficult to find – they go rancid very quickly, so ask to taste one before you buy. If you do find good ones, buy extra and freeze some.

Serves 4

8 scallops
1 oz/30 g/$1/4$ cup pine kernels
3–4 tablespoons olive oil
1–1$1/2$ tablespoons balsamic
vinegar *or* white wine vinegar
salt and freshly ground pepper

$1/2$ teaspoons Dijon mustard
selection of salad leaves, e.g.
lamb's lettuce, radicchio, frizzy
lettuce, watercress
1 ripe avocado

GARNISH
a few sprigs of fresh chervil

DETACH the corals from the scallops. Cut the scallop nuggets in half across the centre and dry well on kitchen paper. Toast the pine kernels under a hot grill or in a moderate oven until golden (approximately 5 minutes). Whisk the olive oil, vinegar and mustard together to make a vinaigrette and season to taste. Wash the lettuces well, shake dry and tear into bite-sized pieces.

Just before serving season the scallops with salt and freshly ground pepper and fry quickly in a non-stick pan for about 1 minute on each side, turning once only. Remove from the pan and keep warm.

Cut the avocado in half. Peel, slice thinly and fan out, putting a quarter on each plate. Put the salad leaves in a deep bowl. Toss with a little of the vinaigrette and place a portion of salad on each plate in a mound beside the avocado, arrange the slices of scallop over the salad and sprinkle with chervil leaves and toasted pine kernels. Serve immediately.

A WARM SALAD WITH BLUE CHEESE

Serves 4

Some ripe, crumbly Cashel Blue cheese – made in Fethard, Co. Tipperary by Jane and Louis Grubb – would be wonderful for this salad.

a selection of lettuces and salad leaves, e.g. iceberg, endive, rocket, oakleaf and butterhead	1¹/₂ oz/45 g/3 tablespoons soft butter
12 round croûtons of bread, ¹/₄ in/7 mm cut from a thin French stick	1 clove garlic, peeled 5 oz/140 g smoked streaky bacon, in one piece 2 oz/55 g blue cheese

VINAIGRETTE DRESSING

1 tablespoon balsamic vinegar *or*
sherry vinegar *or* red wine
vinegar
1 tablespoon arachide *or*
sunflower oil

2 tablespoons olive oil
salt and freshly ground pepper
2 teaspoons chopped chervil and
2 teaspoons chopped tarragon *or*
4 teaspoons chopped parsley

GARNISH

1 heaped tablespoon sprigs of chervil *or* freshly chopped parsley

WHISK the above ingredients together for the dressing.

Wash and dry the mixture of lettuces and salad leaves and tear into bite-sized pieces. Spread both sides of the rounds of bread with softened butter. Put on to a baking sheet and bake in a moderate oven, 180°C/350°F/gas 4, until golden and crisp on both sides, for approximately 20 minutes. Rub them with a cut clove of garlic and keep hot in a low oven with the door slightly open. Cut the rind off the piece of bacon and discard. Cut the bacon into $^1/_4$ in/7 mm lardons (see glossary) and then blanch and refresh in cold water if necessary. Dry well on kitchen paper. Just before serving, sauté the bacon in a little olive oil until golden.

TO SERVE: Dress the lettuces with some vinaigrette in a salad bowl. Use just enough to make the leaves glisten. Crumble the cheese with a fork and add it to the salad, tossing them well together. Divide between 4 plates. Scatter the *hot* crispy bacon over the top, put 3 warm croûtons on each plate and sprinkle sprigs of chervil or chopped parsley over the salad. Serve immediately.

A WARM SALAD OF GOAT'S CHEESE WITH WALNUT OIL DRESSING

Serves 6

1 fresh, soft goat's cheese, e.g. Cléire, Lough Caum *or* St Tola
6 slices toasted French bread
18–24 fresh walnuts
a selection of lettuces and salad leaves, e.g. butterhead, frisée, oakleaf,
radicchio trevisano, rocket, salad burnet, golden marjoram, and
chive *or* wild garlic flowers to garnish

WALNUT OIL DRESSING

2 tablespoons white wine vinegar	2 tablespoons sunflower *or* arachide oil
4 tablespoons walnut oil	salt and freshly ground pepper

WASH and dry the salad leaves and tear all the large leaves into bite-sized bits. Make the dressing by whisking all the ingredients together. Cover each piece of toasted French bread with a ³/₄ in/2 cm slice of goat's cheese. Just before serving, preheat the grill. Place the slices of bread and cheese under the grill and toast for 5 or 6 minutes or until the cheese is soft and slightly golden.

Meanwhile, toss the salad greens lightly in the dressing and drop a small handful on to each plate. Place a hot goat's cheese croûton in the centre of each salad, scatter with a few walnut pieces and serve immediately. We sprinkle wild garlic or chive flowers over the salad in season.

NOTE: This salad may be used either as a starter or as a cheese course.

A Warm Winter Salad with Duck Livers and Hazelnut Oil Dressing

Serves 4

6 fresh duck livers *or*, if
unavailable, chicken livers
1/2 oz/15 g/1 tablespoon butter
12 chicory leaves
2 oz/55 g/1 cup grated celeriac

4 leaves of butterhead lettuce
4 sprigs of watercress
2 large leaves of iceberg lettuce
4 leaves of radicchio trevisano *or*
4 leaves of oakleaf lettuce

2 oz/55 g/1 cup grated carrot

HAZELNUT OIL DRESSING

6 tablespoons hazelnut oil   salt and freshly ground pepper
2 tablespoons wine vinegar

GARNISH
1 tablespoon chopped chives

Wash and dry the salad leaves and tear them into bite-sized pieces. Whisk together the ingredients for the dressing. Toss the grated carrot and celeriac in approximately 3 tablespoons of dressing. Taste and season with salt and freshly ground pepper if necessary. Toss the salad leaves in a little more of the dressing – just enough to make the leaves glisten.

Melt the butter in a sauté pan, season the livers and cook over a gentle heat. While the livers are cooking, arrange 3 leaves of chicory in a star shape on each plate. Put a mound of salad leaves in the centre with some celeriac and carrot on top. Finally, cut the livers in half and while still warm arrange 3 pieces on each salad. Sprinkle with chopped chives and serve immediately.

FISH

I'll never forget the first time I tasted really fresh fish – what a revelation! Tim, who is now my husband, cooked fresh plaice for me the first evening I came to Ballymaloe (the way to a girl's heart and all that!). My home was in a little village called Cullohill in Co. Laois and when I was a child the bus travelling from Dublin to Cork dropped off fish every Thursday evening (ready for Friday!) at the shop in our village. It was usually whiting and smoked haddock and occasionally, when we were lucky, some plaice. Plaice was our great favourite; we looked forward to it, dipped in seasoned flour and cooked in a little butter in the pan. I now know that the 'grand name' for that method is *à la meunière*, but to me then it was simply fried plaice. We thought it was delicious – that was until I tasted really fresh plaice! It was incredible, I simply couldn't believe that it was the same fish. The sad thing is, there must be lots of people, particularly those living far from the sea, who still have never tasted really fresh fish and so can't quite appreciate what all the excitement is about. It's not until you taste fish in season, fresh from the sea that you suddenly realize how exquisite it can be.

We now live only two miles from the fishing village of Ballycotton, so we get the most wonderful fish direct from the fishermen on the pier. Most of this is still caught in small boats and is landed every day, so the quality is superb. Fishing is not an easy life and fishermen often toil in wretched weather to bring us our catches of beautiful silver fish, which makes me all the more determined to cook it as soon, and as well, as possible.

The recipes included in this section have been chosen not only because they are delicious but also because they include techniques that can be used for many different kinds of fish. We pan-grill the mackerel and serve it with maître d'hôtel butter but, of course, fillets or pieces of almost any fresh fish can be cooked in this way. Mackerel is particularly wonderful within hours of being caught – local fishermen always say that for perfection the sun shouldn't set on a mackerel before you eat it.

The technique we use for Baked Plaice or Sole with Herb Butter is one of our favourite ways of cooking flat fish. As a cooking method it has all the advantages because the fish is cooked on the bone for extra flavour, and with the skin on so it will stay moist. The skin is cut so you can peel it off easily and then spoon any sauce you choose over the fish, or if you just like to eat fish absolutely as it is for reasons of diet, then this is also a perfect way to cook it because it's totally fat free. We also cook brill or turbot this way.

I've included a recipe for cooking fish in foil for those who like to cook a whole fish but don't have a fish kettle. Again, many fish – as well as salmon and sea mullet – can be cooked in this way.

Wild Irish salmon, poached gently in boiling salted water and served with a simple Hollandaise Sauce made from good Irish butter, can scarcely be bettered. When wild salmon is out of season, use the best farmed salmon available to you. Bass, cod and the delicious and greatly underestimated grey sea mullet are also wonderful served this way.

Cod Baked with Cream and Bay Leaves is a master recipe which can be used for all kinds of round fish. You can ring the changes by using a different fresh herb or a mixture of herbs, as in Sea Trout with Cream and Fresh Herbs.

I include Hake in Buttered Crumbs for two reasons. The first is that it is one of those terrific dishes that never fails to please adults and children alike (even fish haters!). The second is that this is a master recipe which can be used for any round fish – cod, haddock, pollock, ling or grey sea mullet. This recipe also includes the basic technique for making Béchamel sauce – useful on its own or with many different flavourings (for example, cheese, as in Mornay sauce), and indispensable for making fish pies. The beauty of Béchamel is that anything coated in it can be reheated perfectly. This is not the case, alas, with grander sauces such as Hollandaise.

Hollandaise Sauce does, however, make any fish into a feast

and, believe it or not, can be made well inside five minutes. It's a 'mother' sauce so once you have mastered this technique you can make lots of 'daughter' sauces by just adding different garnishes, for example, the Sauce Mousseline with turbot or brill, or the Cucumber and Tomato Hollandaise that we serve with monkfish.

I've also given a number of lovely recipes using mussels, the cheapest of all shellfish and the most widely available, both farmed and wild. I've noticed that a lot of people love eating mussels in restaurants (huge platefuls of garlicky Mussels Provençale are frequently polished off by individuals who say they can't stand garlic!) – but they are nervous about cooking them at home. Let me reassure any of you who are worried about pollution and possible food poisoning: there really is no cause for concern if you buy from a reliable source, because no fishmonger worth his salt can afford to risk selling unpurified mussels.

As far as freshness is concerned, it's easy to check this yourself. The shells should be tightly shut or should tighten up when tapped against a worktop. This safety rule is simple: if in doubt, throw it out!

Although mussels are available all year round, they are at their best, like oysters, when there is an 'r' in the month. It really is worth learning how to deal with them, because they can be added to so many other fish dishes for variety. And on their own they are divine. What could be nicer for supper than a bowl of freshly-cooked mussels served with a good home-made mayonnaise and some crusty brown soda bread!

In fact, every fish has its season, and there is all the difference in the world between a meltingly tender plaice in summer, and a watery, roe-filled one in January. The variation in flavour can be so dramatic that it is hard to believe you are actually eating the same fish, so train yourself to 'think season', as you would for vegetables.

Both Monkfish Steamed in its Own Juices with Tomato and Dill and Three-minute Fish are favourites of mine, shown to me by the wonderful English cook Jane Grigson who was such an inspiration. The first is useful because it works equally well with monkfish, halibut, sea bass or turbot. The second is simply the fastest fish dish I know. A mixture of pink and white fish looks especially pretty, and a good fruity olive oil gives a marvellous flavour. Timing is crucial, however. The eaters must be at the table, poised, the minute the oven door is opened!

A Note About Buying Fresh Fish

Fresh is the only way to eat fish and that's that, so it's absolutely vital to be able to judge accurately whether fish is fresh or not. You sure as hell can't trust your fishmonger and you can't blame him either: he is dealing with a very perishable product and occasionally needs to have some dummies on whom he can palm off stale fish, otherwise he'd go broke. Just make sure it's not you!

So let me give you a bit of advice on what to look out for. Fresh fish looks bright, slippery and lively – and not at all dull. The white underskin of flat fish should be really white and not yellowing. Stale fish really looks miserable. The eyes will be sunken and the skin can be gritty and dry and sometimes shiny, with a strong fishy smell. That's straightforward enough, but between the time fish is really fresh and the time it is really stale there are several days during which it will be gradually deteriorating. It is in this period that it's difficult to tell just what condition it is in, particularly if the fish has been cut into small pieces. You have to judge by the colour and smell. White fish should be white and the best thing of all to remember is that fresh fish doesn't smell fishy – it just has the merest scent of the sea, reminiscent of fresh seaweed.

It is well worthwhile building up a good relationship with your fishmonger, just as you do with your butcher. Ask for help and take the opportunity to learn every time you go shopping. When you get some delicious fresh fish remember to say how much you enjoyed it, but on the other hand if you get stale fish, hand it back gently but firmly, reminding your fishmonger that he or she must have known perfectly well that it wasn't fresh when they sold it to you.

For those who live far from the sea, frozen fish fillets can be excellent. Good firms freeze their fish within hours of it being caught, so it is far preferable to fresh fish several days old.

POACHED SALMON WITH HOLLANDAISE SAUCE

Serves 8

Most cookbooks you look up will tell you to poach salmon in a 'court bouillon'. This is a mixture of wine and water with perhaps some sliced carrots, onion, peppercorns and a bouquet garni including a bay leaf, but I feel very strongly that a beautiful salmon is at its best poached gently in just boiling salted water.

The proportion of salt to water is very important. We use 1 rounded tablespoon of salt to every 40 fl oz/2 Imperial pints (1.1 litres/5 cups) of water. Although the fish or piece of fish should be just covered with water, the aim is to use the minimum amount of water to preserve the maximum flavour, so you should use a saucepan that will fit the fish exactly.

To Poach a Piece of Salmon

3–3½ lb/1.35–1.6 kg centre-cut of fresh salmon	salt
water	Hollandaise sauce (see below)

GARNISH

fennel, chervil *or* parsley	8 lemon segments

CHOOSE a saucepan that fits the piece of fish exactly: an oval cast-iron saucepan is usually perfect. Half fill with measured salted water, bring to the boil, put in the piece of fish, cover, bring back to the boil and simmer gently for 20 minutes. Turn off the heat, allow to sit in the water and serve within 15–20 minutes.

If a small piece of fish is cooked in a large saucepan of water, much of the flavour will escape into the water, so for this reason we use the smallest saucepan possible. Needless to say we never poach a salmon cutlet because in that case one has the maximum surface exposed to the water and therefore maximum loss of flavour. A salmon cutlet is best dipped in a little seasoned flour and cooked slowly in a little butter in a pan, or alternatively pan-grilled with a little butter. Serve with a few pats of maître d'hôtel butter (see page 83) and a wedge of lemon.

Hollandaise Sauce

Serves 4–6, depending on what it is to be served with

Hollandaise is the 'mother' of all the warm emulsion sauces. The version we use here is easy to make and quite delicious with fish. Like mayonnaise, it takes less than 5 minutes to make and transforms any fish into a 'feast'. Once the sauce is made it must be kept warm: the temperature should not go above 180°C/350°F or the sauce will curdle. A thermos flask can provide a simple solution on a small scale, otherwise put the Hollandaise sauce into a delph or plastic bowl in a saucepan of hot but not simmering water. Hollandaise sauce cannot be reheated absolutely successfully so it's best to make just the quantity you need. If, however, you have a little left over, use it to enrich sauces, such as Cod with Cream and Bay Leaves (page 95), or Duchesse Potato (page 197).

2 egg yolks, free-range	4 oz/110 g butter cut into dice
1 dessertspoon cold water	1 teaspoon lemon juice approx.

Serve with poached fish, eggs and vegetables.

Put the egg yolks in a heavy stainless steel saucepan on a low heat, or in a bowl over hot water. Add the water and whisk thoroughly. Add the butter bit by bit, whisking all the time. As soon as one piece melts, add the next piece. The mixture will gradually thicken, but if it shows signs of becoming too thick or slightly 'scrambling', remove from the heat immediately and add a little cold water if necessary. Do not leave the pan or stop whisking until the sauce is made. Finally add the lemon juice to taste. If the sauce is slow to thicken it may be because you are excessively cautious and the heat is too low. Increase the heat slightly and continue to whisk until the sauce thickens to coating consistency.

It is important to remember that if you are making Hollandaise sauce in a saucepan directly over the heat, it should be possible to put your hand on the side of the saucepan at any stage. If the saucepan feels too hot for your hand it is also too hot for the sauce.

Another good tip if you are making Hollandaise sauce for the first time is to keep a bowl of cold water close by so you can plunge the bottom of the saucepan into it if it becomes too hot.

Keep the sauce warm until serving either in a bowl over warm water, or in a thermos flask.

POACHED WHOLE SALMON OR SEA TROUT TO BE SERVED HOT OR COLD

A whole poached salmon served hot or cold is always a dish for a very special occasion. Long gone are the days when the servants in great houses complained bitterly if they had to eat salmon more than twice a week!

If you want to poach a salmon or sea trout whole with the head and tail on, then you really need access to a 'fish kettle'. This is a long narrow saucepan which will hold a fish of $8^{1}/_{2}$–9 lb/3.7–4 kg weight. If you do not have a fish kettle but want to keep the fish whole the best solution is to bake it in the oven wrapped in tinfoil (see below).

Alternatively, you could cut the salmon into three pieces, and cook them separately in the way I describe for cooking a piece of salmon on page 74. Later, you could arrange the salmon on a board or serving dish, skin it and do a cosmetic job with rosettes of mayonnaise and lots of fresh herbs.

An 8 lb/3.4 kg salmon will feed sixteen people generously and could be enough for twenty. $4^{1}/_{2}$–5 oz/125–140 g cooked salmon is generally plenty to allow per person as salmon is very rich. Use any left-over bits for mousse or Salmon Rillettes (see page 33).

Poached Whole Salmon or Sea Trout
to be served Hot

1 whole salmon *or* sea trout	salt
water	

GARNISH

sprigs of fresh parsley, lemon balm and fennel	Hollandaise sauce (see page 75) 1 lemon segment for each person

fish kettle

CLEAN and gut the salmon carefully; do not remove the head, tail or scales. Carefully measure the water and half fill the fish kettle, adding 1 rounded tablespoon of salt to every 40 fl oz/2 Imperial pints (1.1 litre/5 cups). Cover the fish kettle and bring the water to the boil. Add the salmon or sea trout and allow the water to come back to the boil. Cover and simmer gently for 20 minutes. Then turn off the heat and leave the salmon in the water until you wish to serve. It will keep hot for 20–30 minutes.

TO SERVE: Carefully lift the whole fish out of the fish kettle and leave to drain on the rack for a few minutes. Then slide on to a large hot serving dish, preferably a beautiful long white china dish, but failing that, whatever it will fit on! Garnish with lots of parsley, lemon balm and fennel and the segments of lemon. I don't remove the skin until I am serving it at the table, then I peel it back gradually as I serve; however, if you prefer, remove the skin just at the last second before bringing it to the table. When you have served all the fish from the top, remove the bone as delicately as possible, put it aside and continue as before. Serve with Hollandaise sauce.

Poached Whole Salmon or Sea Trout
to be served Cold

1 whole salmon *or* sea trout   salt
water

GARNISH

crisp lettuce leaves   1 lemon segment
sprigs of watercress, lemon   for each person
balm, fennel and fennel flowers   home-made mayonnaise
if available   (see page 23)

fish kettle

CLEAN and gut the salmon carefully; do not remove the head, tail or scales. Carefully measure the water and half fill the fish kettle, adding 1 rounded tablespoon of salt to every 40 fl oz/2 Imperial pints (1.1 litre/5 cups). Cover the fish kettle and bring the water to the boil. Add the salmon or sea trout and allow the water to come back to the boil. Simmer for just 2 minutes and then turn off the heat. *Keep the lid on* and allow the fish to cool completely in the water (the fish should be just barely covered in the water).

TO SERVE: When the fish is barely cold, remove from the fish kettle and drain for a few minutes. Line a large board or serving dish with fresh crisp lettuce leaves, top with sprigs of watercress, lemon balm and fennel and fennel flowers if available. Carefully slide the salmon on to the board. Just before serving, peel off the top skin, leave the tail and head intact. (We don't scrape off the brown flesh in the centre because it tastes good.) Pipe a line of home-made mayonnaise along the centre of the salmon length-ways, garnish with tiny sprigs of fennel and fennel flowers or very thin twists of cucumber. Put some segments of lemons around the dish between the lettuces and herbs. Resist the temptation to use any tomato or – horror of horrors – to put a slice of stuffed olive over the eye! The pale pink of the salmon flesh against the crisp lettuces and fresh herbs seems just perfect. Serve with a bowl of good home-made mayonnaise.

WHOLE SALMON OR SEA TROUT COOKED IN FOIL

---

1 salmon *or* sea trout, 8–9 lb/ 3.4–4 kg approx.

4 oz/110 g/¹/₂ cup butter approx.

sea salt and freshly ground pepper

sprig of fennel

GARNISH

lemon segments and sprigs of parsley *or* fennel

a large sheet of good quality tinfoil

PREHEAT the oven to 180°C/350°F/gas 4.

Clean and gut the fish if necessary, dry carefully. Put the sheet of tinfoil on a large baking sheet, preferably with edges. Place the salmon in the centre of the sheet of tinfoil. Smear butter on both sides and put a few lumps in the centre. Season with salt and freshly ground pepper and put a sprig of fennel in the centre if you have it. Be generous with the butter; it will mix with the juices to make a delicious sauce to spoon over your cooked fish. Bring the tinfoil together loosely and seal the edges well.

Bake for approximately 90 minutes (allow 10 minutes per 1 lb/450 g). Open the package, be careful of the steam. Test by lifting the flesh off the backbone just at the thickest point where the flesh meets the head. The fish should lift off the bone easily and there should be no trace of blood; if there is, seal again and pop back in the oven for 5 or 10 minutes, but be careful not to overcook it.

Serve hot or cold. If you are serving it hot, spoon the juices over each helping, or use the butter and juice to make a Hollandaise-type sauce by whisking the hot melted butter and salmon juice gradually into 2 egg yolks, and add a little lemon juice to taste. If the fish is to be served cold, serve with some freshly made salads and a bowl of home-made mayonnaise. Garnish with parsley and fennel.

SALMON WITH TOMATO AND FRESH HERB SALSA

Serves 6

This is a refreshing new way of serving salmon with a distinct Californian flavour. This recipe would also be delicious for pan-grilled tuna fish steaks. Remember to cook them rare so they will be moist and juicy.

$2^1/_4$ lb/1.1 kg fresh wild salmon   salt

TOMATO AND FRESH HERB SALSA

6 very ripe tomatoes, peeled, seeded and cut into $^1/_4$ in/7 mm dice

$1-1^1/_2$ tablespoons freshly chopped oregano (annual marjoram)

$1-1^1/_2$ tablespoons basil

$1-1^1/_2$ tablespoons parsley

$1-1^1/_2$ tablespoons thyme leaves

4 fl oz/120 ml/$^1/_2$ cup extra virgin olive oil

1 teaspoon sea salt

freshly ground pepper

FIRST poach the salmon. Choose a saucepan which will barely fit the piece of fish: an oval cast-iron one is usually perfect. Half fill with measured salted water (1 tablespoon salt to every 2 pints water), bring to the boil, put in the piece of fish, bring back to the boil, cover and simmer gently for 20 minutes. Turn off the heat, allow to sit in the water and serve within 15–20 minutes.

Mix together all the ingredients for the salsa, taste and correct seasoning. When the salmon is cooked divide into portions and serve on hot plates surrounded by the cold tomato and fresh herb salsa.

NOTE: The salmon may also be pan-grilled for this recipe.

SEA TROUT WITH CREAM AND FRESH HERBS

Serves 2

1 lb/450 g sea trout fillets
2 teaspoons chopped onion
¹/₂ oz/15 g/1 tablespoon butter
8 fl oz/250 ml/1 cup creamy
milk (we use ¹/₂ cream and
¹/₂ milk)

1 oz/30 g/¹/₂ cup chopped herbs:
fennel, chives, parsley, chervil
and thyme leaves
roux (optional, see glossary)
salt and freshly ground pepper

GARNISH
sprigs of fresh fennel

CHOOSE a frying pan that is just big enough to hold the fish in a single layer. Melt the butter and fry the onion gently in it for 2 minutes. Add the trout and brown on both sides. Season with salt and freshly ground pepper. Cover with creamy milk and 1 tablespoon of chopped herbs; bring it to simmering point. Cover the pan with a tight-fitting lid and cook on a gentle heat for about 5–10 minutes. Keep a good eye on the fish as it's easy to overcook it. Just as soon as the fish is pale pink and no longer opaque, remove it to a serving dish. Bring the pan juices back to the boil, and thicken slightly by whisking in a little roux or by reducing the liquid. Add the remainder of the freshly chopped herbs. Taste and correct seasoning if necessary. Spoon the sauce over the fish. Garnish it with sprigs of fresh fennel and serve immediately.

Trout with Ginger Butter

Serves 6

This fresh ginger butter is also very good with other grilled fish such as salmon, sea bass or grey sea mullet.

6 fresh pink rainbow trout
salt and freshly ground pepper

olive oil for brushing

GINGER BUTTER

3 oz/85 g/6 tablespoons unsalted butter
1 tablespoon finely chopped spring onion (scallion) *or* shallot

1 1/2–2 tablespoons dry vermouth
1 1/2–2 tablespoons fresh ginger, grated

GARNISH
whole chives and chive flowers if available

FIRST make the ginger butter. Melt 1/2 oz/1 tablespoon (15 g) butter and sweat the spring onion or shallot for a few minutes over a gentle heat until it is almost soft. Add the vermouth and cook until it has all been absorbed. Scrape this mixture into a bowl of a food processor and add the grated ginger. Whizz for a few seconds, allow to cool, add the remainder of the butter and whizz until smooth. Taste, season with salt and freshly ground pepper. Put into a bowl and refrigerate until needed.

Gut, fillet, wash and dry the trout carefully and season with salt and freshly ground pepper. Preheat a grill pan, brush the trout with olive oil and cook flesh-side down for about 3 minutes, then turn over carefully and cook on the skin side for a further 3 or 4 minutes, depending on the thickness of the fillets.

Serve on hot plates with a little ginger butter melting on top. Garnish with whole chives and chive flowers if available.

PAN-GRILLED MACKEREL WITH MAÎTRE D'HÔTEL BUTTER

Serves 4

8 fillets of very fresh mackerel
(allow 6 oz/170 g fish for main
course, 3 oz/85 g for a starter)

seasoned flour
small knob of butter

MAÎTRE D'HÔTEL BUTTER

2 oz/55 g/4 tablespoons butter
juice of ½ lemon

4 teaspoons finely chopped
parsley

GARNISH

4 lemon segments

parsley

FIRST make the maître d'hôtel butter. Cream the butter, stir in the parsley and a few drops of lemon juice at a time. Roll into butter pats or form into a roll and wrap in greaseproof paper or tinfoil, screwing each end so that it looks like a cracker. Refrigerate to harden.

Heat the grill pan. Dip the fish fillets in flour which has been seasoned with salt and freshly ground pepper. Shake off the excess flour and then spread a little butter with a knife on the flesh side, as though you were buttering a slice of bread rather meanly. When the grill is quite hot but not smoking, place the fish fillets butter side down on the grill; the fish should sizzle as soon as they touch the pan. Turn down the heat slightly and let them cook for 4 or 5 minutes on that side before you turn them over. Continue to cook on the other side until crisp and golden. Serve on a hot plate with some slices of maître d'hôtel butter and a segment of lemon. Maître d'hôtel butter may be served directly on the fish, or if you have a pretty shell, place it at the side of the plate as a container for the butter. Garnish with parsley.

NOTE: Fillets of any small fish are delicious pan-grilled in this way. Fish under 2 lb/900 g such as mackerel, herring and brown trout can also be grilled whole on the pan. Fish over 2 lb/900 g can be filleted first and then cut across into portions. Large fish 4–6 lb/1.8–2.7 kg can also be grilled whole. Cook them for approximately 10–15 minutes on each side and then put in a hot oven for another 15 minutes or so to finish cooking.

SAUTÉ OF MACKEREL WITH MUSHROOMS AND HERBS

Serves 4

4 very fresh mackerel	4 teaspoons finely chopped fresh
seasoned flour	herbs: thyme, parsley, chives,
½ oz/15 g/1 tablespoon butter	fennel and lemon balm
4 oz/125 g mushrooms	1–2 cloves garlic

FILLET the mackerel, wash, dry and dip in flour which has been seasoned with salt and freshly ground pepper. Melt the butter in a pan large enough to take the fish in a single layer, and sauté the fish until golden on both sides. Meanwhile, chop the mushrooms and herbs finely and crush the garlic.

Remove the fish to a hot serving dish or 4 individual plates. Add the mushrooms and garlic to the pan. Cook for 2 or 3 minutes, add the fresh herbs and season with a little salt and freshly ground pepper if necessary. Serve this mixture as a garnish down the centre of the fish.

NOTE: This mushroom, garlic and herb mixture is also delicious served with sauté chicken livers on toast, as a first course.

Poached Mackerel with Bretonne Sauce

Serves 6

Fresh mackerel cooked like this is exquisite with Bretonne sauce; it may be served as a starter or main course.

6 very fresh mackerel   1 teaspoon salt
              2 pints/1.1 l/5 cups water

BRETONNE SAUCE

2 egg yolks, preferably free-   2 tablespoons mixed finely
              range   chopped chives, fennel, parsley
1 teaspoon French mustard   and thyme
(we use Maille mustard with   6 oz/170 g/3/4 cup butter
        green herbs)

First make the Bretonne sauce. Whisk the egg yolks in a bowl with the mustard and finely chopped herbs. Bring the butter to the boil and pour it in a steady stream on to the egg yolks, whisking continuously until the sauce thickens to a light coating consistency like a Hollandaise. Keep warm in a flask, or place in a pottery or plastic bowl (*not* stainless steel), in a saucepan of hot but not boiling water.

Cut the heads off the mackerel, gut and clean but keep whole. Bring water to the boil and add salt and the mackerel. Bring back to boiling point, cover and remove from the heat.

After about 5–8 minutes, check to see whether the fish are cooked. The flesh should lift off the bone. Remove the mackerel on to a plate, scrape off the skin and carefully lift the fillets off the bones and on to a serving plate. Coat carefully with warm sauce. Serve with a good green salad and perhaps some new potatoes.

MACKEREL WITH CREAM AND DILL

Serves 4 as a main course, 8 as a starter

Dill, which is an annual herb, is particularly good with mackerel. One wouldn't normally think of cream with an oily fish but this combination is surprisingly delicious and very fast to cook.

4 fresh mackerel	6 fl oz/175 ml/³/₄ cup cream
salt and freshly ground pepper	2–2¹/₂ tablespoons fresh dill,
¹/₄ oz/8 g butter	finely chopped

GUT the mackerel, fillet carefully, wash and dry well. Season with salt and freshly ground pepper. Melt the butter in a frying pan, fry the mackerel fillets flesh side down until golden brown, turn over on to the skin side, add the cream and freshly chopped dill. Simmer gently for 3 or 4 minutes or until the mackerel is cooked, taste the sauce and serve immediately.

GREY SEA MULLET BAKED WITH BUTTER

Serves 4

Grey sea mullet is possibly the most under-estimated fish in our waters at present. Its flavour and texture are in my opinion every bit as good as sea bass but it costs a fraction of the price, so search for it in your fish shops before everyone discovers it and the price goes up. Remember how cheap monkfish used to be a few years ago! Grey sea mullet has large scales which must be removed. It is wonderful poached, fried or baked.

1 grey sea mullet,	salt and freshly ground pepper
3¹/₂–4 lb/1.6–1.8 kg approx.	sprig of fennel

2–4 oz/55–110 g/¹/₄–¹/₂ cup butter

GARNISH

4 lemon segments	sprigs of fennel

PREHEAT the oven to 180°C/350°F/gas 4.

Scale the mullet, wash and gut if necessary. Dry the fish well.

Take a large sheet of good-quality tinfoil. Season the fish inside and out. Smear with lots of butter and put a few knobs into the centre with a sprig of fennel if available. Don't put lemon wedges or bay leaf or anything else – it doesn't need it. Place the fish in the centre of the tinfoil, draw up the edges and sides and seal well so that no butter or juices can escape while cooking.

Bake for about 45 minutes in a moderate oven. Test to see if the fish is cooked by lifting up some of the flesh off the bone near the head. There should be no trace of pink and it should lift off the bone easily. Put the whole package on to a serving dish. Garnish with a few sprigs of fennel and 4 lemon segments. Serve right away. Remove the skin as you serve and spoon the buttery cooking juices over the fish.

GREY SEA MULLET WITH GRUYÈRE AND MUSTARD

Serves 6

This is one of the simplest and most delicious fish dishes I know – another gem which Jane Grigson taught us when she came to teach at the Ballymaloe Cookery School in 1989.

6 grey sea mullet fillets weighing
6 oz/170 g each (haddock,
halibut, cod, brill, whiting *or*
monkfish could be used instead)
¼ oz/8 g/½ tablespoon butter
salt and freshly ground pepper

8 oz/250 g/2 cups grated
Gruyère, Gouda *or* Emmental
cheese
1–1½ tablespoons Dijon
mustard
4–5 tablespoons cream

ovenproof dish 8½ × 10 in/21 × 25 cm

PREHEAT the oven to 180°C/350°F/gas 4. Lightly butter the oven-proof dish. Season the fish with salt and freshly ground pepper. Arrange the fillets in a single layer. Mix the grated cheese with the mustard and cream and spread carefully over the fish. Cook in the preheated oven for about 20 minutes or until the fish is cooked and the top is golden brown. Flash under the grill if necessary. Serve with new potatoes and a good green salad.

DEH TA HSIUNG'S CHINESE STEAMED WHOLE FISH

Serves 4

Deh Ta Hsiung, a Chinese chef who came to the school on several occasions to give us a 'Taste of China', was so excited by the flavour of grey sea mullet that he almost emigrated to Ireland! I give you his delicious recipe for steamed fish with his permission.

1 grey sea mullet *or* perch,
1½–2 lb/675–900 g
1 teaspoon salt
1 teaspoon sesame seed oil
4 spring onions (scallions)
2–3 dried mushrooms, soaked
and thinly shredded

2 oz/55 g pork fillet *or* cooked
ham, thinly shredded
2 tablespoons light soy sauce
1 tablespoon rice wine *or* sherry
2 slices peeled ginger root,
thinly shredded
2 tablespoons oil

SCALE and gut the fish, wash it under the cold tap and dry it well both inside and out with a cloth or kitchen paper. Trim the fins and tail if not already trimmed, and slash both sides of the fish diagonally as far as the bone at intervals of about $1/2$ in/1 cm with a sharp knife. (In case you wonder why it is necessary to slash both sides of the fish before cooking, the reason is twofold: first, if you cook the fish whole the skin will burst unless it is scored; and secondly it allows the heat to penetrate more quickly and at the same time helps to diffuse the flavours of the seasoning and sauce. Also, as the Chinese never use a knife at the table, it is much easier to serve the fish if you can pick up the pieces of flesh with just a pair of chopsticks.)

Rub about half the salt and all the sesame seed oil inside the fish, and place it on top of 2 spring onions on an oval-shaped dish.

Mix the mushrooms and pork with the remaining salt, a little of the soy sauce and the rice wine. Stuff about half of this mixture inside the fish and put the rest on top with the ginger root. Place in a hot steamer and steam vigorously for 15 minutes.

Meanwhile, thinly shred the remaining spring onions and heat the oil in a little saucepan until bubbling. Remove the fish dish from the steamer, arrange the spring onion shreds on top, pour the remaining soy sauce over it and then the hot oil from the head to tail. Serve hot.

If you don't possess a steamer big enough to hold a whole fish, it can be wrapped in silver foil and baked in the oven at 230°C/ 450°F/gas 8 for 20–25 minutes.

NOTE: This recipe is taken from *The Home Book of Chinese Cookery* by Deh Ta Hsiung.

BAKED PLAICE OR SOLE WITH HERB BUTTER

Serves 4

This is a master recipe which can be used not only for plaice and sole but for all very fresh flat fish, e.g. brill, turbot, dabs, flounder and lemon sole. Depending on the size of the fish, it may be served as a starter or a main course. It may be served not only with herb butter but with any other complementary sauce, e.g. Hollandaise or Beurre blanc (see pages 75 and 117).

4 very fresh plaice *or* sole on the bone	4 teaspoons mixed finely chopped fresh parsley, chives,
2–4 oz/55–110 g/¹/₄–¹/₂ cup butter	fennel and thyme leaves
	salt and freshly ground pepper

PREHEAT the oven to 190°C/375°F/gas 5.

Turn the fish on its side and remove the head. Wash the fish and clean the slit very thoroughly. With a sharp knife, cut through the skin right round the fish, just where the 'fringe' meets the flesh. Be careful to cut neatly and to join the side cuts at the tail or it will be difficult to remove the skin later on.

Sprinkle the fish with salt and freshly ground pepper and lay them in 7 mm/¹/₄ in of water in a shallow baking tin. Bake in a moderately hot oven for 20–30 minutes according to the size of the fish. The water should have just evaporated as the fish is cooked. Check to see whether the fish is cooked by lifting the flesh from the bone at the head; it should lift off the bone easily and be quite white with no trace of pink.

Meanwhile, melt the butter and stir in the freshly chopped herbs. Just before serving, catch the skin down near the tail and pull it off gently (the skin will tear badly if not properly cut). Lift the fish on to hot plates and spoon the herb butter over them. Serve immediately.

Plaice or Sole with Mussels

Serves 6

6 large fillets of black sole *or* plaice, 2¼ lb/1 kg approx.	2½ fl oz/60 ml/generous ¼ cup dry white wine
1 oz/30 g/2 tablespoons butter	6 oz/170 g/2 cups sliced mushrooms
salt and freshly ground pepper	salt and freshly ground pepper
24 mussels	

BÉCHAMEL SAUCE

½ pint/300 ml/1¼ cups milk	a small sprig of parsley
a few slices of carrot	3 peppercorns
a few slices of onion	1½ oz/45 g/scant ⅓ cup roux
a small sprig of thyme	(see glossary)

LIAISON

1 egg yolk	3 fl oz/75 ml/scant ½ cup cream

MAKE the Béchamel sauce in the usual way (see below). Skin the fillets of fish. Smear half the butter over the base of an ovenproof dish. Tuck in the ends of the fish fillets and arrange in a single layer on the dish. Season with salt and freshly ground pepper. Put the washed mussels into a stainless steel saucepan, add the wine, cover and place on a low heat just until the mussels open, 2–3 minutes. Take the mussels from the shells, remove the beard and keep the mussels aside. Pour the liquid over the fish, cover with tinfoil and bake in a moderate oven, 180°C/350°F/gas 4, until the fish is almost cooked, approximately 10–15 minutes.

Meanwhile sauté the mushrooms in the remaining butter in a hot pan, season with salt and freshly ground pepper. Strain off the cooking liquor and add it to the Béchamel. Bring it to the boil. Make the liaison by mixing the egg yolks with the cream, add some of the hot liquid to the cold liaison and then mix into the rest of the sauce; taste and correct the seasoning. Sprinkle the mushrooms and mussels over the fish in the serving dish and coat with the sauce (may be made ahead to this point). Return to the oven

(160°C/325°F/gas 3) for 15–20 minutes or until the fish is hot and the sauce is golden on top.

Béchamel Sauce

¹/₂ pint/300 ml/1¹/₄ cups milk	a small sprig of parsley
a few slices of carrot	1¹/₂ oz/45 g/scant ¹/₃ cup roux
a few slices of onion	(see glossary)
3 peppercorns	salt and freshly ground pepper
a small sprig of thyme	

THIS is a marvellous quick way of making this sauce if you already have roux made. Put the cold milk into a saucepan with the carrot, onion, peppercorns, thyme and parsley. Bring to the boil, simmer for 4–5 minutes, remove from the heat and leave to infuse for ten minutes. Strain out the vegetables, bring the milk back to the boil and thicken with roux to a light coating consistency. Season with salt and freshly ground pepper, taste and correct the seasoning if necessary.

BAKED PLAICE WITH CHANTERELLES

Serves 4

Chanterelles are in season from July to the end of September. We get ours from the old pine woods on the Beara Peninsula in West Cork. This dish can be served as a first course or as a main course, depending on the size of the fish. If chanterelles aren't available, just serve the plaice with the herb butter.

4 very fresh plaice on the bone
8 oz/225 g fresh chanterelles
2–4 oz/55–110 g/¹/₄–¹/₂ cup
butter

4 teaspoons fresh parsley *or* a
mixture of parsley, chives,
fennel and lemon thyme leaves,
finely chopped

salt and freshly ground pepper

PREHEAT the oven to 190°C/375°F/gas 5.

Turn the fish on its side and remove the head. Wash the fish and clean the slit very thoroughly. With a sharp knife, cut through the skin right round the fish, just where the 'fringe' meets the flesh. Be careful to cut neatly and to join the side cuts at the tail or it will be difficult to remove the skin later on.

Sprinkle the fish with salt and pepper and lay them in ¹/₄ in/7 mm of water in a shallow baking tin. Bake in the preheated oven for 20–30 minutes according to the size of the fish. The water should have just evaporated as the fish is cooked. Check to see if the fish is ready by lifting the flesh from the bone at the head: it should lift off easily and be quite white with no trace of pink.

Pick over the chanterelles carefully and cut off the tough end bits. Wash quickly, drain on absorbent paper and cut into pieces. Melt ¹/₂ oz/15 g/1 tablespoon butter and when it foams toss in the chanterelles and season with salt and freshly ground pepper. Cook on high heat for 3–4 minutes or until soft.

Melt the remaining butter and stir in the freshly chopped herbs and chanterelles. Just before serving, catch the skin of the plaice down near the tail and pull it off gently (the skin will tear badly if not properly cut). Lift the fish on to hot plates and spoon the herb butter and chanterelles over it. Serve immediately.

NOTE: All flat fish are delicious cooked in this way, e.g. black sole, lemon sole, brill, turbot, dab and flounder. The sauce can be varied – Hollandaise or Beurre blanc (see pages 75 and 117) are both very good.

SOLE STUFFED WITH PRAWNS AND GARLIC BUTTER

Serves 4

This recipe would be perfect for a 'slightly grand' dinner party, and most of the preparation can be done in advance. It is delicious with plaice and lemon sole also.

8 fillets of sole, each 2^1/$_2$ oz/70 g approx.

2–2^1/$_2$ tablespoons garlic butter (see page 120)

salt and freshly ground pepper

16 large *or* 24 small cooked prawns (see page 45 for cooking method)

2^1/$_2$–3^1/$_2$ tablespoons home-made fish stock (see page 11)

Hollandaise sauce (see page 75)

GARNISH
sprigs of chervil *or* fennel

PREHEAT the oven to 180°C/350°F/gas 4.

Put the fillets skin side uppermost on the work surface, season with salt and freshly ground pepper and spread 1 teaspoon of garlic butter over each fillet. Put 2 or 3 cooked prawns on the narrow end of each fillet and roll up towards the wide end.

Put the rolled fillets on to a large pyrex or ovenproof plate, add the fish stock, cover with tinfoil and tuck it in well underneath the plate. Bake in the preheated oven for 15–18 minutes, depending on the thickness of the fillets; the fish should be beautifully soft and moist.

Meanwhile, make a Hollandaise sauce. When the fish is cooked whisk in some or all of the cooking juices to make a light fluffy sauce. Pour a little sauce on to each individual hot plate. Place two fish rolls on top, garnish with sprigs of chervil or fennel and serve immediately.

NOTE: If you find garlic butter a little strong with sole use Maître d'hôtel butter (see page 83).

COD WITH DIJON MUSTARD SAUCE

Serves 6

2 lb/900 g fresh cod fillets
2 oz/55 g/4 tablespoons butter
8 oz/225 g/2 cups chopped onions
1 pint/600 ml/2½ cups milk
2 fl oz/55 ml/¼ cup cream
1 oz/30 g/scant ¼ cup flour

2–3 tablespoons Dijon *or* English mustard
1 tablespoon chopped parsley
1¾ lb/800 g Duchesse potato (optional, see page 197)
salt and freshly ground pepper

MELT the butter and sweat the onions in a covered saucepan until golden brown. Skin the cod and cut into portions. Season with salt and freshly ground pepper. Put into a wide saucepan or frying pan, cover with milk and cream, bring to the boil and simmer gently for 4–6 minutes, depending on the thickness of the fish. Remove the fish carefully to a serving dish. Add the flour to the onions, stir and cook for 2 minutes. Add in the hot milk and bring back to the boil, then simmer for 3–4 minutes. Add the mustard and chopped parsley; taste and correct the seasoning, then pour over the fish and serve.

Duchesse potato may be piped around this dish. It may be allowed to cool and then reheated later in a moderate oven, 180°C/350°F/gas 4, for approximately 20 minutes.

COD BAKED WITH CREAM AND BAY LEAVES

Serves 6

This master recipe can be used for most round fish, e.g. haddock, pollock, grey sea mullet, ling, hake, etc. Salmon and sea trout are delicious done in this way or with a mixture of fresh herbs, e.g. parsley, fennel, lemon balm and chives.

6 portions of cod (allow 6 oz/ 170 g approx. filleted fish per person)

1 oz/30 g/2 tablespoons butter

1 tablespoon finely chopped onion

3–4 fresh bay leaves

light cream to cover the fish, approx. ¹/₂ pint/300 ml/1¹/₄ cups

roux (see glossary)

salt and freshly ground pepper

ENRICHMENT

¹/₂ oz/15 g butter *or* 1–2 tablespoons Hollandaise sauce
(optional, see page 75)

MELT the butter in a pan. Fry the onion gently for a few minutes until soft but not coloured. Put the cod in the pan and cook on both sides for 1 minute. Season with salt and freshly ground pepper. Add bay leaves. Cover with cream or creamy milk and simmer with the lid on for 5–10 minutes, until the fish is cooked. Remove the fish to a serving dish. Bring the cooking liquid to the boil and lightly thicken with roux. Whisk in the remaining butter or Hollandaise as an enrichment, check the seasoning. Coat the fish with sauce and serve immediately.

This dish can be prepared ahead and reheated, and it also freezes well. Reheat in a moderate oven 180°C/350°F/gas 4, for anything from 10–30 minutes, depending on the size of the container.

For a delicious starter, put the cod with its sauce into scallop shells which have been piped around the edge with a little ruff of Duchesse potato (see page 197). For a dinner party the Duchesse potato can be piped around a large serving dish with the cod in the centre. Garnish with bay leaves before serving.

TURBOT, BRILL, COD OR MONKFISH WITH BLACK PEPPERCORNS

Serves 8

This recipe for fish with peppercorns sounds most unlikely. It is an adaptation of a recipe in Jane Grigson's *Fish Cookery*, and even though it is a little extravagant the delicious result makes it worthwhile.

8 turbot, brill, cod *or* monkfish steaks, 1 in/7 mm thick (allow about 5 oz/140 g per person)
salt
1¹/₂–2 tablespoons whole black peppercorns
1¹/₂–2 tablespoons flour
1¹/₂ oz/45 g/3 tablespoons unsalted butter

1 generous tablespoon olive oil
2 fl oz/55 ml/¹/₄ cup brandy
2 fl oz/55 ml/¹/₄ cup port
¹/₄ pint/150 ml/generous ¹/₂ cup fish stock (see page 11) *or* light chicken stock (see page 137)
¹/₄ pint/150 ml/generous ¹/₂ cup cream

GARNISH
flat-leaf parsley *or* watercress sprigs

SEASON the fish steaks with salt. Crush the peppercorns coarsely in a pestle and mortar and mix with the flour. Coat the fish on both sides with this mixture. Melt one-third of the butter with the olive oil in a wide frying pan and fry the steaks on a gentle heat until golden on both sides. When the fish is almost cooked add the brandy and port and flame, then add the stock, bring to the boil and simmer for 3–4 minutes or until the fish is just cooked through.

Lift the fish carefully on to a serving dish. Add the cream to the pan and reduce until the sauce thickens to a light coating consistency. Whisk in the remaining butter. Taste and correct seasoning. Spoon over the fish and serve immediately. Garnish with flat-leaf parsley or watercress sprigs.

NOTE: This fish dish reheats surprisingly well.

TURBOT OR BRILL WITH CARROT AND CHIVES

Serves 6

Another delicious recipe which I managed to extract out of my brother Rory O'Connell!

6 fillets turbot *or* brill weighing
4–5 oz/110–140 g each
1/2 oz/15 g butter

few sprigs of fennel
salt and freshly ground pepper

CARROT PURÉE

1 lb/450 g carrots
1/4 pint/150 ml/generous 1/2 cup water
salt and freshly ground pepper

pinch of sugar
1 oz/30 g/2 tablespoons butter
2 fl oz/50 ml/1/4 cup cream

Hollandaise sauce (see page 75)

GARNISH

1 tablespoon chives, finely chopped

WASH the carrots and peel thinly if necessary. Bring the water to the boil. Cut the carrots in 1/4 inch/5 mm thick slices and add to the boiling water. Season with salt, pepper and a pinch of sugar. Cover and cook until soft. Remove the carrots with a perforated spoon, reserve the liquid, purée the carrots with the butter and cream, taste and correct seasoning.

Preheat the oven to 180°C/350°F/gas 4. Bake the fish fillets in one large foil packet with fennel, salt and freshly ground pepper (it will take 10–15 minutes).

Meanwhile make the Hollandaise sauce by the usual method (see page 75). Thin out the sauce by whisking in a little of the reserved carrot cooking liquid. Taste and season the sauce, adding more lemon juice if necessary; it should be the consistency of light pouring cream.

When the fish is cooked, remove the skin and lift each fillet on to a hot serving plate. Put 4 or 5 teaspoons of purée around each plate in 'quenelle' shapes (little ovals), coat the fish with the sauce, sprinkle a ring of finely chopped chives around each piece of fish and serve immediately.

SKATE WITH BLACK BUTTER

Serves 2

This classic recipe is one of the most delicious ways of serving a piece of really fresh skate wing.

1 medium skate (ray) wing, $1\frac{1}{4}$–$1\frac{1}{2}$ lb/560–675 g	1 onion, sliced
2–3 tablespoons white wine vinegar	few sprigs of parsley
	a little salt

BLACK BUTTER

2 oz/55 g/4 tablespoons butter
2–3 tablespoons white wine vinegar

GARNISH
chopped parsley

CHOOSE a pan wide enough for the skate to lie flat while cooking. Put the skate in, cover completely with cold water, add the onion, parsley, salt and wine vinegar. Bring to the boil gently, cover and barely simmer for 15–20 minutes. If the flesh lifts easily from the cartilage the skate is cooked. Turn off the heat and transfer the fish on to a large serving plate. Skin and lift the flesh on to hot plates, first from one side of the cartilage, then the other scraping off the white skin. Cover and keep hot.

Next make the black butter. Melt the butter immediately on a hot pan, allow it to foam and just as it turns brown add the wine vinegar, allow to bubble up again and then pour sizzling over the fish. Sprinkle with chopped parsley and serve immediately.

WARM RAY WING WITH CORIANDER

Serves 2 as a main course, 4 as a starter

The French are very fond of serving warm fish with a cold dressing. The coriander makes this dressing particularly delicious.

1 medium ray wing
1 onion
2–3 sprigs of parsley

2–2¹/₂ tablespoons white wine vinegar
pinch of salt

DRESSING

4–5 tablespoons olive oil
2–2¹/₂ tablespoons sunflower *or* arachide oil
2–2¹/₂ tablespoons sherry vinegar *or* balsamic vinegar

2–2¹/₂ tablespoons white wine vinegar
salt and freshly ground pepper
¹/₂ teaspoon Dijon mustard
1 teaspoon coriander seeds

1–1¹/₂ tablespoons green spring onion (scallion) cut at an angle

POACH the ray wing (see Skate with black butter, page 99, for method). Lift the flesh off the bone and divide it into 2 or 4 portions.

Meanwhile make the dressing by combining the oils, sherry vinegar, salt, freshly ground pepper and mustard. Warm the coriander seed for a few minutes, crush in a pestle and mortar and add to the dressing. Just before serving add the spring onion tops and spoon over the warm ray wing.

Serve immediately on warm plates. This dish is best eaten lukewarm.

RAY AND MUSHROOM TART

Serves 6

This is an absolutely delicious tart, again inspired by a recipe in Jane Grigson's *Fish Cookery*. Skate or ray wing cooked this way could be served as a filling for vol au vents or surrounded by a border of potato in scallop shells, or simply as a fish pie with a top of potato or overlapping croûtons.

1 medium ray wing

1 onion, sliced

2–3 sprigs of parsley

2–2¹/₂ tablespoons white wine vinegar

3 oz/85 g/1 cup chopped mushrooms

¹/₂ clove garlic, crushed

1 oz/30 g/2 tablespoons butter

¹/₂ tin anchovy fillets, chopped

2¹/₂ fl oz/60 ml/generous ¹/₄ cup double cream

chopped parsley

salt and freshly ground pepper

SHORTCRUST PASTRY

4 oz/110 g/generous ³/₄ cup flour

pinch of salt

2–3 oz/55–85 g/4–6 tablespoons butter

1 egg yolk

2 teaspoons cold water

BÉCHAMEL SAUCE

1 oz/30 g/2 tablespoons butter

1 generous tablespoon flour

salt and freshly ground pepper

¹/₂ pint/300 ml/1¹/₄ cups hot milk

TOPPING

1 generous tablespoon Gruyère cheese, grated

1 generous tablespoon buttered crumbs (see page 103)

7 in/18 cm flan ring

FIRST make the pastry. Sieve the flour with the salt and rub in the butter. Beat the egg yolk with the cold water and bind the mixture with this. You may need a little more water, but do not make the pastry too wet – it should come away cleanly from the bowl.

Wrap in clingfilm and rest for 15–30 minutes. Roll out thinly on a floured board and use it to line the flan ring. Line with greaseproof paper, fill with dried beans and bake blind in a preheated moderate oven, 180°C/350°F/gas 4, for about 20–25 minutes or until almost cooked. Remove the beans and paper and allow to cool.

Take a pan sufficiently wide for the ray wing to lie flat while cooking. Cover it completely with cold water, add onion, parsley, wine vinegar and a pinch of salt. Bring gently to the boil, cover and let barely simmer for 15–20 minutes or until the flesh will lift off the bone easily. Lift the ray wing out on to a plate with a slotted spoon. Remove the skin, lift the flesh off the bone and cut it into 1 in/2.5 cm pieces.

Meanwhile melt the butter for the béchamel, stir in the flour and gradually add the hot milk, beating well between additions. Leave to cook very slowly for 20 minutes, stirring now and then until you have a thick, creamy sauce (use a heat diffuser mat if you have one).

Sauté the mushrooms and garlic in the butter for 5 minutes. Add the anchovies, stir well and add the cream. Reduce to a fairly thick sauce. Add to the béchamel and leave to simmer over a low heat for a couple of minutes. Season and add the parsley.

Put a thin layer of sauce into the pastry case, arrange the fish on top, then spoon enough sauce over to cover it well. Sprinkle the top with the Gruyère cheese mixed with the buttered crumbs. Reheat in a fairly hot oven, 200°C/400°F/gas 6, for 10–15 minutes. Serve with a green salad.

HAKE IN BUTTERED CRUMBS

Serves 6–8

This dish is particularly good served with buttered leeks (see page 192). This is a master recipe which may be used for almost any round fish, e.g. cod, pollock, ling, haddock and grey sea mullet. My children particularly love fish cooked in this way.

2¹/₄ lb/1.1 kg hake   ¹/₂ oz/15 g/1 tablespoon butter
salt and freshly ground pepper

MORNAY SAUCE

1 pint/600 ml/2¹/₂ cups milk
a few slices of carrot and onion
3 or 4 peppercorns
a sprig of thyme and parsley
2 oz/55 g/¹/₃ cup roux (see
glossary) approx.
¹/₄ teaspoon mustard, preferably
Dijon

5–6 oz/140–170 g/1¹/₄–1¹/₂ cups
grated Cheddar cheese or
3 oz/85 g/³/₄ cup grated
Parmesan cheese
1 tablespoon chopped parsley
(optional)
salt and freshly ground pepper

BUTTERED CRUMBS

2 oz/55 g/4 tablespoons butter   4 oz/110 g/2 cups soft, white
breadcrumbs

³/₄ lb/800 g Duchesse potato approx. (optional, see page 197)

FIRST make the sauce. Put the cold milk into a saucepan with the carrot, onion, peppercorns and a sprig of thyme and parsley. Bring to the boil, simmer for 4–5 minutes, remove from the heat and leave to infuse for 10 minutes if you have enough time. Strain out the vegetables, bring the milk back to the boil and thicken with roux to a light coating consistency. Add the mustard and two-thirds of the grated cheese; keep the remainder of the cheese for sprinkling over the top. Season with salt and freshly ground pepper, taste and correct the seasoning if necessary. Add optional parsley.

Next make the buttered crumbs. Melt the butter in a pan and stir in the white breadcrumbs. Remove from the heat immediately and allow to cool.

Skin the fish and cut into portions: 6 oz/170 g for a main course, 3 oz/85 g for a starter. Season with salt and freshly ground pepper. Lay the pieces of fish in a lightly buttered ovenproof dish, coat with the Mornay sauce, mix the remaining grated cheese with the buttered crumbs and sprinkle over the top. Pipe a ruff of fluffy Duchesse potato round the edge if you want to have a whole meal in one dish.

Cook in a moderate oven, 180°C/350°F/gas 4, for 25–30 minutes or until the fish is cooked through and the top is golden brown and crispy. If necessary, place under the grill for a minute or two before you serve, to brown the edges of the potato.

NOTE: You can serve this in individual dishes; scallop shells are particularly attractive, are completely ovenproof and may be used over and over again.

POACHED MONKFISH WITH RED PEPPER SAUCE

Serves 6

This is by far the most popular monkfish dish in our restaurant. Serve it sparingly for a special occasion and don't compromise the recipe!

1 1/2 lb/675 g monkfish tails, carefully trimmed of skin and membrane	2 pints/1.1 l/5 cups water 1 dessertspoon salt

SAUCE

1 red pepper	5 oz/140 g/generous 1/2 cup
8 fl oz/250 ml/1 cup cream	butter

GARNISH
sprigs of flat-leaf parsley *or* chervil

CUT the monkfish tails into 1 1/2 in/1 cm collops (see glossary) and refrigerate until needed. Seed the red pepper and dice the flesh into 1/8 in/3 mm cubes. Sweat gently in 1 teaspoonful of butter in a covered pot until soft (it's really easy to burn this so turn off the heat after a few minutes and it will continue to cook in the pot).

Put the cream into a saucepan and gently reduce to about 3 tablespoons or until it is in danger of burning, then whisk in the butter bit by bit as though you were making a Hollandaise sauce. Finally stir in the diced red pepper. Thin with warm water if necessary and keep warm.

Bring the water to the boil and add the salt. Add the collops of monkfish and simmer for 4–5 minutes or until completely white and no longer opaque. Drain well. Arrange in a warm serving dish or on individual plates, coat with the red pepper sauce, garnish with sprigs of flat parsley or chervil and serve immediately.

MONKFISH WITH CUCUMBER AND TOMATO HOLLANDAISE

Serves 4

1 ¹/₂ lb/675 g monkfish tail cut into ¹/₂ in/1 cm collops

POACHING LIQUID

4 pints/2.3 l/10 cups water   1 tablespoon salt

CUCUMBER AND TOMATO HOLLANDAISE

2 egg yolks, free-range
1 dessertspoon cold water
4 oz/110 g/¹/₂ cup butter cut into dice
1 teaspoon lemon juice approx.
¹/₄ oz/8 g/¹/₂ tablespoon butter

2 very ripe firm tomatoes to yield 2 tablespoons tomato concassé approx.
1 teaspoon finely chopped fennel
salt, freshly ground pepper and sugar

¹/₃ of a cucumber, peeled and cut into tiny dice

GARNISH
sprigs of fresh fennel

FIRST make the sauce. Put the egg yolks in a heavy stainless steel saucepan on a very low heat, or in a bowl over hot water. Add water and whisk thoroughly. Add the butter bit by bit, whisking all the time. As soon as one piece melts, add the next piece. The mixture will gradually thicken, but if it shows signs of becoming too thick or slightly 'scrambling', remove from the heat immediately and add a little cold water if necessary. Do not leave the pan or stop whisking until the sauce is made. Finally add the lemon juice to taste. If the sauce is slow to thicken it may be because you are excessively cautious and the heat is too low. Increase the heat slowly and continue to whisk until the sauce thickens to coating consistency. Pour into a bowl and keep warm.

Melt the small amount of butter and toss the tiny dice of cucumber in it for 1–2 minutes. Add to the Hollandaise sauce.

Pour boiling water over the tomatoes, count to ten, pour off the water and peel. Cut in half and remove the seeds with a teaspoon or melon baller, and cut the flesh into the same size dice as the cucumber. Sprinkle with salt, freshly ground pepper and sugar and keep aside.

Just before serving, bring the 4 pints/2.3 l/10 cups of water to the boil and add 1 tablespoon of salt. Add the monkfish collops, bring back to the boil and *simmer* for 4–5 minutes or until the pieces are no longer opaque, but completely white and tender. Drain the monkfish thoroughly.

TO SERVE: Put into a serving dish or arrange overlapping slices on individual plates. Drain the tomato concassé and add to the sauce with the finely chopped fennel. Taste. Add a little hot water if the sauce is too thick. Spoon carefully over the fish. Garnish with sprigs of fennel and serve immediately.

MONKFISH STEAMED IN ITS OWN JUICES WITH TOMATO AND DILL

Serves 4

This is another superb recipe originally shown to me by Jane Grigson. She used halibut, but we have found that it may be adapted to many kinds of fish, e.g. sea bass, grey sea mullet, turbot or brill.

1½ lb/675 g monkfish tail	1 oz/30 g/2 tablespoons butter
2 very ripe tomatoes, peeled, seeded and flesh cut into ¼ in/7 mm dice (concassé)	1 tablespoon finely chopped dill
	1 tablespoon finely chopped parsley
1 small, very finely chopped shallot	salt, freshly ground pepper and sugar

1 × 14 in/35 cm sauté pan *or* frying pan with a lid

TRIM the monkfish tail of all skin and membrane. Cut the flesh into ¼ in/7 mm collops.

Prepare the tomato concassé (see glossary), and season with salt, freshly ground pepper and sugar.

Grease the base of the sauté pan with half of the butter, scatter with the finely chopped shallot, then arrange the pieces of fish in a single layer. Sprinkle with tomato concassé, chopped dill and parsley. Season with salt and freshly ground pepper. Cut a circle of greaseproof paper to fit inside the pan exactly; smear it with the rest of the butter and place butter side down on top of the fish. Cover with a tight-fitting saucepan lid. Cook on a medium heat for about 8 minutes. Test, taste, correct the seasoning if necessary and serve right away on 4 hot plates; no garnish is needed.

Serve with a good green salad and perhaps some new potatoes.

SMOKED HADDOCK WITH PARMESAN

Serves 6

Smoked haddock is widely available. Try to find smoked Finnan haddock which has not been dyed as well as smoked.

1 ½ lb/675 g smoked Finnan haddock
1 pint/600 ml/2½ cups milk
a few slices of carrot
a few slices of onion
bouquet garni
2 oz/55 g/⅓ cup roux (see glossary)

2 tablespoons chopped parsley
4 oz/110 g/1¼ cups grated cheese (preferably Parmesan but mature Cheddar would be wonderful too)
buttered crumbs (see page 103)
1¾ lb/800 g Duchesse potato approx. (see page 197)

PUT the cold milk into a saucepan with the carrot, onion and bouquet garni. Bring slowly to the boil and simmer for 3–4 minutes; remove from the heat and leave to infuse for 10–15 minutes. Strain. Meanwhile cover the smoked haddock with cold water, bring slowly to the boil, then discard the water. Cover the haddock with the flavoured milk and simmer for 10 minutes approx. or until just cooked. Remove the haddock to the serving dish with a perforated spoon.

Bring the milk back to the boil, thicken with roux to a light coating consistency, add the parsley and half the cheese, taste and pour over the haddock in the dish. Sprinkle with a mixture of buttered crumbs and the remainder of the grated cheese. Pipe Duchesse potato around the outside of the dish (may be prepared ahead to this point). Reheat in a moderate oven 180°C/350°F/gas 4, for 15–20 minutes or until the top is crispy and bubbly and the potato edges are golden.

OMELETTE ARNOLD BENNETT

Serves 1–2

This delicious omelette would also be very good made with smoked salmon or smoked mackerel.

2–3 oz/55–85 g smoked haddock
a little milk
1 oz/30 g/2 tablespoons butter
¼ pint/150 ml/generous ½ cup cream

3 eggs, preferably free-range
2–4 tablespoons grated Parmesan cheese
salt and freshly ground pepper

GARNISH
freshly chopped parsley

10 in/25 cm omelette pan, preferably non-stick

PUT the smoked haddock into a small saucepan. Cover with milk and simmer gently until it is cooked enough to separate into flakes (about 10 minutes). Drain. Toss the haddock over a moderate heat with half the butter and 2 tablespoons of the cream and keep aside. Separate the eggs, beat the yolks with a tablespoon of the cream and season with salt and freshly ground pepper. Whip the egg whites stiffly. Fold into the yolks with the haddock and add half the grated Parmesan cheese.

Melt the remaining butter in the omelette pan. Pour the mixture in gently and cook over a medium heat until the base of the omelette is golden. Spoon the remaining cream over the top and sprinkle with the rest of the finely grated Parmesan. Pop under a hot grill for a minute or so until golden and bubbly on top. Slide on to a hot dish, sprinkle with chopped parsley and serve immediately accompanied by a good green salad.

PROPER BREAKFAST KIPPERS

Serves 2

Our neighbour Mrs Schwartau smokes the very best kippers I have ever tasted. I like them best cooked for breakfast by what I call the jug method.

2 undyed kippers

maître d'hôtel butter
(see page 63)

GARNISH

2 lemon segments

2 sprigs of parsley

PUT the kippers head downwards into a deep jug. Cover them with boiling water right up to their tails as though you were making tea. Leave for 5–10 minutes to heat through. Lift them out carefully by the tail and serve immediately on hot plates with a pat of maître d'hôtel butter melting on top. Garnish each with a segment of lemon and a sprig of parsley.

SALTED FISH WITH OLIVE OIL AND HERBS

Serves 4

Anne Willan of La Varenne Cookery School in Paris told me about salting fish in this Japanese way; it intensifies the flavour and makes it even tastier.

4 whole fish weighing 1 lb/450 g
each approx. *or* 4 × 6 oz/170 g
fillets of white fish, e.g. bass,
bream, grey sea mullet *or*
mackerel

4 fl oz/130 ml/½ cup olive oil
2 tablespoons mixed freshly
chopped chives, basil and
parsley *or* chives, fennel, lemon
balm and parsley

1½ oz/45 g coarse sea salt

IF you are using whole fish, gut them carefully, scale if necessary and wash and dry well with kitchen paper. Cut 3 or 4 deep slashes diagonally on each side, almost to the bone. Put the fish on a tray and sprinkle it on both sides with coarse sea salt. Leave in the fridge for 2–3 hours, turning occasionally.

If you are using fish fillets there is no need to slash them, but salt them and leave for approximately 30 minutes. When the fish is ready, wash off the salt, dry well, brush lightly with olive oil and cook on a heavy grill pan until brown on each side and cooked through.

Mix the olive oil with chopped herbs and spoon over the hot fish. Serve immediately on hot plates with a good green salad and perhaps some new potatoes.

MOULES PROVENÇALES

Serves 6–8

Mussels are a perennial favourite; don't skimp on the garlic in this recipe or they will taste rather dull and 'bready'.

48 mussels, approx. 3½–4 lb/1.6–1.8 kg

PROVENÇALE BUTTER

3 oz/85 g/6 tablespoons soft butter

2 large cloves garlic

2 tablespoons (¼ cup) finely chopped parsley

fresh, white breadcrumbs

1 tablespoon olive oil

CHECK that all the mussels are closed. If any are open, tap the mussel on the worktop; if it does not close within a few seconds, discard. (The rule with shellfish is always, 'If in doubt, throw it out'.) Scrape off any barnacles from the mussel shells. Wash the mussels well in several changes of cold water. Then spread them in a single layer in a pan, cover with a folded tea-towel or a lid and cook over a gentle heat. This usually takes 2–3 minutes; the mussels are cooked just as soon as the shells open. Remove them from the pan immediately or they will shrink in size and become tough.

Remove the beard. Discard one shell and loosen the mussel but leave it in the other shell. Allow to get quite cold.

Meanwhile make the Provençale butter. Peel and crush the garlic and pound it in a mortar with the parsley and olive oil. Gradually beat in the butter (this may be done either in a bowl or a food processor). Spread the garlic butter over the mussels in the shells and dip each one into the soft, white breadcrumbs. They may be prepared ahead to this point and frozen in a covered box lined with clingfilm or tinfoil.

Arrange in individual serving dishes. Brown under the grill and serve with crusty white bread to mop up garlicky juices.

COCKLES OR PALOURDES PROVENÇALES

For those of you unfamiliar with the word palourdes, it is a type of clam which grows off the West Cork coast, around Kenmare Bay.

48 cockles *or* palourdes   fresh, white breadcrumbs
Provençale butter (see above)

PREPARE in the same way as Moules Provençales.

Mushroom Soup

Purée of Onion Soup with Thyme Leaves

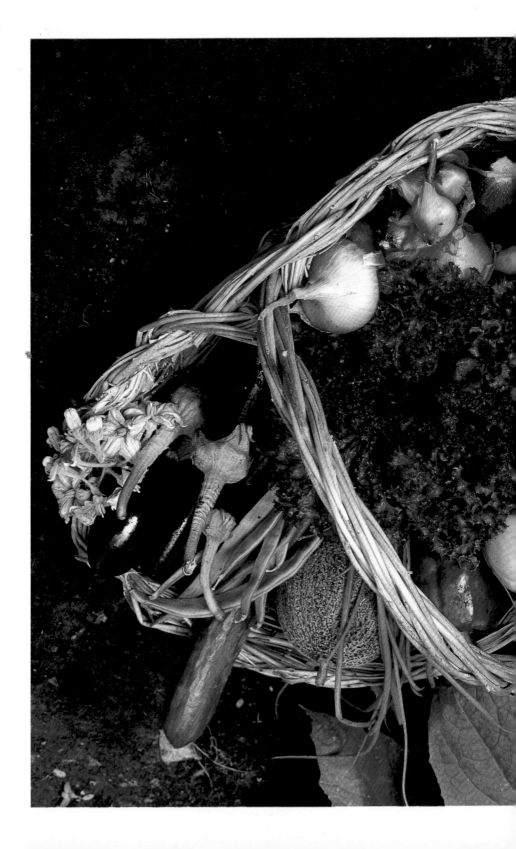

Salade Tiède with Chicken Livers, Bacon and Croûtons

Salad of Carrot and Apple with Honey and Vinegar Dressing

Crab Pâté

Ballycotton Bay

Hake in Buttered Crumbs

Ivan Allen's Dressed Crab

Dingle Pie

A Leg of Lamb with Rosemary and Garlic, ready for the oven

Ballymaloe Bacon Chop

Ballymaloe Cheese Fondue

Glazed Loin of Bacon

Ballymaloe Vanilla Ice-cream served in an Ice Bowl

Crème Caramel

Orange Mousse with Chocolate Wafers

Clockwise from right: Brown Soda Bread, Mummy's Sweet White Scones, Raspberry Jam, Ballymaloe Brown Yeast Bread

GRATIN OF MUSSELS AND POTATO

Serves 4–6

Everyone loves this gratin recipe. It's cheap to make and very tasty – and you could do variations on the theme.

3 lbs/1.35 kg mussels

8–10 tablespoons olive oil

8 oz/225 g/2 cups onion, chopped

10 fl oz/300 ml/1¼ cups dry white wine

1–1⅓ tablespoons shallot *or* spring onion (scallion), chopped

2 sprigs of parsley

2 sprigs of thyme

sea salt and freshly ground pepper

2 oz/55 g/½ cup buttered crumbs (see page 103)

2 large cloves garlic, peeled and crushed

2–2½ tablespoons chopped parsley

1 oz/30 g/¼ cup finely grated Parmesan cheese

1¼ lb/560 g cooked potatoes

SWEAT the onions in half the olive oil in a heavy-bottomed saucepan until soft and golden brown (about 7–8 minutes).

Meanwhile check that all the mussels are tightly closed, wash them and put them into a stainless steel saucepan with the wine, shallot and herbs, cover and cook on a medium heat. As soon as the shells open remove to a tray to cool. Strain the mussel cooking liquor, take the mussels out of the shells, remove the beards and put the mussels into the liquid.

Slice the potatoes, toss in the remaining olive oil in a frying pan, season with sea salt and freshly ground pepper, then layer the potatoes, mussels and onions in a gratin dish and pour on some of the mussel liquor to come a quarter way up the dish. Mix the buttered crumbs with the garlic, chopped parsley and cheese. Sprinkle over the top.

Bake in a moderate oven, 180°C/350°F/gas 4, until hot and bubbly – 15–20 minutes. Flash under a grill to crisp the top if necessary. Serve with a good green salad.

IVAN ALLEN'S DRESSED CRAB

Serves 5–6

When I first came to Ballymaloe my father-in-law always prepared the dressed crab for dinner. This is his recipe and very delicious it is too.

15 oz/425 g/3 cups crab meat, brown and white mixed (2 or 3 crabs should yield this – see page 41 for cooking method; keep shells intact for later)
3–3 1/2 oz/85–100 g/1 1/2–1 3/4 cups) soft white breadcrumbs
2 teaspoons white wine vinegar

2–2 1/2 tablespoons ripe tomato chutney (see page 189)
1 oz/30 g/2 tablespoons butter generous pinch of dry mustard *or* 1 level teaspoon French mustard
6–8 fl oz/175–250 ml/3/4–1 cup béchamel sauce (see page 92)

salt and freshly ground pepper

TOPPING

4 oz/110 g/1 cup buttered crumbs (see page 103)

SCRUB the crab shells, mix all the ingredients except the buttered crumbs together, taste carefully and correct the seasoning. Fill into the shells and sprinkle the tops with the buttered crumbs. (The dish may be prepared ahead to this point and refrigerated for 1–2 days or frozen.)

Bake in a moderate oven, 180°C/350°F/gas 4, until heated through and brown on top (approximately 15–20 minutes). Flash under the grill if necessary to crisp the crumbs.

NOTE: 1 lb/450 g cooked crab in the shell yields approximately 6–8 oz/170–225 g crab meat depending on the time of the year.

BALLYMALOE HOT BUTTERED LOBSTER

Serves 4 as a main course

One of the most exquisite ways to eat fresh lobster, but for perfection the lobster must come straight from the sea.

4 lb/1.8 kg live lobster

COURT BOUILLON

1 carrot	1 pint/600 ml/2½ cups dry
1 onion	white wine
1 pint/600 ml/2½ cups water	bouquet garni
4 oz/110 g/½ cup butter	squeeze of lemon

GARNISH

lemon segments
sprigs of watercress, flat-leaf parsley *or* fennel

COOK the lobsters following the method on page 116, steaming them until they are just beginning to change colour and are speckled with red.

As soon as they are cool enough to handle, split them in half and extract all the meat from the body, tail and large and small claws. Scrape out all the soft, greenish tomalley (liver) from the part of the shell nearest the head and put it with the firmer meat into a warm bowl wrapped in a tea-towel.

Heat the lobster shells. Cut the meat into chunks, melt half the butter and when it is foaming toss the meat and tomalley in it until the meat is cooked through and the juices turn pink.

Spoon the meat into the hot shells. Put the remaining butter into the pan, heat and scrape up any bits. Add a squeeze of lemon juice. Pour the buttery juices into small heated ramekins and serve beside the lobster on hot plates. Garnish with sprigs of watercress, flat parsley or fennel, and lemon segments. Hot buttered lobster should be eaten immediately.

How to Cook Lobster or Crayfish

Serves 2–4

THE method described here is considered by the RSPCA to be the most humane way to cook lobster and certainly results in deliciously tender and juicy flesh. When we are cooking lobster we judge by colour, but if you are uneasy about that allow 15 minutes for the first lb/450 g and 10 minutes per lb/450 g after that.

2 × 2 lb/900 g live lobsters *or* crayfish

COURT BOUILLON

1 carrot	bouquet garni: parsley stalks,
1 onion	sprig of thyme, celery stalks and
1 pint/600 ml/2½ cups water	a small bay leaf
1 pint/600 ml/2½ cups dry	6 peppercorns
white wine	*no* salt

COVER the lobsters or crayfish with lukewarm salted water (6 oz/170 g/⅞ cup salt to every 4 pints/2.3 l/10 cups water). Put the saucepan on a low heat and bring slowly to simmering point: lobster die at about 44°C/112°F. By this stage the lobsters will be changing colour so remove them and discard all the cooking water.

Slice the carrot and onion and put with the wine, fresh water, herbs and peppercorns into a stainless steel saucepan and bring to the boil; replace the lobsters and cover with a tight-fitting lid. Steam them until they change colour to bright red, and remove them from the pot. Strain the cooking liquid and reserve for a sauce.

SCALLOPS WITH BEURRE BLANC AND CHERVIL

Serves 4 as a main course, 8 as a starter

This is the most exquisite way to eat really fresh scallops. A non-stick pan is essential for this recipe.

12 large scallops   salt and freshly ground pepper

BEURRE BLANC SAUCE

3–4 tablespoons white wine   1 generous tablespoon cream

3–4 tablespoons white wine   6 oz/170 g cold unsalted butter,
vinegar   cut into cubes

1–1½ tablespoons shallots,   salt
finely chopped   freshly squeezed lemon juice

pinch of ground white pepper

GARNISH
fresh fennel *or* chervil sprigs

FIRST make the beurre blanc. Put the wine, wine vinegar, shallots and pepper into a heavy-bottomed stainless steel saucepan and reduce down to about ½ tablespoon. Add the cream and boil again until it thickens. Whisk in the cold butter in little pieces, keeping the sauce just warm enough to absorb the butter. Strain out the shallots, season with salt, white pepper and lemon juice and keep warm in a bowl over hot but not simmering water.

Just before serving, slice the white part of each scallop in half so that you have two round pieces of equal thickness, and keep the coral intact. Dry on kitchen paper. Just before cooking season the scallops with salt and freshly ground pepper. Heat the non-stick pan and put the scallops directly on to it in a single layer, not too close together. Allow to cook on one side until golden before turning over, then cook the other side.

Spoon a little very thin beurre blanc on to a large hot (preferably white) plate for each person (thin it if necessary by whisking in warm water), arrange the slices of scallop and coral on top of the sauce, garnish with fennel or chervil and serve immediately.

THREE-MINUTE FISH

Serves 4

This is the fastest fish recipe I know and certainly one of the most delicious. It can be fun to mix pink- and white-fleshed fish on the same plate, e.g. salmon and sea bass.

1 lb/450 g very fresh fish, e.g. wild Irish salmon, cod, turbot, large sole, sea bass *or* grey sea mullet	finely chopped parsley, thyme, chives
olive oil *or* melted butter	finely grated rind of 1 small lemon
	salt and freshly ground pepper

4 ovenproof main course plates

GARNISH
a few scattered chive flowers, if available

SEASON the fillet of fish with salt and freshly ground pepper about half an hour before cutting; chill in the fridge to stiffen it.

Preheat the oven to 230°C/450°F/gas 8.

While the oven is heating, brush the plates with olive oil or melted butter. Put the fillet of fish on a chopping board skin-side down; cut the flesh into scant ¼ in/7 mm thin slices down on to the skin. Arrange the slices on the base of the plate but don't allow them to overlap or they will cook unevenly. Brush the fish slices with more olive oil or melted butter, season with salt and freshly ground pepper and sprinkle each plate with a little freshly chopped herbs and lemon zest. Put the plates in the *fully preheated oven* and cook for 3 minutes; you might like to check after 2 minutes if the slices are exceptionally thin. The fish is cooked when it looks opaque. Sprinkle with chive flowers.

Rush it to the table, served with crusty white bread, a good green salad and a glass of dry white wine.

BALLYCOTTON FISH PIE

Serves 6–8

Many different types of fish may be used for a fish pie, so feel free to adapt this recipe a little to suit your needs. Periwinkles would be a good and cheap addition and a little smoked haddock is tasty also.

2¼ lb/generous 1 kg fillets of cod, haddock, ling, hake *or* pollock *or* a mixture
18 cooked mussels (optional, see page 91)
1 pint/600 ml/2½ cups milk and a very little cream (optional)
4 oz/110 g/1 cup onions
3 *or* 4 slices of carrot
1 small bay leaf
a sprig of thyme
3 peppercorns

6 oz/170 g/2 cups sliced mushrooms
roux made with 1 oz/30 g/ 2 tablespoons butter and 1 oz/30 g/2 tablespoons flour (see glossary)
4 hard-boiled eggs
2 tablespoons chopped parsley
2 lb/900 g Duchesse potato *or* soft mashed potato (see page 197)
salt and freshly ground pepper

ACCOMPANIMENT

Maître d'hôtel butter (see page 83) *or* garlic butter (see below) (optional)

PUT the onions, carrot, bay leaf, thyme and peppercorns into the milk, bring to the boil and simmer for 3–4 minutes. Remove from the heat and leave to infuse for 10–15 minutes. Strain.

Meanwhile, sauté the sliced mushrooms in a little butter in a hot pan, season with salt and freshly ground pepper and set aside.

Put the fish into a wide pan or frying pan and cover with the flavoured milk. Season with salt and freshly ground pepper. Cover and simmer gently until the fish is cooked. Take out the fish, carefully removing any bones or skin. Bring the liquid to the boil and thicken with roux; add a little cream (optional) and the chopped parsley, roughly chopped hard-boiled eggs, mushrooms, pieces of fish and the mussels. Stir gently, taste and correct the seasoning. Spoon into 1 large or 6–8 small dishes and pipe Duchesse potato on top. The pie may be prepared ahead to this point.

Put into a moderate oven 180°C/350°F/gas 4 to reheat and slightly brown the potato on top, 10–15 minutes if the filling and potato are warm, or about 30 minutes if reheating the dish from cold.

Serve with garlic butter or maître d'hôtel butter. For garlic butter just add 2 large crushed cloves to the recipe for maître d'hôtel butter, and omit the lemon juice.

POULTRY

Chicken used to be the greatest luxury about twenty years ago. My grandfather would bring us chickens that he specially reared on his farm, but they were always for festive occasions, and later at boarding school – delight of delights – we used to get chicken for lunch on Mother Prioress's feast day. The excitement, I remember it still! Perhaps it's just nostalgia but I'm quite sure that chicken tasted much more delicious then. Nowadays, chicken is less expensive and is arguably the most popular meat of all. The birds are intensively reared and produced on a large scale in not very humane conditions, so while the price has come down considerably, flavour has suffered correspondingly. As a result, there is inevitably a small but steadily growing demand for free-range chickens and eggs. These are more expensive to produce so the consumer must be prepared to pay a little extra for the naturally reared bird with superior flavour.

When you are buying a chicken make sure to choose a good plump bird with unblemished skin. Just about every bit of a chicken can be used, so ask for the giblets also. The heart, neck and gizzard may be added to your stock pot and the chicken liver may form the basis of the delicious Ballymaloe Chicken Liver Pâté. The little lump of fat just inside the vent needn't be wasted either; if the chicken is free-range, this fat can be rendered down in a low oven and the resulting chicken fat is wonderful for roasting or sautéing potatoes. In a battery-reared chicken this fat can taste nasty, so just discard it.

The other thing you might like to seek out is an 'old hen', cheaper and even better suited to the Chicken Pilaff recipe than a chicken. Hens are undeservedly scorned nowadays. They have actually been rechristened 'casserole roasters' by the poultry trade to give them an air of respectability! This is one recipe that proves how tasty they can be. It also proves that it is possible to feed a large crowd of people easily and economically. My mother-in-law, Myrtle Allen, used to cook this Chicken Pilaff recipe when her children were hungry teenagers, given to inviting other hungry teenagers home for impromptu parties.

Poached Turkey with Mushrooms shows how successfully turkey can be treated in a similar way, with mushrooms added to the sauce for extra excitement – but the turkey should be free-range too, because that special flavour comes through in the poaching.

Equally comforting is Farmhouse Chicken, a recipe from my childhood. A big black roasting tin of this, taken from the Aga, would feed our whole family – once we had stopped fighting over the crispy potatoes on top! It could, of course, be put in something more glamorous than a roasting tin, but that's the way it still tastes best to me.

Casserole roasting which is the method we use for Casserole Roast Chicken with Tarragon is a tremendously useful technique. It can be used not only to cook chicken, but also for turkey, pheasant and guinea fowl. The herb we use here is French tarragon but you could use marjoram or thyme or a mixture of fresh herbs or even watercress. You can also cook the chicken on a bed of vegetables, for example in the recipe for Casserole Roast Chicken with Leeks and Bacon, or Pheasant with Celery and Port. Again, this technique can also be used for turkey or guinea fowl, and is particularly good for pheasant which can sometimes be dry. So you see there are many variations on this theme. The sauce is made from the skimmed juices in the bottom of the casserole, with or without the addition of cream.

For the days when you simply haven't time for any of these recipes, Chicken Breasts with Cream and Lemon Juice is the answer. You can rush into the shops on your way home to buy the chicken breasts and have them on the table, tasting delectable, in fifteen minutes – just long enough to rustle up Tomato Fondue (see page 188) or a simple green salad to set them off.

Casserole Roast Chicken with Tarragon

Serves 4–6

There are two kinds of tarragon, French and Russian, but we prefer to use French in this recipe because it has a better flavour than the Russian variety. Unfortunately French tarragon is more difficult to come by than Russian because it is propagated by root cuttings: you can't just grow it from seed like the Russian tarragon. French tarragon grows to a height of about 9 in/23 cm, whereas the Russian will grow to about 4 ft/1.25 m in the summer.

1 × 3¹/₂ lb/1.6 kg chicken, free-range if possible
1 tablespoon freshly chopped French tarragon and 1 sprig of tarragon
1 oz/30 g/2 tablespoons butter
¹/₄ pint/150 ml/generous ¹/₂ cup cream

¹/₂–1 tablespoon freshly chopped French tarragon (for sauce)
¹/₄ pint/150 ml/generous ¹/₂ cup home-made chicken stock (optional, see page 137)
roux (optional, see glossary)
salt and freshly ground pepper

GARNISH
sprigs of fresh tarragon

PREHEAT the oven to 190°C/375°F/gas 5.

Remove wing tips and wishbone and keep for stock. Season the cavity of the chicken with salt and freshly ground pepper and stuff a sprig of tarragon inside. Chop the remaining tarragon and mix with two-thirds of the butter. Smear the remaining butter over the breast of the chicken, place breast-side down in a casserole and allow it to brown over a gentle heat. Turn the chicken breast-side up and smear the tarragon butter over the breast and legs. Season with salt and freshly ground pepper. Cover the casserole and cook in a moderate oven for 1¹/₄–1¹/₂ hours.

Test to see if the chicken is cooked, remove to a carving dish and allow to rest for 10–15 minutes before carving. (To test if the chicken is cooked, pierce the flesh between the breast and thigh. This is the last place to cook, so if there is no trace of pink here and the juices are clear, the chicken is certainly cooked.) Spoon off the surplus fat from the juices, blend in the cream and boil up the sauce to thicken it. Alternatively, just bring the liquid to the boil and whisk in a little roux until the sauce thickens slightly. Add a little freshly chopped tarragon if necessary, taste and correct seasoning.

Carve the chicken into 4 or 6 helpings; each person should have a portion of white and brown meat. Arrange on a serving dish, nap with the sauce and serve.

NOTE: Some chickens yield less juice than others. If you need more sauce, add a little home-made chicken stock with the cream. If the sauce is thickened with roux this dish can be reheated.

CASSEROLE ROAST CHICKEN WITH LEEKS AND BACON

Serves 4–6

1 × 3½ lb/1.6 kg chicken, preferably free-range
8 oz/225 g streaky bacon, in one piece
1 lb/450 g/2 cups leeks, trimmed
½ oz/15 g/1 tablespoon butter
splash of sunflower oil

8 fl oz/250 ml/1 cup home-made chicken stock (see page 137) or water
8 fl oz/250 ml/1 cup light cream
roux (optional, see glossary)
salt and freshly ground pepper

GARNISH
1 tablespoon chopped parsley

PREHEAT the oven to 180°C/350°F/gas 4.

Cut the white part of the leeks into rounds and wash them well. Remove the rind from the bacon and cut into ½ in/1 cm cubes.

Remove the lumps of fat from inside the vent end of the

chicken. Season with salt and freshly ground pepper. Rub the butter over the breast and legs of the chicken and put it breast-side down into a casserole. Allow it to brown on a gentle heat; this can take 5 or 8 minutes. As soon as the breast is golden, remove from the casserole and keep aside. Add the pieces of bacon to the casserole with a splash of oil. Cook the bacon until the fat runs and the bacon is golden. Then add the sliced leeks and toss together in the bacon fat. Season with freshly ground pepper, but no salt as the bacon will probably be salty enough. Then replace the chicken on top of the leeks and bacon. Cover the casserole and put into a moderate oven for $1\frac{1}{4}-1\frac{1}{2}$ hours.

When the chicken is cooked, remove to a serving dish. Lift out the leeks and bacon with a perforated spoon and put into the centre of a hot serving dish.

Skim the juices of all fat, add the chicken stock and cream, and bring to the boil. Thicken by whisking in a little roux. The sauce should not be too thick, just thick enough to coat lightly the back of a spoon. Allow to simmer on a low heat while you carve the chicken.

Carve the chicken into 4 or 6 helpings, depending on how hungry you all are; everyone should get a portion of white and brown meat. Arrange the leeks and bacon around the chicken. Taste the sauce and add a little more salt and freshly ground pepper if necessary. If the sauce has become too thick, add a little water. Spoon the hot sauce over the chicken, sprinkle with chopped parsley and serve.

CHICKEN WITH ROSEMARY AND TOMATOES

Serves 4–6

1 × 3½ lb/1.6 kg chicken, preferably free-range
3 medium-sized onions
3 medium-sized potatoes
5–6 medium-sized very ripe tomatoes

1 oz/30 g/1 tablespoon butter
1 tablespoon olive oil
sprig of rosemary *or* 1 teaspoon thyme leaves
salt and freshly ground pepper

PREHEAT the oven to 180°C/350°F/gas 4.

If possible, remove the wishbone from the neck end of the chicken for ease of carving. Remove the lump of fat from inside the vent end of the chicken and put aside. Season the cavity with salt and freshly ground pepper. Smear the breast with half the butter, put the chicken breast-side down into a casserole (preferably an oval one that will just fit the chicken) and allow to brown on a *gentle heat* for 5 or 6 minutes.

Meanwhile, peel and thickly slice the onions, potatoes and tomatoes. Chop the rosemary finely. Remove the chicken to a plate, add the remaining butter and the olive oil to the casserole. Toss the potatoes, onions and tomatoes in the fat and oil. Sprinkle with chopped rosemary, salt and freshly ground pepper. Cover and cook for 5–6 minutes. Put the chicken on top of the vegetables and cover. Cook in a moderate oven for approximately 1¼ hours.

Carve the chicken and serve surrounded with the potatoes, tomatoes and onions. De-grease the juices, bring to the boil and spoon over the chicken and vegetables; sprinkle with chopped parsley.

CHICKEN PILAFF

Serves 8

This delicious chicken recipe can be a very economical way to serve large numbers for a party. Serve with a Pilaff Rice (see below) and Tomato Fondue (see page 188) and garnish with sprigs of parsley or watercress. It may be prepared ahead of time and reheats well but do not add the liaison until just before serving.

1× 4–4¹/₂ lb/1.8–2 kg approx. boiling fowl *or* good free-range chicken
1 large sliced carrot
1 stick celery
1 large sliced onion
a bouquet garni made up of a sprig of thyme, parsley stalks, a tiny bay leaf, a stick of celery

5 peppercorns
³/₄ pint/450 ml/scant 2 cups approx. water *or* water and white wine mixed *or* light home-made chicken stock (see page 137)
1 oz/30 g roux approx. (see glossary)
6 fl oz/175 ml/³/₄ cup cream
salt and freshly ground pepper

LIAISON

1 egg yolk   2 fl oz/55 ml/¹/₄ cup cream

SEASON the chicken with salt and freshly ground pepper; put into a heavy casserole with the carrot, celery, onion, peppercorns and bouquet garni. Pour in water, water and wine or stock. Cover and bring to the boil and simmer either on top of the stove or in the oven for 1¹/₂–3 hours, depending on the age of the bird. When the bird is cooked, remove from the casserole.

Strain and de-grease the cooking liquid and return to the casserole. Discard the vegetables: they have already given their flavour to the cooking liquid. Reduce the liquid in an uncovered casserole for a few minutes. If it tastes a little weak, add cream and reduce again; thicken to a light coating consistency with roux. Taste, add salt, correct the seasoning. Skin the chicken and carve the flesh into 2 in/5 cm pieces; add the meat to the sauce and allow it to heat through and bubble (the dish may be prepared ahead to this point).

Finally, just before serving, mix the egg yolk and cream to make a liaison. Add some of the hot sauce to the liaison then carefully stir into the chicken mixture. Taste, correct the seasoning and stir well but do not allow to boil further or the sauce will curdle.

Pilaff Rice

2 tablespoons finely chopped onion *or* shallot

14 oz/400 g/2 cups long-grain rice, preferably Basmati

1 oz/30 g/2 tablespoons butter

32 fl oz/900 ml/4 cups home-made chicken stock (see page 137)

salt and freshly ground pepper

Melt the butter in a casserole, add the finely chopped onion and sweat for 2–3 minutes. Add the rice and toss for a minute or two until the grains change colour. Season with salt and freshly ground pepper, add the chicken stock, cover and bring to the boil. Simmer either on top of the stove or in the oven for approximately 10 minutes, or until the rice is just cooked and all the water is absorbed.

NOTE: Basmati rice cooks quite quickly; other types of rice may take up to 15 minutes.

FARMHOUSE CHICKEN

Serves 8

A whole meal in a dish, this was a favourite family supper in our house. We used to serve it in a big black roasting tin.

1 × 3¹/₂ lb/1.6 kg free-range chicken

1¹/₄ lb/560 g streaky bacon in one piece

2 tablespoons sunflower *or* arachide oil

14 oz/400 g/3¹/₂ cups finely sliced *or* chopped onions

seasoned flour

12 oz/340 g/3¹/₂ cups thinly sliced carrots

5 lb/2.3 kg large 'old' potatoes

salt and freshly ground pepper

2 pints/1.1 l/5 cups chicken stock, made from the giblets and carcass (see page 137)

GARNISH

1 tablespoon freshly chopped parsley

deep roasting tin 15 in/38 mm square approx.

PREHEAT the oven to 230°C/450°F/gas 8.

Joint the chicken into 8 pieces; separate the wing joints so they will cook evenly. Cut the rind off the bacon; cut a little less than half of it into $\frac{1}{2}$ in/1 cm lardons (see glossary) and the remainder into $\frac{1}{4}$ in/7 mm thick slices. If salty, blanch, refresh and dry on kitchen paper. Heat the oil in a wide frying pan and cook the lardons until the fat begins to run and they are pale golden; transfer to a plate. Toss the chicken joints in seasoned flour, sauté in the bacon fat and oil until golden on both sides, remove from the pan and put with the bacon. Finally toss the onions and carrots in bacon fat for 1–2 minutes.

Peel the potatoes and slice a little less than half of them into $\frac{1}{4}$ in/7 mm rounds. Arrange a layer of potato slices on the bottom of the deep roasting tin. Season with salt and freshly ground pepper. Sprinkle the carrots, onions and bacon over the potatoes and arrange the chicken on top. Season again with salt and freshly ground pepper. Cut the remaining potatoes into thick slices lengthways, $1\frac{1}{2}$ in/4 cm, and arrange cut side up on top of the chicken (the whole top of the dish should be covered with potato slices). Season with salt and freshly ground pepper. Pour in the chicken stock.

Bake in the preheated oven for 1 hour approx. After 30 minutes put the strips of bacon on top so they get deliciously crisp with the potatoes. Test after 1 hour – it may take a little longer. Cover loosely with greaseproof paper or foil near the end of cooking; if it is getting too brown, sprinkle with chopped parsley and serve.

CHICKEN BREASTS WITH CREAM AND LEMON JUICE

Serves 4

4 chicken breasts

1 lemon

1/2 oz/15 g/1 tablespoon butter

1/4 pint/150 ml/generous 1/2 cup cream

1/4 pint/150 ml/generous 1/2 cup home-made chicken stock (see page 137)

1–2 tablespoons chopped parsley

salt and freshly ground pepper

GRATE the rind from the lemon on the finest part of the grater; keep aside. Squeeze the juice from half of the lemon, dip the chicken breasts in it and keep the rest for later. Season with salt and freshly ground pepper. Melt a little butter in a sauté pan which is wide enough to take the breasts in a single layer. Toss the breasts in butter, cover with a butter wrapper or greaseproof-paper round and lid and cook gently on top or in a moderate oven, 180°C/350°F/gas 4, for about 10 minutes (depending on the size of the breasts). Be careful not to overcook them or they will be dry.

Remove the breasts to a warm dish, de-glaze the pan with the stock and stir to dissolve any little crusty bits remaining. Add the cream and reduce, taste and season if necessary. Add a little lemon rind, a squeeze of lemon juice and the chopped parsley, then taste again. Spoon the sauce over the chicken breasts and serve immediately with Tomato Fondue (see page 188) and a good green salad.

Poached Turkey with Mushrooms

Serves 20–25

A great dish for a party, it can be made up ahead and reheated.

1 × 10 lb/4.5 kg turkey, preferably free-range
2 large carrots, sliced
2 large onions, quartered
2 sticks of celery
a bouquet garni made up of 6 parsley stalks, 2 sprigs of thyme, 1 small bay leaf, 1 sprig of tarragon
10 peppercorns

6 pints/3.4 l/15 cups home-made light chicken stock (see page 137) *or* water
2 lb/900 g mushrooms, sliced
1–2 oz/30–55 g/2–4 tablespoons butter
32 fl oz/900 ml/4 cups cream *or* cream and milk
4 oz/110 g roux approx. (see glossary)

GARNISH
flat-leaf parsley

Put the turkey into a large saucepan. Pour in the chicken stock or water, add the carrots, onions, celery, bouquet garni and some peppercorns. Season with salt and freshly ground pepper. Bring to the boil, cover and simmer on top of the stove or in a moderate oven, 180°C/350°F/gas 4, for 2–2½ hours. When the turkey is cooked, remove from the pot, strain and de-grease the cooking liquid. Discard the vegetables – they will have given their flavour to the cooking juices already. Reduce the liquid by one-half.

Meanwhile sauté the sliced mushrooms in a little butter on a very hot pan and keep aside. Add the cream or creamy milk to the turkey poaching liquid, reduce again for 5–10 minutes, and thicken with the roux to a light coating consistency. Add the mushrooms and taste. Skin the turkey, carve the flesh into 2 in/5 cm pieces and add to the sauce. Bring back to the boil, taste and correct the seasoning if necessary. Put into a hot serving dish and garnish with flat-leaf parsley.

Alternatively, put it into several large serving dishes, pipe a ruff of Duchesse potato around the edges (see page 197) and reheat later in a moderate oven, 180°C/350°F/gas 4, for 20–30 minutes.

Serve with a good green salad. Pilaff rice would also be delicious instead of potato (see page 128).

Turkey Baked with Marjoram

Serves 12–14

1 × 10–12 lb/4.5–5.4 kg turkey
4 oz/110 g/½ cup butter
2 tablespoons finely chopped marjoram and 2–3 sprigs of marjoram

32 fl oz/900 ml/4 cups light cream
2 heaped tablespoons freshly chopped marjoram
salt and freshly ground pepper

GARNISH

sprigs of marjoram

PREHEAT the oven to 180°C/350°F/gas 4.

If possible remove the wishbone from the neck end of the turkey for ease of carving. Also remove the fat from the vent end, season the cavity with salt and freshly ground pepper and stuff with 2 or 3 sprigs of fresh marjoram.

Smear the breast of the turkey with half of the butter. Put the turkey breast-side down into a large saucepan and cook on a gentle heat for 6–8 minutes, or until the skin on the breast turns golden. Turn the other way up and smear with 2 tablespoons of chopped marjoram mixed with the remaining butter. Season with salt and freshly ground pepper. Cover with greaseproof paper and a tight-fitting lid. Cook in a moderate oven for 2–2½ hours. Test to see if the turkey is cooked: the juices should be clear and there should be no trace of pink between the thigh and the breast.

Remove the turkey to a carving dish, allow to rest while the sauce is being made. De-grease the cooking juices, add the light cream, bring to the boil, taste, and reduce if necessary to strengthen the flavour. Add 2 more tablespoons of freshly chopped marjoram. Add the juices from the carving dish to the sauce. Taste, correct seasoning.

Carve the turkey and nap with the sauce. Garnish with sprigs of fresh marjoram.

NOTE: Use the turkey carcass to make stock on exactly the same principle as the chicken stock (see page 137). Use for soups.

There are several varieties of marjoram; the one we use for this recipe is the annual sweet marjoram – *Origanum marjorana*.

PHEASANT WITH APPLES AND CALVADOS

Serves 4

Chicken or guinea fowl may also be used.

1 plump young pheasant	1 oz/30 g/2 tablespoons butter
1/2 oz/15 g/1 tablespoon butter	2 dessert apples, e.g. Golden
2 fl oz/55 ml/1/4 cup Calvados	Delicious, peeled and diced
8 fl oz/250 ml/1 cup cream	salt and freshly ground pepper

GARNISH

sprigs of watercress *or* chervil

PREHEAT the oven to 180°C/350°F/gas 4.

Choose a casserole, preferably oval, just large enough to take the bird. Season the cavity, spread 1/2 oz/15 g of butter over the breast and legs of the pheasant and place breast-side down into the casserole. Allow it to brown on a gentle heat, turn over and sprinkle with salt and freshly ground pepper. Cover with a tight-fitting lid and cook in a moderate oven for 40–45 minutes. Check to see that the pheasant is cooked (there should be no trace of pink between the leg and the breast). Transfer the pheasant to a serving dish and keep warm.

Carefully strain and de-grease the juices in the casserole. Bring to the boil, add the Calvados and ignite with a match. Shake the pan and when the flames have subsided, add the cream. Reduce until the sauce thickens, stirring occasionally; taste for seasoning.

Meanwhile, carve the pheasant and arrange on a hot serving dish. Mask with the sauce.

Fry the diced apple in butter until golden. Put the apple in the centre and garnish the dish with watercress or chervil.

PHEASANT WITH CELERY AND PORT

Serves 4

Chicken or guinea fowl may also be used.

1 plump pheasant	4 oz/110 g streaky bacon in one
1½ oz/45 g/3 tablespoons butter	piece
1 finely chopped onion	salt and freshly ground pepper
4 fl oz/130 ml/½ cup port	½ or 1 small head of celery
½ pint/300 ml/1¼ cups home-	6 fl oz/175 ml/¾ cup cream
made chicken or pheasant giblet	squeeze of lemon juice
stock (see page 137)	if necessary

roux (optional, see glossary)

GARNISH
chopped parsley

PREHEAT the oven to 180°C/350°F/gas 4.

Cut the rind off the bacon and cut into ¼ in/7 mm cubes. Melt the butter in a casserole, add the bacon and onion and cook for a few minutes. Remove to a plate.

Smear a little butter on the breast of the pheasant and brown it in the casserole over a gentle heat. Return the onion and bacon to the casserole, then add port and stock. Bring to the boil, cover and cook in a moderate oven for 30 minutes.

Meanwhile, slice the celery into ½ in/10 mm pieces, at an angle. Add to the casserole, packing it all around the pheasant. Season with salt and freshly ground pepper and replace the lid. Cook for a further 30–35 minutes. Remove the pheasant as soon as it is cooked, strain and de-grease the cooking liquid. Arrange the celery and bacon in a serving dish, carve the pheasant into 4 portions and arrange on top of the celery.

Bring the cooking liquid back to the boil, add cream and simmer for 4 or 5 minutes to intensify the flavour. Thicken with a little roux if necessary. Taste for seasoning and sharpen with a little lemon juice. Spoon the sauce over the pheasant and celery, and serve scattered with chopped parsley.

BALLYMALOE CHICKEN LIVER PATÉ WITH MELBA TOAST

Serves 10–12, depending on how it is served

This has been our *pâté maison* at Ballymaloe since the opening of the restaurant. We serve it in several different ways.

1. In little ramekins accompanied by hot crusty white bread.
2. In tiny pottery pots as part of a second course called 'Little pots of pâté'.
3. We fill the pâté into a loaf tin lined with clingfilm and, when it is set, slices are arranged on individual plates with a little well-seasoned tomato concassé and garnished with chervil or lemon balm.
4. For a buffet, the loaf-shaped pâté is covered with a thin layer of soft butter, which is decorated with tiny rosettes of butter and thyme flowers. The whole pâté is then arranged on a bed of lettuces and garnished with herbs in flower.
5. Rosettes of pâté can be piped on to tiny triangles of Melba Toast, tiny Ballymaloe Cheese Biscuits (page 236) or slices of cucumber. These rosettes must be served within an hour of being prepared and are very pretty. Garnish with a spot of tomato concassé and a little chervil.
6. Pâté can be formed into a roll, wrapped in clingfilm or grease-proof paper and refrigerated. Later the paper is removed and the roll of pâté is decorated with rosettes of butter and thyme leaves and flowers.

8 oz/225 g fresh chicken livers	1 large clove garlic
8–10 oz/225–340 g/1–1½ cups butter (depending on how strong the chicken livers are)	1 teaspoon fresh thyme leaves clarified butter (see page 46) to seal the top
1½–2 tablespoons brandy	salt and freshly ground pepper

WASH the livers and remove any membrane or green tinged bits. Melt a little butter in a frying pan; when the butter foams add in the livers and cook over a gentle heat. Be careful not to overcook them or the outsides will get crusty; all traces of pink should be gone. Put the livers through a sieve or into a food processor. De-glaze the pan with brandy, allow to flame, add garlic and then scrape off with a spatula and add to the livers. Purée for a few seconds. Allow to cool, then add 8 oz/225 g/1 cup butter and fresh thyme leaves. Season carefully, taste and add more butter if necessary. This pâté should taste fairly mild and be quite smooth in texture.

Clarify some butter (see below) and run a little over the top of the pâté which can then be put into little pots or into one large terrine. Serve with Melba Toast or hot white bread. This pâté will keep for 4 or 5 days in a refrigerator.

NOTE: It is essential to cover the pâté with a layer of clarified, or even just melted butter, otherwise it will oxidise and become bitter in taste and grey in colour.

Melba Toast

Serves 4

2 thin slices of white bread

TOAST the bread on both sides. Cut the crusts off immediately and then split the slice in half. Scrape off any soft crumb, cut into triangles and put back under the grill, untoasted side up, for a few seconds until the edges curl up.

CHICKEN STOCK

Home-made chicken stock is a wonderfully useful thing to have in your fridge or freezer. *Fond* is the name for stock in French; *fond* means foundation, which just sums up stock: stocks are the foundation of so many things – soups, sauces, casseroles, etc. Making stock is really just an attitude of mind! Instead of absent-mindedly flinging things into the bin, keep your carcasses, giblets and vegetable trimmings and use them for your stock pot.

2–3 raw *or* cooked chicken carcasses *or* a mixture of both *or* 1 × 4 lb/1.8 kg boiling fowl, disjointed	1 sliced onion
	1 leek, split in two
	1 stick of celery *or* 1 lovage leaf
giblets from the chicken, i.e. neck, heart, gizzard	1 sliced carrot
	few parsley stalks
	sprig of thyme
6 pints/3.4 l/15 cups cold water	6 peppercorns

BREAK up the carcasses as much as possible. Put all the ingredients in a saucepan and cover with cold water. Bring to the boil and skim the fat off the top with a tablespoon. Simmer for 3–5 hours. Strain and remove any remaining fat. If you need a stronger flavour, boil down the liquid in an open pan to reduce by one-third or one-half the volume. Do not add salt.

NOTE: Stock will keep several days in the refrigerator. If you want to keep it for longer, boil it up again for 5–6 minutes every couple of days; allow it to get cold and refrigerate again. Stock also freezes perfectly. For cheap containers use large yogurt cartons or plastic milk bottles, then you can cut them off the frozen stock without a conscience if you need to defrost it in a hurry!

In restaurants the stock is usually allowed to simmer uncovered so it will be as clear as possible but I usually advise people making stock at home to cover the pot, otherwise the whole house will smell of stock and that may put you off making it on a regular basis.

The above recipe is just a guideline. If you have just one carcass and can't be bothered to make a small quantity of stock, why not freeze the carcass and save it up until you have 6 or 7 carcasses plus giblets, then you can make a really good-sized pot of stock and get best value for your fuel.

Chicken liver shouldn't go into the stock pot because it will cause a bitterness in the stock, but the livers make a wonderful smooth pâté which can be served in lots of different ways.

There are some vegetables which should not be put in the stock: potatoes because they soak up flavour and make the stock cloudy; parsnips – they are too strong; beetroot – they are too strong and the dye would produce a red stock. Cabbage or other brassicas give an off-taste on long cooking. A little white turnip is sometimes an asset, but it is very easy to overdo it. I also ban bay leaf in my chicken stocks because I find that the flavour of bay can predominate easily and add a sameness to soups made from the stock later on.

Salt is another ingredient that you will find in most stock recipes, but not in mine. The reason I don't put it in is because if I want to reduce the stock later to make a sauce, it very soon becomes oversalted.

BEEF AND LAMB

BEEF

Ireland with its lush green pastures has one of the very best climates anywhere in the world for the production of superb quality beef and as a nation we are very fond of beef. Wherever you live, however, make sure you choose a butcher who buys his meat not only for tenderness, but also for flavour. Fillet of beef is really never tough, but it can be virtually tasteless. What you are looking for is a piece of *fresh* fillet of beef with a really 'beefy' flavour. It seems to me that the best-flavoured beef comes from well-reared Aberdeen Angus and Shorthorn. I personally very much regret the growing popularity of the continental breeds, e.g. Limousin and Charollais, which produce leaner meat with less flavour. That, we are told by the powers that be, is what the consumer wants: well, it's certainly not what I want and I strongly question that it's what anyone else wants either! We have been brainwashed into believing that meat with any litttle bit of fat will kill us 'stone dead'. I doubt that too, but one thing I do know for certain is that meat must have a little bit of fat if it is to have a really good flavour. Cook the meat with the fat on, then leave it to the side of your plate if you don't want to eat it, but your lean meat will at least taste wonderful.

The recipe for Fillet of Beef with Mushrooms and Thyme Leaves is a recipe for a special occasion and makes the most of a nice piece of fillet of beef. The Fillet of Beef with Black, White and Pink Peppercorns is also delicious and takes even less time to make. I also wanted to include the great old favourite Boeuf Bourguignon, because nothing can surpass this classic French beef stew when it's made with really good stewing beef and a bottle of wine. Everyone loves it and it's really warming fare for a winter day. Carpaccio on the other hand, which is the famous Italian raw beef recipe, may not instantly appeal to you, but try it and you will be surprised at how appetising it is; 1 lb/450 g of beef can feed about 14–16 people served this way.

Italian Beef Stew is a warming winter dish, full of flavour and a great favourite of my children and their friends. Add the mushrooms at the end of cooking; if you add them at the beginning they will taste and look like bitter little black rags by the end! The great thing about stews like these is that they can, indeed *should*, be prepared in advance, because they taste better the next day.

Pan-grilled Steak with Béarnaise Sauce and Pommes Allumettes uses a classic warm French emulsion sauce. Béarnaise Sauce is really worth mastering and besides being delicious with steak it is very good indeed with plain roast beef, or even fish or poached eggs. The crispy little Pommes Allumettes are a perfect accompaniment to the steak. I cook them in olive oil to make them taste, yes, simply delicious!

It's a great shame that so many people seem to have decided that they just don't like any kind of offal – they don't know what they are missing. I've converted several determined offal-haters by twisting their arms to taste a bit of calf's liver before they write off offal completely. Lightly cooked calf's liver is a revelation – it just melts in your mouth. It also has the advantage of cooking very quickly; in fact it is vital not to overcook it, otherwise it can, like any liver, become tough and leathery. In this recipe we add a little Irish whiskey to the sauce to make it extra special and it's one of the great favourites on the menu at Ballymaloe. Young lamb's liver can be used instead if you cannot find calf's liver.

LAMB

Irish lamb particularly has a wonderful flavour because most is still reared naturally outdoors on grass and, in the case of my butcher, on old pastures full of herbs and wild flowers. I've discovered that the flavour of meat comes not only from the breed of animal and the way it is reared, but also from what the animal feeds on. There are still local butchers who choose their own meat and understand about flavour, so shop around, and when you find a really good butcher ask him to point out the various cuts of meat to you because it's absolutely vital that you 'know your meat'. Otherwise, human nature being what it is, you may just be taken advantage of. When you do get a particularly good piece of meat, don't forget to tell your butcher it was good and then he will know that you're really interested and you will get an even better piece the next time.

My own marvellous butcher has a great saying that 'there's no such thing as bad meat to a good cook'. In other words if someone complains about tough meat, it usually means that they haven't cooked it properly or else they have cooked it when the meat was too fresh. Lamb should be hung for seven to ten days, beef for ten to fourteen days, depending on the cut and the weather.

For Lamb Roast with Rosemary and Garlic or Lamb Roast with Garden Herbs, you can use not only the leg but also loin, or indeed shoulder (except it's a little tricky to carve on the bone). The former is wonderful served with a home-made red currant jelly. The technique for Lamb Roast with Garden Herbs is very similar. Myrtle Allen came up with this recipe when she had her restaurant in Paris; she called it Lamb Roast with Irish Garden Herbs, and the French absolutely loved it served pink and cut in quite thick slices.

Both Myrtle Allen and I are interested in collecting traditional Irish recipes which we believe should be saved from oblivion while there is still time. Sometimes they can be difficult to find: people may have cooked from instinct, putting in a fist of this and a pinch of that, or they may have begun to lose confidence, feeling that in some strange way their old-fashioned, home-cooked food was inferior to newer foods bought in tins or packets. The Dingle Pie recipe is Myrtle Allen's adaptation of a traditional mutton pie recipe made on the Dingle Peninsula. We are convinced that it is a variation of the Cornish Pasty introduced to the south-west of Ireland by Cornish miners who came over in the early nineteenth century to help the locals to mine copper. Myrtle added cumin to the filling – with magical results. The hot water crust pastry which absolutely anyone can master was originally made with mutton fat, but Myrtle substituted butter which results in a light crisp pastry with a delicious flavour. This pastry can of course be used for other pies and it is a great stand-by for people who feel that they absolutely cannot make pastry. The Dingle Pie can be made in advance, eaten hot or cold and frozen cooked or uncooked.

Perhaps the most famous Irish recipe is Irish Stew. This is the version we serve at Ballymaloe. We don't claim that this is the only authentic version, because there are many variations on the theme. Feelings run high on this point! People seem to divide into two main camps: those who believe that real Irish Stew should include carrots, and those who feel that it should have only mutton, onions and potatoes. We add carrots because they enhance the flavour and I like to add a sprig of thyme too. Other people add some pearl barley and still others slice some of the potatoes into the bottom of the pot to thicken the juices. I don't do this because, while the potato does indeed thicken the juices, it is rather inclined to soak up the flavour too; instead, I cover the top of the stew with the potatoes so they can steam. They taste wonderful and are flavoured with the meat juices.

Irish Stew is a marvellous dish for a chilly day – what I call 'comfort food'. When I think of Irish Stew I feel all warm inside. I remember sitting by the fire eating stew from a deep plate and I'm transported back to my childhood. Such a pity that Irish Stew is so seldom seen on restaurant menus. It deserves to be served more, particularly in restaurants on the tourist routes, because visitors in Ireland ask over and over again where they can find an Irish Stew.

Spiced Lamb with Aubergines on the other hand is a completely different flavour. The smoky taste of the aubergines and the nutty taste of the cumin evoke images of the Middle East.

FILLET OF BEEF WITH MUSHROOMS AND THYME LEAVES

Serves 6

Fillet of Beef is always a treat nowadays and this delicious recipe for a special occasion makes a little beef go as far as possible.

2¼–2½ lb/1–1.2 kg fillet steak (allow 6–8 oz/170–225 g sirloin *or* fillet steak per person)

½ oz/15 g/1 tablespoon butter
1 dessertspoon olive oil

FOR THE SAUCE

1 oz/30 g/2 tablespoons butter
3–4 tablespoons finely chopped shallot *or* spring onion
8 oz/225 g/4 cups sliced button mushrooms
¼ pint/150 ml/generous ½ cup red wine *or* dry vermouth

¼ pint/150 ml/generous ½ cup home-made brown beef stock (see page 150)
½ pint/300 ml/1¼ cups cream roux (optional, see glossary)
½ teaspoon fresh thyme leaves
a few drops of lemon juice
salt and freshly ground pepper

GARNISH

tomato concassé (see glossary)
salt, freshly ground pepper and sugar

flat-leaf parsley
or watercress
or chervil

FIRST prepare the sauce. Melt the butter in a frying pan and sweat the finely chopped shallot on a gentle heat until soft but not coloured; remove from the pan. Increase the heat and sauté the mushrooms in small batches; season each batch and add to the onions as soon as they are cooked. Add the wine or vermouth and stock to the pan and boil rapidly until the liquid has reduced to about 2½ fl oz/60 ml. Add the cream and allow to simmer for a few minutes to thicken (whisk in a tiny bit of roux if you like), add the mushroom and onion mixture and the thyme leaves. Simmer for 1 or 2 minutes; don't allow the sauce to thicken too much or it will be heavy and cloying. Correct seasoning if necessary. If the sauce tastes too rich, add a squeeze of lemon juice. This sauce can be prepared several hours in advance and reheated later.

Trim the beef of any fat or membrane, cut into 2 oz/55 g pieces. Melt the butter and olive oil in a hot pan and when the foam subsides sauté the beef. Remember not to overcrowd the pan; the pieces of beef will only take 1–3 minutes on each side, depending on how you like it cooked. As soon as the beef is cooked, place the pieces on an upturned plate which rests on a larger plate to catch any juices.

To serve: Reheat the sauce, place the pieces of beef on individual plates or on a large serving plate and coat with the mushroom sauce. Garnish with tomato concassé and flat-leaf parsley, watercress or chervil.

FILLET OF BEEF WITH BLACK, WHITE AND PINK PEPPERCORNS

Serves 4

The pink peppercorn is a reasonably new arrival in our speciality shops. Also called *poivre rose* and *baie rose*, it is a soft bright pink peppercorn with a peppery but sweet flavour. It is sold dried and can be ground in a mill. In fact it's not a true pepper at all, but the berry of a plant related to poison ivy. Some people are allergic to it, so use with caution!

4 fillet steaks, 6–8 oz/170–225 g each	¼ pint/150 ml/generous ½ cup cream
1–1½ tablespoons olive oil	salt
2 tablespoons brandy	

PEPPER

1 teaspoon black peppercorns
(mignonette, see note below)

1 teaspoon green peppercorns
(washed)

2 teaspoons pink peppercorns

HEAT a heavy pan until very hot, add oil and sauté the steaks to the required degree: approximately 3 minutes each side for medium rare, about 5 minutes each side for well done. Remove the steaks and leave to relax on a warm plate while you make your sauce.

De-glaze the pan with brandy, then flame or reduce. Add green and black peppercorns. Crush the green peppercorns slightly with a wooden spoon in the pan. Add the cream and reduce for a few minutes, then add the juices from the steaks on the plate. Season with salt and add the pink peppercorns; taste. Return the steaks to the pan and turn them in the sauce, then transfer to a warm plate and nap with the sauce. Serve at once.

NOTE: If you would like a little more sauce, add 3–4 tablespoons of home-made beef stock (see page 150) to the pan with the brandy and continue as above.

Mignonette of peppers means that the peppercorns should be roughly crushed, preferably in a pestle and mortar, but use whatever means are at your disposal – even if it involves putting them into a plastic bag and banging them with the bottom of a saucepan! Pepper ground in a pepper mill is too fine for this recipe.

CARPACCIO WITH MUSTARD AND HORSERADISH SAUCE

Serves 12

Carpaccio is the ultimate recipe to make a little beef go a very long way. This sophisticated dish was invented in Harry's Bar in Venice and named after the great fifteenth-century Venetian painter.

1 lb/450 g fillet of beef (fresh not frozen)

SAUCE

2 egg yolks, preferably free-range	$^1/_4$ pint/150 ml/generous $^1/_2$ cup light olive oil *or* sunflower oil
2 tablespoons Dijon mustard	1 tablespoon grated fresh horseradish
1 tablespoon sugar	
2–2$^1/_2$ tablespoons wine vinegar	1 good teaspoon chopped parsley

1 good teaspoon chopped tarragon

GARNISH

24 tiny spring onions   watercress *or* flat-leaf parsley

FIRST make the sauce. Put the egg yolks into a bowl and add the mustard, sugar and wine vinegar and mix well. Whisk in the oil gradually as though you were making mayonnaise. Finally, add the grated horseradish and chopped parsley and tarragon. Taste and season if necessary.

Chill the meat. Slice the beef fillet with a very sharp knife, as thinly as possible. Place each slice on a piece of oiled clingfilm and cover with another piece of oiled clingfilm. Roll gently with a rolling pin until almost transparent and double in size. Peel the clingfilm off the top, invert the meat on to a chilled plate, and gently peel away the other layer of film.

TO SERVE: Spoon a little sauce on to the side of each plate, garnish with tiny spring onions and some flat-leaf parsley or sprigs of watercress.

Carpaccio may be served as a starter or main course, depending on the size of the helping.

Pan-grilled Steak with Béarnaise Sauce and Pommes Allumettes

Serves 6

Of all the sauces to serve with steak, Béarnaise is my absolute favourite. We find a heavy-ridged cast-iron grill pan the best to cook the steaks when you don't need to make a sauce in the pan.

6 × 6 oz/170 g sirloin *or* fillet steaks
1 clove garlic
a little olive oil
salt and freshly ground pepper

Béarnaise sauce (see below)
pommes allumettes (see below)

GARNISH
fresh watercress (optional)

PREPARE the steaks about 1 hour before cooking. Cut a clove of garlic in half; rub both sides of each steak with the cut clove of garlic, grind some black pepper over the steaks and sprinkle on a few drops of olive oil. Turn the steaks in the oil and leave aside. If using sirloin steaks, score the fat at 1 in/2.5 cm intervals. Make the Béarnaise sauce and keep warm. Heat the grill pan, season the steaks with a little salt and put them down on to the hot pan.

The approximate cooking times for *each side* of the steaks are:

	Sirloin	*Fillet*
RARE	2 minutes	5 minutes
MEDIUM RARE	13 minutes	6 minutes
MEDIUM	4 minutes	7 minutes
WELL DONE	5 minutes	8–9 minutes

Turn a sirloin steak over on to the fat and cook for 1–2 minutes or until the fat becomes crisp. Put the steaks on to a plate and leave them to rest for a few minutes in a warm place while you cook the pommes allumettes.

TO SERVE: Put the steaks on hot plates. Serve the Béarnaise sauce over one end of the steak or in a little bowl on the side of the plate. Garnish with pommes allumettes and fresh watercress.

Béarnaise Sauce

One of the great classics! Use French rather than Russian tarragon if you can find it.

2 fl oz/55 ml/¹/₄ cup tarragon vinegar	2 egg yolks, preferably free-range
2 fl oz/55 ml/¹/₄ cup dry white wine	4–6 oz/110–170 g/¹/₂–³/₄ cup butter approx., salted or
2 teaspoons finely chopped shallots	unsalted depending on what it is being served with
a pinch of freshly ground pepper	1 tablespoon freshly chopped French tarragon leaves

IF you do not have tarragon vinegar to hand, use a wine vinegar and add some extra chopped tarragon. Boil the first four ingredients together until completely reduced and the pan is almost dry but not browned. Add 1 tablespoon of cold water immediately. Pull the pan off the heat and allow to cool for 1 or 2 minutes; whisk in the egg yolks and add the butter bit by bit over a very low heat, whisking all the time. As soon as one piece melts, add the next piece; it will gradually thicken. If it shows signs of becoming too thick or slightly 'scrambling', remove from the heat immediately and add a little cold water if necessary. Do not leave the pan or stop whisking until the sauce is made. Finally add 1 tablespoon of freshly chopped French tarragon and taste for seasoning.

If the sauce is slow to thicken it may be because you are excessively cautious and the heat is too low. Increase the heat slightly and continue to whisk until the sauce thickens to a coating consistency. It is important to remember, however, that if you are making Béarnaise sauce in a saucepan directly over the heat, it should be possible to put your hand on the side of the saucepan at any stage. If the saucepan feels too hot for your hand it is also too hot for the sauce.

Another good tip if you are making Béarnaise sauce for the first time is to keep a bowl of cold water close by so that you can plunge the bottom of the saucepan into it if it becomes too hot.

Keep the sauce warm in a bowl over warm water or in a thermos flask until you want to serve it.

Pommes Allumettes

Serves 6

Pommes allumettes are matchstick potatoes. They are particularly delicious cooked in olive oil.

1 lb/450 g 'old', 'floury' potatoes
olive oil for deep-fat frying salt

WASH and peel the potatoes. Cut them into tiny, even matchsticks and soak in cold water for 15 minutes. This will remove the excess starch and prevent the potatoes from sticking together. Dry them thoroughly with a tea-towel.

Heat the oil, 190°C/375°F. Fry the potatoes until they are golden brown and very crisp. Drain on kitchen paper. Sprinkle with salt and serve.

NOTE: If the pommes allumettes are very crisp they will keep in the oven for 10 minutes or even longer.

BROWN BEEF STOCK

Brown beef stock is used for beef and game stews and for sauces.

5–6 lb/2.3–2.7 kg beef bones, preferably with some scraps of meat on, cut into small pieces
2 large onions, quartered
2 large carrots, quartered
2 stalks celery, cut in ¹/₂ in/2.5 cm pieces
10 peppercorns
2 cloves
4 unpeeled cloves garlic
1 teaspoon tomato purée
8 pints/4.6 l/20 cups water
large bouquet garni, including parsley stalks, bay leaf, sprigs of thyme and a sprig of tarragon

PREHEAT the oven to 230°C/450°F/gas 8.

Put the bones into a roasting tin and roast for 30 minutes or until the bones are well browned. Add the onions, carrots and celery and return to the oven until the vegetables are also browned. Transfer the bones and vegetables to the stock pot with a metal spoon. Add the peppercorns, cloves, garlic, tomato purée and bouquet garni. De-grease the roasting pan and de-glaze with some water, bring to the boil and pour over the bones and vegetables. Add the rest of the water and bring slowly to the boil. Skim the stock and simmer gently for 5–6 hours. Strain the stock, allow it to get cold, and skim off all the fat before use.

This stock will keep for 2–3 days in the refrigerator. If you want to keep it for longer, boil it for 10 minutes, and then chill again. It can also be frozen.

BOEUF BOURGUIGNON

Serves 6

In this country, stew is generally regarded as something you feed the family but not your honoured guests. Not so in France, where this recipe for the most famous of all beef stews, Boeuf Bourguignon, might be served for a special Sunday lunch or dinner with friends. After all it is not cheap to make: you need best-quality well-hung stewing beef and almost a bottle of red wine. As the name suggests it used to be made with Burgundy, but with current Burgundy prices I think I might settle for a good Beaujolais or a full-bodied Côtes du Rhône wine!

6 oz/170 g streaky bacon in one piece
1½–2½ tablespoons olive oil
3 lb/1.35 kg stewing beef cut into 2 in/5 cm cubes
1 carrot, sliced
1 onion, sliced
1¼ pints/750 ml/3 cups red wine: a full-bodied young wine, e.g. a Burgundy, Beaujolais or Côtes du Rhône would be perfect
1 tablespoon tomato paste

¾ pint/450 ml/generous 2 cups home-made brown beef stock (see page 150)
a 2 in/5 cm piece of dried orange peel
1 bay leaf
1 sprig of thyme
2–3 cloves garlic
roux (optional, see glossary)
18–24 button onions, depending on size
1 lb/450 g fresh mushrooms, cut in quarters

salt and freshly ground pepper

REMOVE the rind from the bacon and cut into ½ in/1 cm cubes. Blanch and refresh if salty. Dry well on kitchen paper. Heat 1–2 tablespoons of olive oil in a frying pan, sauté the bacon until crisp and golden, and transfer it to a casserole. Turn up the heat so that the oil and bacon fat is almost smoking. Dry off the beef. Sauté it, a few pieces at a time, until nicely browned on all sides, and add to the casserole with the bacon. Toss the sliced carrot and onion in the remaining fat and add these too. If there is any fat left on the pan at this stage pour it off, then de-glaze the pan with the wine, scraping the little bits of sediment on the pan until they dissolve. Bring to the boil and pour over the beef.

The casserole may be prepared ahead to this point. Allow it to get cold, cover and refrigerate overnight, or at least for a few hours. The wine will have a tenderising effect on the meat, and the herbs and other ingredients will add extra flavour as the meat marinades.

Bring the casserole to the boil, add enough stock to cover the meat, add in the tomato paste, dried orange peel, bay leaf, thyme and the whole cloves of garlic. Season with salt and freshly ground pepper. Bring to the boil, cover and simmer very gently either on top of the stove or in a low oven, 160°C/325°F/gas 3 for 2–3 hours, depending on the cut of meat used. The meat should not fall apart, but it should be tender enough to eat without too much chewing.

Meanwhile cook the small onions and mushrooms. Peel the onions. This task is made easier if you drop them in boiling water for 1 minute and then run them under the cold tap. 'Top and tail' them and then slip off the skins. Simmer gently in a covered casserole with about ½ in/1 cm of water or beef stock – they will take about 30–35 minutes depending on size. A knife should pierce them easily.

Toss the quartered mushrooms a few at a time in a little olive oil in a hot pan. Season with salt and freshly ground pepper.

When the meat is tender, pour the contents of the casserole into a strainer placed over a saucepan. Discard the herbs, sliced carrot and onion and orange peel. Return the meat to the casserole with the onions and mushrooms. Remove the fat from the liquid. There should be about 1 pint/600 ml of sauce. Taste, bring back to the boil and simmer. If the sauce is too thin or too weak, reduce for a few minutes, otherwise thicken slightly by whisking in a little roux. Pour over the meat, mushrooms and onions, bring back to the boil, simmer for a few minutes until heated through, and correct seasoning if necessary.

Sprinkle with chopped parsley and serve.

Boeuf Bourguignon may be made a few days ahead and, within reason, the flavour even improves with keeping.

ITALIAN BEEF STEW

Serves 6–8

3 lb/1.35 kg well-hung stewing
beef *or* lean flank
1 tablespoon olive oil
10 oz/300 g/2½ cups sliced
onions
2 large carrots cut into ½ in/1
cm slices
1 rounded tablespoon flour

8 fl oz/250 ml/1 cup red wine
8 fl oz/250 ml/1 cup brown beef
stock (see page 150)
8 fl oz/250 ml/1 cup home-made
tomato purée
5 oz/140 g/1½ cups sliced
mushrooms
1 tablespoon chopped parsley

TRIM the meat of any excess fat and cut into 1½ in/4 cm cubes. Heat the olive oil in a casserole; sweat the sliced onions and carrots on a gentle heat with the lid on for 10 minutes. Heat a little more olive oil in a frying pan until almost smoking. Sear the pieces of meat on all sides, reduce the heat, stir in flour; cook for 1 minute; mix the wine, stock and tomato purée together and add gradually to the casserole. Cook gently for 2½–3 hours in a low oven, depending on the cut of meat, 160°C/325°F/gas 3. Meanwhile sauté the mushrooms and add to the casserole with the parsley, approximately 30 minutes before the end of cooking. Serve with potatoes or noodles and a good green salad.

Tomato Purée

2 lb/900 g very ripe tomatoes
1 small onion, chopped
2 teaspoons sugar

a good pinch of salt and a few
twists of black pepper

CUT the tomatoes into quarters; put into a stainless steel saucepan with the onion, sugar, salt and freshly ground pepper. Cook on a gentle heat until the tomatoes are soft (no water is needed). Put through the fine blade of the mouli-legume or a nylon sieve. Allow to get cold, then refrigerate or freeze.

NOTE: Tomato purée is one of the very best ways of preserving the flavour of ripe, summer tomatoes for winter. Use for soups, stews, casseroles, etc.

SAUTÉ OF CALF'S LIVER WITH WHISKEY AND TARRAGON

Serves 2

8–12 oz/225–340 g calf's liver, cut into ¹/₂ in/1 cm slices
seasoned flour
¹/₂ oz/15 g/1 tablespoon butter
3 tablespoons whiskey
1 small clove garlic
salt and freshly ground pepper

4 fl oz/130 ml/¹/₂ cup concentrated home-made brown beef stock (see page 150)
2 teaspoons chopped fresh tarragon
3–4 tablespoons cream

GARNISH
2 sprigs of fresh tarragon

HEAT the butter in a heavy frying pan until it foams. Dip the slices of liver in seasoned flour and fry gently on both sides. While the liver is still pink in the centre remove to a warm serving plate. Pour the whiskey into the pan; if cooking on gas, tilt the pan towards the heat, allowing the flame to leap in to ignite the whiskey. Light with a match otherwise. When the flames have died down, add the stock, garlic and tarragon. Reduce until the sauce thickens slightly, add the cream and boil again until the sauce lightly coats the back of a spoon. Taste for seasoning and add a little freshly ground pepper and salt if necessary. Spoon the sauce over the liver, garnish with a sprig of tarragon and serve *immediately*.

LAMB ROAST WITH ROSEMARY AND GARLIC

Serves 8–10

1 × 6 lb/2.7 kg leg of lamb (a 6–7 lb/2.7–3.2 kg leg of lamb will have
about 1 lb 6oz/620 g bone)
2 sprigs of rosemary
4–5 cloves garlic
salt and freshly ground pepper

FOR GRAVY

1/2 pint/300 ml/1 1/4 cups stock
(preferably home-made lamb
stock, see page 158)

roux (optional, see glossary)
red currant jelly
(optional, see page 241)

CHOOSE a good leg of lamb with a thin layer of fat. With the point of a sharp knife or skewer, make deep holes all over the lamb, about 1 in/2.5 cm apart. It is a good idea not to do this on the underside of the joint, in case somebody insists on eating their lamb unflavoured. Divide the rosemary sprigs into tufts of three or four leaves together.

Peel the garlic cloves and cut them into little spikes about the same size as a matchstick broken into three. Stick a spike of garlic into each hole with a tuft of rosemary. Cover and refrigerate for up to 24 hours if you have time.

Heat the oven to 200°C/400°F/gas 6. Sprinkle the joint with salt and freshly ground pepper and put it into a roasting tin in the oven. Reduce the heat to 180°C/350°F/gas 4 after 20 minutes. Cook for about 1 hour more for rare lamb, 1 1/2 hours if it is to be well done. Remove the joint to a serving dish and allow it to rest while you make the gravy.

Spoon the fat off the roasting tin. Pour stock into the cooking juices remaining in the tin. Boil for a few minutes, stirring and scraping the pan well, to dissolve the caramelised meat juices

(I find a small whisk ideal for this). Thicken with a very little roux if you like. Taste and add salt and freshly ground pepper if necessary. Strain and serve the gravy separately in a gravy boat.

Serve with roast potatoes (see page 198).

LAMB ROAST WITH GARDEN HERBS

An average weight leg of lamb 7¹/₂–8 lb/3.3–3.4 kg will serve 8–10 people. Allow 6 oz/170 g approx. per person.

1 leg of lamb

HERB MARINADE

1¹/₄ oz/38 g/1 cup chopped herbs: parsley, thyme, lemon balm, mint, tarragon, chives, rosemary and marjoram★

3 large cloves garlic
4–8 fl oz/130–250 ml/¹/₂–1 cup olive oil
salt

GRAVY

1 pint/600 ml/2¹/₂ cups home-made lamb (see page 158) *or* chicken stock (see page 137)
a little roux (see glossary)

2 teaspoons freshly chopped herbs as above
a little butter
salt and freshly ground pepper

GARNISH

sprigs of fresh mint and parsley

★ If you don't have access to this variety, use whatever fresh herbs you have, e.g. parsley, chives, thyme and mint.

FIRST make the herb marinade. Peel the garlic cloves and make them into a paste. Put them with the olive oil, salt and fresh herbs into a food processor and whizz them round for about 1 minute or until it becomes a soft green paste, otherwise just mix in a bowl.

If possible remove the aitch bone from the top of the leg of lamb so that it will be easier to carve later, then trim the end of the leg. Score the fat lightly, rub in the herb mixture and leave to marinade for several hours if possible.

Preheat the oven to 180°C/350°F/gas 4 and roast for approximately 1¹/₄ hours for rare, 1¹/₂ hours for medium and 1³/₄ hours for well done. When the lamb is cooked to your taste, remove the joint to a carving dish. Rest the lamb for 10 minutes before carving.

De-grease the juices in the roasting tin, add stock, bring to the boil, season with salt and freshly ground pepper, thicken with a little roux if desired, taste and correct seasoning. Just before serving, whisk in some knobs of butter to enrich the gravy and add some freshly chopped herbs.

NOTE: A 6–7 lb/2.7–3.2 kg leg of lamb will have about 1 lb 6 oz/620 g of bone.

MINT SAUCE

---

¹/₂ oz/15 g/¹/₄ cup finely chopped fresh mint

2 teaspoons sugar

3–4 teaspoons white wine vinegar *or* lemon juice

2 fl oz/55 ml/¹/₄ cup boiling water

PUT the sugar and freshly chopped mint into a sauce boat. Add the boiling water and vinegar or lemon juice. Allow to infuse for 5–10 minutes before serving.

DINGLE PIE

Serves 6

This is a favourite, adapted by my mother-in-law, Myrtle Allen, from an old traditional recipe. It is wonderful served either hot or cold and makes marvellous picnic food. The secret is the cumin seed, a widely available spice which is particularly good with lamb.

1 lb/450 g boneless lamb *or*
mutton (from the shoulder *or*
leg; keep bones for stock)
9 oz/255 g/2¼ cups chopped
onions
1 good teaspoon cumin seed

9 oz/255 g/1¾ cups chopped
carrots
2 tablespoons flour
½ pint/300 ml/1¼ cups mutton
or lamb stock
salt and freshly ground pepper

STOCK

lamb bones from the meat
1 carrot
1 onion
outside stalk of celery

a bouquet garni
made up of a sprig of thyme,
parsley stalks,
a small bay leaf

PASTRY

1 lb/450 g/3½ cups flour
9 oz/255 g/generous 1 cup butter

6 fl oz/175 ml/¾ cup water
a pinch of salt

EGG WASH

1 egg

a pinch of salt

2 tins 6 in/15 cm in diameter, 1¼ in/4 cm high

IF no stock is available, put the bones, carrot, onion, celery and bouquet garni into a saucepan. Cover with cold water and simmer for 3–4 hours to make a stock.

Cut all the surplus fat away from the meat and then cut the meat into small, neat pieces about the size of a small sugar lump. Render down the scraps of fat in a hot, wide saucepan until the fat runs. Discard the pieces. Cut the vegetables into slightly smaller dice than the meat and toss them in the fat, leaving them to cook for 3–4 minutes. Remove the vegetables and toss the meat in the remaining fat over a high heat until the colour turns.

Heat the cumin seed in the oven for a few minutes and crush lightly. Stir the flour and cumin seed into the meat. Cook gently for 2 minutes and blend in the stock gradually. Bring to the boil, stirring occasionally. Add back the vegetables, season with salt and freshly ground pepper and leave to simmer in a covered pot. If using young lamb, 30 minutes will be sufficient; an older animal may take up to 1 hour.

Meanwhile, make the pastry. Sieve the flour and salt into a mixing bowl and make a well in the centre. Dice the butter, put it into a saucepan with the water and bring to the boil. Pour the liquid all at once into the flour and mix together quickly; beat until smooth. At first the pastry will be too soft to handle but as it cools it may be rolled out 1/8–1/4 in/3–7 mm thick, to fit the two tins. The pastry may be made into individual pies or one large pie. Keep back one-third of the pastry for lids.

Fill the pastry-lined tins with the meat mixture which should be almost, but not quite, cooked and cooled a little. Brush the edges of the pastry with water and egg wash and put on the pastry lids, pinching them tightly together. Roll out the trimmings to make pastry leaves or twirls to decorate the tops of the pies; make a hole in the centre, egg-wash the lid and then egg-wash the decoration also.

Bake the pies for approximately 40 minutes at 200°C/400°F/gas 6. Serve with a good green salad (see page 55).

BALLYMALOE IRISH STEW

Serves 4–6

2¹/₂–3 lb/1.2–1.35 kg mutton
or lamb chops
(gigot *or* rack chops) not less
than 1 in/2.5 cm thick
5 medium *or* 12 baby onions
5 medium *or* 12 baby carrots
8 potatoes *or* more if you like

1 pint/600 ml/2¹/₂ cups stock
(mutton stock if possible)
or water
1 sprig of thyme
1 tablespoon roux
(optional, see glossary)
salt and freshly ground pepper

GARNISH

1 tablespoon freshly chopped
parsley

1 tablespoon freshly chopped
chives

PREHEAT the oven to 180°C/350°F/gas 4.

Cut the chops in half and trim off some of the excess fat. Set aside. Render down the fat on a gentle heat in a heavy pan (discard the rendered down pieces).

Peel the onions and scrape or thinly peel the carrots (if they are young you could leave some of the green stalk on the onion and carrot). Cut the carrots into large chunks, or if they are young leave them whole. If the onions are large, cut them small; if they are small they are best left whole.

Toss the meat in the hot fat on the pan until it is slightly brown. Transfer the meat into a casserole, then quickly toss the onions and carrots in the fat. Build the meat, carrots and onions up in layers in the casserole, carefully season each layer with freshly ground pepper and salt. De-glaze the pan with mutton stock and pour into the casserole. Peel the potatoes and lay them on top of the casserole, so they will steam while the stew cooks. Season the potatoes. Add a sprig of thyme, bring to the boil on top of the stove, cover and transfer to a moderate oven or *allow to simmer* on top of the stove until the stew is cooked, 1–2$^1/_2$ hours, depending on whether the stew is being made with lamb or mutton.

When the stew is cooked, pour off the cooking liquid, de-grease and reheat in another saucepan. Slightly thicken it with a little roux if you like. Check seasoning, then add chopped parsley and chives and pour it back over the stew. Bring it back up to boiling point and serve from the pot or in a large pottery dish.

SPICED LAMB WITH AUBERGINES

Serves 6

2 lb/900 g shoulder of lamb	8 oz/225 g very ripe tomatoes *or*
2 aubergines	1 tin of tomatoes
1 large onion, sliced	1 large clove garlic, crushed
2–2$^1/_2$ tablespoons olive oil	1 heaped teaspoon crushed
3 teaspoons chopped mint	cumin seed
3 teaspoons chopped marjoram	salt and freshly ground pepper

PREHEAT the oven to 180°C/350°F/gas 4.

Cut the meat into 1 in/2.5 cm cubes. Cut the aubergines into cubes about the same size as the lamb. Sprinkle them with salt and put in a colander to drain with a plate on top of them to weigh them down.

Heat the olive oil in a pan and sweat the sliced onion. Add the meat and allow it to colour, sprinkle with mint and marjoram and season. Transfer the meat and onions to a casserole.

Wash off the aubergines and drain them in kitchen paper; toss them in olive oil in the pan, season with salt and freshly ground pepper and cook for 10 minutes. Add to the meat and cover. Skin the tomatoes, chop them up and put them in the casserole with the meat mixture. Add crushed garlic. Heat the cumin for a few minutes either in a bowl in the oven or in a frying pan, crush in a mortar and add to the casserole. Cook on a gentle heat or in a moderate oven for about $1\frac{1}{2}$ hours. Taste, correct the seasoning and de-grease the cooking liquid if necessary. Serve with rice.

LAMB WITH TOMATO AND HARICOT BEANS

Serves 6

Hearty lamb, tomato and bean casseroles are a great favourite in France.

8 oz/225 g haricot beans

2 fl oz/55 ml/$\frac{1}{4}$ cup olive oil

8 oz/225 g piece of streaky bacon, cut into $\frac{1}{2}$ in/1 cm cubes

2 cloves garlic, crushed

10 oz/300 g/$2\frac{1}{2}$ cups sliced onions

9 oz/255 g carrots, diced

4 sticks celery, diced

2 lb/900 g lamb, leg *or* shoulder

1 tin of tomatoes *or* 1 lb/450 g very ripe tomatoes, peeled

a bouquet garni made up of a sprig of thyme, several sprigs of parsley, a large sprig of rosemary

salt, freshly ground pepper and sugar

GARNISH
2 tablespoons chopped parsley

SOAK the beans in plenty of cold water overnight. Next day heat the olive oil in a casserole, add the bacon and fry until crisp. Add the garlic and onions, toss for a minute or two, then add the diced carrots and celery, cover and sweat for a few minutes.

Meanwhile cut the lamb into 1½ in/4 cm cubes; toss in a little olive oil in a hot pan until the meat changes colour, add to the vegetables with the chopped tomatoes and drained beans. Season with salt, freshly ground pepper and sugar. Add the bouquet of herbs, bring to the boil, cover and simmer for 1–1½ hours depending on the age of the lamb. Taste, correct the seasoning, remove the bouquet garni and serve in an earthenware dish. Sprinkle with chopped parsley.

PORK AND BACON

I absolutely love Irish bacon. It has a unique flavour quite unlike bacon from any other country, yet somehow it is looked on as the 'poor relation' of other meats and considered by many to be 'fine' for a family meal, but nothing like 'grand' enough for entertaining. I don't agree. I quite often serve Glazed Loin of Bacon for a dinner party with Piperonata or Tomato Fondue and either Colcannon or Champ (see pages 188, 190, 195 and 196) and every scrap disappears! It never fails to re-convert people to the most traditional of Irish meats. However, a word of caution: if you want to find really good bacon you have to search carefully. I buy my bacon from several sources, one being a pork and bacon shop in Cork which has been in the same family for three generations. They choose their bacon carefully and exact a high standard from their suppliers so that the bacon and pork is not tainted with strong flavours or cured with too much salt. The result is delicious sweet bacon that leaves one licking one's lips and wishing for more.

Bacon is also extremely versatile. The Glazed Loin of Bacon recipe can be used not only for a loin, but also for a ham or oyster cut (that lovely piece between the loin and the ham). The ham looks very splendid in all its glory and will feed fifteen to twenty people, but can be tricky to carve. The advantage of the loin is that carving it is easy and the piece of meat can be as large as you like.

Ballymaloe Bacon Chop is unbelievably easy and surprisingly delicious served with Fried Banana and even better with an accompaniment of Irish Whiskey Sauce. Ham Morvandelle, on the other hand, is a special party piece, perfect for a large number of people. It requires the best part of a bottle of Chablis (any old wine will, alas, *not* do for cooking!), but the flavour is quite superb.

163

The pork dishes are equally varied, starting with another favourite, Roast Pork with Garlic and Thyme Leaves and (the classic accompaniment) good Apple Sauce. We quite often use streaky pork in this but you could, of course, use loin instead. I've included Roast Kassler, too, because I think this type of pork, which has been marinated with juniper berries and spices and then smoked, is one of the most delicious new products to come on the market in the last few years.

For something entirely different, I hope you will try Filipino Pork with Peppers and Fresh Ginger – a simple and not too spicy oriental recipe which one of my assistants tested in the cookery school at lunchtime recently and was duly rewarded with empty plates.

GLAZED LOIN OF BACON

Serves 12–15

This recipe turns bacon into a feast – grand enough for any dinner party. It is particularly good served with Tomato Fondue, Piperonata, Colcannon or Ulster Champ (see pages 188, 190, 195 and 196).

4–5 lb/1.8–2.3 kg best-quality loin of bacon, either smoked or unsmoked, off the bone	12 oz/340 g/1¾ cups brown Demerara sugar
	20–30 whole cloves approx.
1 × 14 oz/400 g tin pineapple	

COVER the bacon in cold water and bring slowly to the boil. If the bacon is very salty there will be a white froth on top of the water; in this case it is preferable to discard the water. It may be necessary to change the water several times depending on how salty the bacon is. Finally, cover the bacon with hot water and then simmer until almost cooked. Allow approximately 15 minutes to 1 lb/450 g. Remove the rind, cut the fat into a diamond pattern and stud with cloves. Blend brown sugar to a thick paste with a little pineapple juice, approximately 3–4 tablespoons Be careful not to make it too liquid. Spread this over the bacon. Bake in a fully preheated hot oven, 250°C/475°F/gas 9, for 20–30 minutes or until the top has caramelised. While it is glazing, baste with juices every few minutes.

This is delicious on a cold buffet when cooked the same day. Cold buffet food is best freshly cooked and not too cold. Glazed Loin of Bacon may be served hot or cold.

BALLYMALOE BACON CHOP

Serves 4–5

In the restaurant at Ballymaloe we serve this with Irish whiskey sauce (see below), but it is also delicious served just with fried banana (see below).

2 lb/900 g loin of bacon (boneless and without the streaky end)

4 oz/110 g/scant 1 cup seasoned flour

1 egg and some milk

fresh, white breadcrumbs

FOR FRYING

1 oz/30 g/2 tablespoons clarified butter (see page 46) *or*

1/2 oz/15 g/1 tablespoon butter and 1–2 tablespoons olive oil

USE freshly cured green bacon. Cover the piece of bacon with cold water. Bring to the boil. If the bacon is salty, throw out the water and start again; you may need to do this twice or in extreme cases three times. Boil for approximately 30 minutes or until it is three-quarters cooked. Remove the rind and trim away any surplus fat. Slice into chops 1/2–3/4 in/1–2 cm thick. Dip in seasoned flour, then in beaten egg and milk, and finally coat with white breadcrumbs. Heat clarified butter and oil in a heavy frying pan; fry the chops gently until they are cooked through and golden on both sides.

NOTE: For a cheaper version, streaky bacon could be used instead of loin.

Fried Banana

2 bananas $^1/_2$ oz/15 g/1 tablespoon butter

MELT the butter in a frying pan, peel the bananas. Split the bananas in half lengthways or cut in thick slices diagonally. Fry gently in the melted butter until soft and slightly golden. Serve hot with Ballymaloe Bacon Chop.

Irish Whiskey Sauce

8 oz/225 g/1 cup caster $2^1/_2$ fl oz/60 ml/generous $^1/_4$ cup
sugar   hot water
3 fl oz/75 ml/$^1/_3$ cup $2–2^1/_2$ fl oz/55–60 ml/$^1/_4$ cup
cold water   Irish whiskey

PUT the caster sugar into a bowl with the water; stir over a gentle heat until the sugar dissolves and the syrup comes to the boil. Remove the spoon and do not stir. Continue to boil until it turns a nice chestnut-brown colour. Remove from the heat and immediately add the hot water. Allow to dissolve again and then add the Irish whiskey. Serve hot or cold.

HAM MORVANDELLE

Serves 16–20

This is another recipe suitable for a party, but rather more extravagant than Chicken Pilaff (see page 127). It freezes well and reheats
perfectly. The recipe comes from the Burgundy area of France and
takes its name from the Morvan forests.

1 × 8–10 lb/3.4–4.5 kg ham
1 oz/30 g/2 tablespoons butter
1 tablespoon oil
8 oz/225 g carrots, sliced
8 oz/225 g onions, sliced
12 parsley sprigs
1 bay leaf

a sprig of thyme
4 cloves
1/2 bottle of white Burgundy,
e.g. Chablis *or* Pouilly Fuissé
(we use a Petit Chablis)
32 fl oz/900 ml/4 cups home-
made chicken stock
(see page 137)

12 peppercorns

SAUCE

4 tablespoons chopped onion *or*
shallot
a little butter

2 lb/900 g mushrooms, sliced
16 fl oz/500 ml/2 cups cream
salt and freshly ground pepper

ROUX

4 oz/110 g/1/2 cup butter

4 oz/110 g/1 cup flour

LIAISON

3 egg yolks, preferably free-range
2 fl oz/55 ml/1/4 cup cream

SOAK the ham in cold water overnight and discard the water the
next day. Place the ham in a large saucepan and cover with fresh,
cold water. Bring it slowly to the boil and discard the water.
Repeat the process once or twice more, depending on how salty
the ham is. (This is particularly important if the dish is to be frozen
because freezing seems tc intensify the salty taste.)

Meanwhile, melt the butter and oil in a casserole large enough
to take the ham. Toss the sliced carrots and onions in the fat and

sweat for approximately 10 minutes. Place the ham on top of the vegetables and add the parsley, bay leaf, peppercorns, thyme and cloves. Pour over the wine and stock; cover, bring to the boil and simmer on top of the stove or in a moderate oven, 180°C/350°F/gas 4, until the ham is cooked, approximately 2¹/₂–3 hours. You can test when it is cooked by lifting the skin: if it peels off easily, the ham is cooked. (Allow about 15 minutes per 1 lb/450 g and 15 minutes over.)

To make the sauce cook the onion or shallot in a little butter on a low heat until soft. Remove from the pan. Sauté the mushrooms on a high heat and add to the shallot. When the ham is cooked, strain and de-grease the cooking liquid. Return the liquid to the casserole with the cream and bring to the boil. Thicken with roux (see glossary) to a light coating consistency and simmer for 5 minutes. Add the mushrooms and shallots and taste for seasoning. Skin the ham and slice carefully, arranging in one or more serving dishes.

To make the liaison, mix the egg yolks with the cream and add a ladleful of the simmering sauce to the liaison, mix well and add into the remaining sauce. Do not allow to boil again or it may curdle.

Spoon the sauce over the slices of ham in the serving dish (may be prepared ahead to this point). Reheat in a moderate oven, 180°C/350°F/gas 4, for approximately 20–30 minutes. It should be bubbling and slightly golden on top.

For a dinner party, you may want to pipe a border of Duchesse potato (see page 197) around the outside of the serving dish. Tomato Fondue (see page 188), Piperonata (see page 190) and a good green salad (see page 55) make nice accompaniments.

NOTE: Loin or oyster cut of bacon may be used for this recipe.

ROAST KASSLER

Serves 10–12

The delicious German speciality, Kassler, is fresh loin of pork marinated with pepper, cloves and juniper berries for 12–24 hours and then oak-smoked for a further 12 hours. It used to be quite difficult to find but is now becoming more widely available as many pork butchers produce their own. It is best roasted rather than boiled. It may be served hot, warm or cold.

1 × 5 lb/2.3 kg Kassler

PREHEAT the oven to 180°C/350°F/gas 4.

Weigh the joint and calculate 20 minutes per 1 lb/450 g. Put the piece of Kassler on to a roasting tin; during cooking, baste once or twice with the fat which will render out. Test the meat. The juices should run clear. When cooked, turn off the oven or set to a very low heat; leave the meat to relax for approximately 20 minutes before carving. De-grease the pan and serve the sweet juices with the Kassler. Keep the pork fat to roast or sauté potatoes.

ROAST PORK WITH GARLIC AND THYME LEAVES AND APPLE SAUCE

Serves 10–12

Streaky pork makes the sweetest and juiciest roast of pork; make sure to buy it with the skin on to get the crackling.

1 × 5 lb/2.3 kg joint of streaky pork

HERB PASTE

3 cloves finely chopped garlic
4 tablespoons parsley

2 tablespoons fresh thyme leaves
1 teaspoon salt

1 tablespoon olive oil (add more if needed to make a thick paste)

1 teaspoon freshly ground black pepper

GRAVY

1 pint/600 ml/2½ cups home-made chicken stock (see page 137)

roux (optional, see glossary)

SCORE the skin at ¼ in/7 mm intervals – let your butcher do this if possible because the skin is quite tough. (This will also make it easier to carve later.) Mix or liquidise the ingredients for herb paste and rub into the pork.

Preheat the oven to 190°C/375°F/gas 5. Roast on a rack, allowing 25–28 minutes per lb/450 g.

NOTE: Just before the end of cooking turn up temperature to very hot, 230°C/450°F/gas 8, to get crisp crackling.

To make gravy, de-grease the roasting pan and add the chicken stock to de-glaze the pan. Bring to the boil. Season and thicken with a little roux if desired. Freshly chopped herbs may be added to the gravy. Serve with crispy, roast potatoes and apple sauce.

Apple Sauce

Serves approximately 10

The trick with apple sauce is to cook it uncovered on a low heat with very little water.

1 lb/450 g cooking apples, e.g. Bramley Seedling *or* Grenadier 1–2 dessertspoons water

2 oz/55 g/¼ cup sugar, depending on how tart the apples are

PEEL, quarter and core the apples. Cut the pieces into two and put in a stainless steel or cast-iron saucepan with sugar and water. Cover and put over a low heat. As soon as the apple has broken down, beat into a purée, stir and taste for sweetness. Serve warm.

NOTE: Apple sauce freezes perfectly, so make more than you need and freeze in tiny, plastic cartons. It is also a good way to use up windfalls.

FILIPINO PORK WITH PEPPERS AND FRESH GINGER

Serves 6

Oriental meat recipes make the most of a little meat. This delicious pork dish was cooked for me by Susie Noriega.

1 lb/450 g pork fillet
2–2½ tablespoons light soya sauce
1½ oz/45 g unsalted peanuts
1 fresh red *or* green chilli
1½ oz/45 g bamboo shoots
2 small green peppers
1 × 1 in/2.5 cm fresh ginger root

4 large spring onions (scallions)
2–2½ tablespoons arachide oil
1 teaspoon tapioca
2½ fl oz/60 ml/generous ¼ cup water approx.
1 tablespoon tabasco *or* oyster sauce
a pinch of sugar
salt and freshly ground pepper

1 large clove garlic

1 wok

CUT the pork into ¼ in/7 mm strips, marinate in light soya sauce, season with freshly ground pepper and leave aside. Put the peanuts on a baking sheet and roast for approximately 20 minutes in a moderate oven, 180°C/350°F/gas 4, until golden. Rub off the loose skins.

Halve the chilli and remove the seeds. Cut into small dice. Cut the bamboo shoots into pieces the same size as the pork. Halve and quarter the green pepper, remove the seeds and cut into similar-sized pieces.

Peel the ginger root and garlic and chop finely. Also chop the spring onions finely on the bias.

Heat the wok, add half the oil and fry the garlic, ginger and spring onions for a few seconds. Remove to a plate. Heat the wok to very hot, add the oil, toss the pork for 2 minutes maximum and then add in the remaining peppers and bamboo shoots. Season with salt and freshly ground pepper, add a drop of water, cover and cook for 3–4 minutes until the vegetables are cooked but still crunchy. Then add the chilli and roasted peanuts. Dissolve the tapioca in the water, add a dash of tabasco or oyster sauce and a pinch of sugar. Add to the wok, bubble up again and serve immediately in a hot serving dish with plain boiled rice.

VEGETARIAN
DISHES

There is no doubt about it, more and more people are turning to vegetarian or part-vegetarian food – some for moral reasons, others because a wider range of tempting vegetables are available than ever before and some for the good of their health. There is also a general unease about the presence of hormones and antibiotics in meat and the apparent failure to implement stringent enough controls to restrict their use. This is unfortunate for those producers whose meat is beyond reproach, as it is very difficult for the consumer to tell which is which. Apart from that, there is a general move away from the meat-laden diet of old with the growing realisation that we don't actually need to eat huge quantities of meat to be healthy.

In tandem with this, vegetarian cooking, which used to have a deadly dull boiled-rice-and-lentils image, has recently become much more adventurous. Many restaurants now offer vegetarian alternatives which are every bit as tempting as the other dishes on the menu – if not more so! So for these reasons I am including a few vegetarian recipes in this book.

I begin with Provençale Bean Stew and Green Lentil and Bean Salad because dried beans and pulses are such a rich and cheap source of protein, making them an indispensable part of a vegetarian diet. They also keep indefinitely. Some were found intact in the Pyramids – but from the cook's point of view this is rather pushing things! The longer they are kept, the drier they become and consequently the longer they take to cook, so it's as well to use them within a year. For any bean recipes, you have to think ahead, since soaking for eight hours or so is essential. Once the beans are cooked, however, you can freeze them very satisfactorily and so save time.

Pasta, too, is becoming more and more popular, and is a quick and tasty accompaniment to many vegetarian dishes. This is also true of rice, while bulgar and couscous provide flavoursome alternatives to such staples as potatoes: they have the added useful- ness of forming a background for colourful assemblies of vege- tables, spices, beans and even fruit.

The other great protein-rich vegetarian mainstay is cheese. We use the delicious mature Irish Cheddar both for cooking and nibbling. It is slightly more expensive and less in evidence than ordinary Cheddar but I feel its nuttier, richer taste make the quest and the extra cost worthwhile. The mature Irish Cheddar that I buy from my local creamery comes in big 'truckles' wrapped in muslin; it has marvellous flavour for both cooking and eating. It is the basis of the Ballymaloe Cheese Fondue, a recipe to keep up your sleeve for an evening when you get home late and exhausted. With crusty bread dipped in, it's the fastest, most deliciously nutritious meal you could ever hope to find and even more delicious with a glass of wine. Don't just save it to eat on your own because it's also great for a party – but just be careful where you sit. According to fondue tradition, she who drops her bread into the pot must kiss the gentleman on her left! (This could be your great chance to give fate a helping hand!) Fondue parties are always fun and children love them too.

Baked Eggs can also be a splendid vegetarian dish and are wonderfully fast and infinitely versatile too. They can be absol- utely plain, as in the basic recipe, or can be transformed with a tablespoon of Tomato Fondue (page 188), Piperonata (page 190), or cooked mushrooms.

Many of the *salades tièdes* in the section on Starters can of course be adapted for vegetarians. Further proof that when you learn one or two techniques you can do any number of wonderful things with them. Vegetarian cooking need not mean a complete break with traditional recipes or methods. Soups, for example, can become an important part of the vegetarian's diet, and all one needs to make many soups acceptable is to use water or vegetable stock (fresh whenever possible) instead of a meat- or fish-based liquid.

Provençale Bean Stew

Serves 8

This is a delicious rustic bean stew, cheap to make yet wonderfully filling and nutritious, and a particularly good dish for vegetarians. Do not add the salt to the beans until near the end of the cooking time, otherwise they seem to harden.

12 oz/340 g/2 cups approx. dried haricot, kidney *or* black-eyed beans *or* a mixture of all three
1–3 carrots
1–3 onions
1–3 bouquet garni
2–2¹/₂ tablespoons virgin olive oil
8 oz/225 g/2 cups sliced onions
1 large red pepper, cored, seeded and sliced
1 large green pepper, cored, seeded and sliced

2 cloves garlic, crushed
1 × 14 oz/400 g tin of tomatoes *or* 1 lb/450 g peeled, very ripe tomatoes, chopped
2–3 tablespoons concentrated tomato purée
1 teaspoon chopped marjoram, thyme *or* basil
1 bouquet garni
2 oz/55 g/¹/₃ cup black olives
2 tablespoons chopped parsley
salt, freshly ground pepper and sugar

THE day before cooking, pick over the beans, cover with plenty of cold water and leave overnight (soak each type of bean separately). Next day, drain the beans, place in a saucepan or saucepans (cook each type of bean separately) and cover with fresh cold water. Add a chunk of carrot, a small onion and a bouquet garni to each pot. Bring to the boil, boil rapidly for 10 minutes, then cover and simmer until almost tender. The cooking time varies according to the variety and age of the beans, so for this reason it is better to cook the beans in separate pots and mix them later. Add a pinch of salt towards the end of cooking.

When the beans are tender but not mushy, strain and reserve ¹/₂ pint/300 ml/1¹/₄ cups of the liquid and discard the vegetables and bouquet garni. Heat the oil in a casserole and sweat the onions on a low heat for about 5 minutes. Add the peppers and garlic, cover and continue to sweat gently for 10 minutes. Add the tomatoes with their juice, tomato purée, herbs, beans, bouquet garni, reserved cooking liquid, salt, freshly ground pepper and a pinch of sugar. Cover and simmer for approximately 20 minutes, or until the beans and peppers are cooked. 5 minutes before the end of cooking time, add the olives and freshly chopped parsley. Remove the bouquet garni, taste and correct the seasoning.

NOTE: 1 lb/450 g streaky bacon, blanched and de-rinded, cut into ¹/₂ in/1 cm cubes, may be added to this stew. Brown the cubes in olive oil before adding the peppers. If this bean stew is being eaten without meat, then rice should be eaten in the same meal in order to get maximum food value from the beans.

GREEN LENTIL AND BEAN SALAD

Serves 8

This salad may be eaten on its own or as part of a selection of salads. (Warm crispy bacon *or* pickled pork is good with it also.)

2 oz/55 g/¹/₃ cup haricot beans

2 oz/55 g/¹/₃ cup kidney beans

2 oz/55 g/¹/₃ cup green lentils

3 bouquet garni

3 small carrots

3 small onions, each stuck with 2 cloves

FRENCH DRESSING

9 fl oz/275 ml/generous 1 cup extra virgin olive oil

3 fl oz/75 ml/scant ¹/₂ cup red *or* white wine vinegar

1 dessertspoon Dijon mustard

1 teaspoon chives

3 large cloves garlic

1 teaspoon thyme

1 teaspoon parsley

salt and freshly ground pepper

GARNISH

2 teaspoons freshly chopped parsley

2 teaspoons fresh basil

SOAK the beans in cold water *separately* overnight. Lentils do not need to be soaked. Cook the pulses in separate saucepans; cover each with cold water and add a carrot, onion and bouquet garni to each saucepan. Do not add salt to the beans until almost cooked. Beans take anything from 20–60 minutes to cook depending on variety and age. Lentils take about 10 minutes. They should be soft, but still hold their shape. (Keep the cooking liquids – they may be used as a base for a bean or lentil soup and are full of vitamins.)

Whisk or liquidise ingredients for French dressing together; it should be very well seasoned and quite sharp. Make sure the pulses are well drained. While they are *still warm*, toss the beans and lentils in the French dressing, using enough just to coat the pulses. Taste and season well with salt and freshly ground pepper, and fold in the chopped parsley and basil.

NOTE: This salad must be carefully seasoned, otherwise it will taste bland.

COUSCOUS WITH VEGETABLES AND CORIANDER

Serves 8

8–12 oz/225–340 g couscous
10 tablespoons olive oil *or* 6 tablespoons olive oil and 4 tablespoons melted butter
12 oz/340 g onions, chopped
12 oz/340 g carrots, diced into ¼ in/7 mm dice
2 cloves garlic, crushed
½–1 tablespoon whole coriander, freshly ground
lb/450 g very ripe tomatoes, peeled and chopped, *or* 1 14-oz tin tomatoes including the juice

1–2 fresh chillies, cut into thin slices
12 oz/340 g courgettes, sliced into ¼ in/5 mm rounds
¼ pint/150 ml/generous ½ cup vegetable stock *or* water
4–6 oz/110–170 g peas
2 tablespoons freshly chopped parsley
2 oz/55 g black olives, optional
2–3 tablespoons fresh basil, oregano or coriander leaves

MÉASURE the volume of couscous and soak in an equal volume of warm water for about 15 minutes or until all the water has been absorbed. Heat 4 tablespoons olive oil in a saucepan, add the onions, carrots, garlic and coriander, cover and sweat over a gentle heat until soft but not coloured. Add the tomatoes and the sliced chillies, season with salt and freshly ground pepper and cook, uncovered, for a further 10 to 15 minutes. Meanwhile, toss the sliced courgettes in 2 tablespoons of olive oil, add to the vegetable mixture and take off the heat.

Season the couscous with salt and freshly ground pepper and stir in about 4 tablespoons olive oil or 4 tablespoons melted butter, put into an ovenproof dish, cover with foil and a tight fitting lid. Put into a moderate oven, 180°C/350°F/gas 4, for about 20 minutes or until cooked through.

Cook the peas in about ¼ pint/150 ml/generous ½ cup of boiling salted water or vegetable stock and add both the peas and liquid to the vegetables, add 1 tablespoon of chopped parsley, taste and correct seasoning. Taste the vegetables and add 1 tablespoon of fresh basil or oregano or coriander.

TO SERVE: spread the couscous on a hot serving dish, make a well in the centre, add two tablespoons of fresh coriander to the hot vegetables and fill into the centre. Sprinkle with the remainder of the basil, oregano or coriander, chopped parsley and the black olives, if using, and serve immediately.

TABBOULEH

Serves 6 as a main course, 12 as a starter

This refreshing and highly nutritious Middle Eastern salad can be served as a starter or as a main dish. I like to serve it with lots of well-seasoned cucumber and tomato dice.

4 oz/110 g bulgar
(cracked wheat)
3 fl oz/75 ml/¹/₃ cup extra virgin
olive oil
freshly squeezed juice of 2
lemons or more if you need it

salt and freshly ground pepper
3–4 oz/85–110 g freshly chopped
parsley
2 oz/55 g freshly chopped mint
8 oz/225 g spring onions, green
and white parts, chopped

GARNISH

small crisp lettuce leaves, e.g.
Cos or Iceberg
1 firm crisp cucumber, cut into
¹/₄ in/7 mm dice

6 very ripe firm tomatoes,
seeded, diced and sprinkled with
a little salt, pepper and sugar
sprigs of parsley

black olives, optional

SOAK the bulgar in cold water for about 30 minutes, drain and squeeze well to remove any excess liquid. Stir in the olive oil and some of the freshly squeezed lemon juice, season with salt and freshly ground pepper, and leave aside to absorb the dressing while you chop the parsley, mint and spring onions. Just before serving, mix the herbs with the bulgar, taste and add more lemon juice if necessary. It should taste fresh and lively.

TO SERVE: Arrange on a serving plate surrounded by lettuce leaves and little moulds of well seasoned tomato and cucumber dice. Garnish with sprigs of flat parsley – a few black olives wouldn't go amiss either if you enjoy them.

BALLYMALOE CHEESE FONDUE

Serves 2

Myrtle Allen devised this recipe made from Irish Cheddar cheese. It's a great favourite at Ballymaloe and even though it's a meal in itself it may be made in minutes and is loved by adults and children alike. A fondue set is obviously an advantage but not essential.

2–2½ tablespoons white wine
1 small clove garlic, crushed
2 teaspoons
Easy Tomato Chutney
(see page 189)

2 teaspoons freshly chopped
parsley
6 oz/170 g/2 cups grated mature
Cheddar cheese
crusty white bread

PUT the white wine and the rest of the ingredients into a small saucepan or fondue pot and stir. Just before serving put over a low heat until the cheese melts and begins to bubble. Put the pot over the fondue stove and serve immediately with fresh French bread or cubes of ordinary white bread crisped up in a hot oven.

NOTE: Ballymaloe Country Relish (available in shops throughout Ireland) is a delicious alternative to Easy Tomato Chutney.

LEEK, POTATO AND CHEDDAR CHEESE PIE

Serves 8

A cheap and cheerful winter lunch or supper dish, which can also be served as a vegetable.

1 lb/450 g leeks
1 lb/450 g 'old', 'floury' potatoes
1/2 clove garlic, crushed
2 tablespoons grated cheese

2 oz/55 g/4 tablespoons butter
1 pint/600 ml/2 1/2 cups Cheddar cheese sauce
(see Mornay sauce, page 183)
salt and freshly ground pepper

1 × 2 pint/1.1 l capacity pie dish

COOK the potatoes in salted boiling water. Cut the green parts off the leeks, wash the white parts well and cut into 1/2 in/1 cm rounds. Melt the butter in a casserole, toss in the leeks, season with salt and freshly ground pepper, cover and cook for 20 minutes on a very low heat. Make the cheese sauce but add the crushed garlic; it should be a light coating consistency. When the potatoes are cooked, peel and cut into 1/2 in/1 cm cubes and mix gently with the leeks and sauce. Turn into a pie dish. Sprinkle with grated Cheddar cheese. This pie may be prepared ahead and reheated later in a moderate oven, 180°C/350°F/gas 4, until golden and bubbly on top, for about 20 minutes.

MACARONI CHEESE

Serves 6

This is one of my children's favourite supper dishes. They prefer it without the onion, but I often add some cubes of cooked bacon or ham to the sauce when I'm adding in the macaroni.

8 oz/225 g/2½ cups macaroni
4 pints/2.3 l/10 cups water
1 teaspoon salt
4 oz/110 g/1 cup chopped onion
or spring onion, including green
stalks (optional)
2 oz/55 g/4 tablespoons butter
2 oz/55 g/½ cup flour

32 fl oz/900 ml/4 cups boiling
milk
¼ teaspoon Dijon mustard
1 tablespoon chopped parsley
(optional)
4½ oz/125 g/1½ cups grated
mature Cheddar cheese
salt and freshly ground pepper

1 x 2 pint/1.1 l capacity pie dish

BRING the water to the boil with the teaspoon of salt. Sprinkle in the macaroni and stir to make sure it doesn't stick together; cook until just soft, for about 15 minutes. Meanwhile melt the butter and sweat the onions gently until soft, for 8–10 minutes or so. Add in the flour and cook, stirring occasionally for 1–2 minutes. Blend in the milk gradually and bring back to the boil; keep stirring. Add the mustard, parsley, salt and freshly ground pepper to taste, and half of the cheese. Stir in the cooked macaroni and turn into a pie dish. Sprinkle the top with the remaining cheese. Reheat in a hot oven, 200°C/400°F/gas 6, or under the grill until the top is brown and bubbly.

This is also good served with cold meat, particularly ham.

CAULIFLOWER CHEESE

Serves 6–8

1 medium-sized cauliflower with green leaves
salt

MORNAY SAUCE

1 pint/600 ml/2½ cups milk
with a dash of cream
a slice of onion
3–4 slices of carrot
6 peppercorns
a sprig of thyme *or* parsley
1 oz/30 g/2 tablespoons butter
1 oz/30 g/¼ cup flour

4 oz/110 g/generous 1 cup
grated cheese, e.g. Cheddar *or* a
mixture of Gruyère, Parmesan
and Cheddar
¼ teaspoon mustard
4 oz/110 g/1 cup grated mature
Cheddar cheese for top
salt and freshly ground pepper

REMOVE the outer leaves and wash well both the cauliflower and the leaves. Put not more than 1 in/2.5 cm of water in a saucepan just large enough to take the cauliflower, add a little salt. Chop the leaves into small pieces and either leave the cauliflower whole or cut in quarters; place the cauliflower on top of the green leaves in the saucepan, cover and simmer until the cauliflower is cooked, approximately 15 minutes. Test by piercing the stalk with a knife: there should be just a little resistance. Remove the cauliflower and leaves to an ovenproof serving dish.

Meanwhile make the sauce. Put the cold milk into a saucepan with the onion, carrot, peppercorns and thyme or parsley. Bring to the boil, simmer for 3–4 minutes, remove from the heat and leave to infuse for 10 minutes. Strain out the vegetables, bring the milk back to the boil and thicken with roux (see glossary) to a light coating consistency. Add the grated cheese and mustard. Season with salt and freshly ground pepper, taste and correct the seasoning if necessary. Spoon the sauce over the cauliflower and sprinkle with more grated cheese. The dish may be prepared ahead to this point.

Put into a hot oven, 230°C/450°F/gas 8, or under the grill to brown. If the dish is allowed to get completely cold, it will take 20–25 minutes to reheat in a moderate oven, 180°C/350°F/gas 4. Serve sprinkled with chopped parsley.

NOTE: If the cauliflower is left whole, cut a deep cross in the stalk.

VEGETARIAN LASAGNE

Serves 12

13 oz/375 g approx. plain *or* spinach lasagne
1 × Piperonata recipe (see page 190)
Mushroom à la Crème recipe (see page 194, make twice the amount)
1 × Tomato Fondue recipe (see page 188)

3 pints/1.7 l/7½ cups milk made into well-seasoned béchamel sauce (not too thick, see page 92)
8 oz/225 g/2 cups grated cheese, Parmesan *or* mature Cheddar *or* Cheddar and Parmesan mixed
salt and freshly ground pepper

1 large *or* 2 medium-sized lasagne dishes

FIRST taste each component; make sure it is delicious and well seasoned.

Blanch the lasagne as directed on the packet; some of the 'easy cook' lasagne may be used without blanching. Spread a little béchamel sauce on the base of each dish, cover with strips of lasagne and a layer of piperonata. Next put another layer of lasagne. Spread with béchamel sauce and sprinkle with grated cheese; add the mushroom à la crème next, then more lasagne, béchamel sauce, cheese, tomato fondue, another layer of lasagne and so on. (See resumé at end of recipe.) Finally cover with a layer of sauce and a good sprinkling of Parmesan cheese. (Make sure all the lasagne is under the sauce.)

Bake in a moderate oven, 180°C/350°F/gas 4, for approximately 30 minutes or until golden and bubbly on top. If possible, leave to stand for 10–15 minutes before cutting to allow the layers to compact. Serve with a good green salad (see page 55).

Resumé

1.	Béchamel sauce	8.	Lasagne
2.	Lasagne	9.	Béchamel sauce
3.	Piperonata	10.	Cheese
4.	Lasagne	11.	Tomato Fondue
5.	Béchamel sauce	12.	Lasagne
6.	Cheese	13.	Béchamel sauce
7.	Mushroom à la Crème	14.	Cheese

BAKED EGGS AND VARIATIONS

Serves 4

These may be served as a starter or snack and there are many variations on the theme.

4 fresh eggs,
preferably free-range

6–8 tablespoons cream
salt and freshly ground pepper

1/2 oz/15 g/1 tablespoon butter

4 small ramekins (see glossary)

LIGHTLY butter the 4 ramekins. Heat the cream; when it is hot, spoon about 1 tablespoon into each ramekin and break an egg into the cream. Season with salt and freshly ground pepper. Spoon the remainder of the cream over the top of the eggs. Place the ramekins in a bain-marie (see glossary) of hot water, cover with tinfoil or a lid and bring to simmering point on top of the stove. Continue to cook either gently on top of the stove, or in a moderate oven, 180°C/350°F/gas 4, about 12 minutes for a soft egg, 15 minutes for a medium egg and 18–20 minutes for a hard egg. Serve immediately.

Baked Eggs with Cheese

Sprinkle ¹/₂–1 tablespoon of finely grated cheese on top of each egg. Bake uncovered in a bain-marie in the oven if preferred.

Baked Eggs with Tomato Fondue

Put 1 tablespoon of Tomato Fondue (see page 188) underneath each egg in the ramekins. Proceed as in the basic recipe, with or without the addition of cheese.

Baked Eggs with Piperonata

Put 1 tablespoon of Piperonata (see page 190) underneath each egg in the ramekins. Spoon 1 tablespoon of cream over each egg. Sprinkle ¹/₂–1 tablespoon of finely grated cheese on top of each egg; a little cooked bacon or crispy rasher may also be added. Bake uncovered in a bain-marie in the oven if preferred.

Baked Eggs with Fresh Herbs and Dijon Mustard

Use 3 tablespoons in total of parsley, tarragon, chives and chervil. Mix 2 teaspoons of mustard and the freshly chopped herbs into the cream and proceed as for the basic recipe.

VEGETABLES

Every year more and more people buy a few tomato plants at their local garden centre, bring them home, plant them and look after them all summer long – yet it is about 3 to 3½ months before they get a single fruit. Why go to all that bother – watering, feeding and side-shooting – you might wonder, when you could just pop into a shop and buy what you need? Well, if you taste a home-grown tomato fully ripened on the plant you'll understand why: the flavour is sweet and intense and worth every minute of the hard work. Commercial growers need to pick off their tomatoes green or semi-green to allow for distribution and shelf life, so the fruit ripens in the box and never quite develops that sun-ripened flavour.

Something else that bothers me are grading systems, which I know were introduced for the most noble reasons. Growers are required to grade their fruit and vegetables, and quite rightly so, but as a result only 'standard' sizes find their way into the shops. This means that small tomatoes, tiny onions or apples are difficult to find, although often they are the ones with the best flavour. I think we should at least be offered the choice.

Only the very dark red, ripe tomatoes have enough flavour for soups, stews, sauces and dishes, such as Tomato Fondue – a quick and deliciously juicy vegetable recipe which goes wonderfully well with roast or grilled meat but can also be used as a sauce for pasta dishes, a base for Baked Eggs (page 186) or a filling for omelettes, pancakes or vol-au-vents. Both this and Piperonata are two marvellous stand-bys to have in your fridge. They re-heat perfectly, unlike most vegetables, which suffer unless they are cooked at the last moment.

My recipe for cooking leeks usually converts even the most determined sceptic – toss them in a little butter and braise them in a covered casserole. This method works very well with parsnips, globe artichokes and cucumber as well, so if you've looked on cucumber only as a salad vegetable until now, try hot Cucumber with Fennel: there's a new treat in store. You can serve it also as an accompaniment to fish, and with mint as the ideal partner for lamb.

I've also included two traditional Irish potato recipes because these lovely homely dishes have a soft spot in my heart. My mother used to make Colcannon for us every Friday when we ran home up the hill from school for lunch and I still think it's comfort food at its best. The Ulster Champ recipe I've just come across recently – Deborah Shorley, a friend from Ulster who has a great knowledge of traditional food, particularly the food of Ulster introduced me to it and it's absolutely gorgeous, even made with frozen peas in winter.

Some of you may feel that Duchesse Potato is not so much old-fashioned as old hat, but I must include it because it is a vital element in so many meals, and if it's piped around the edge, it makes a whole meal in one dish. I think you will agree it deserves its space.

TOMATO FONDUE

Serves 6

This wonderful tomato stew, literally 'melted tomatoes', is best made during the summer months when tomatoes are very ripe.

2 lb/900 g very ripe tomatoes	1 tablespoon of any of the
4 oz/110 g/1 cup sliced onions	following, chopped: thyme,
1 clove garlic, crushed	parsley, mint, basil, lemon
(optional)	balm, marjoram
1 dessertspoon oil	salt, freshly ground pepper and
	sugar to taste

SWEAT the sliced onions and garlic (if used) in oil on a gentle heat. It is vital for the success of this dish that the onions are completely soft before the tomatoes are added. Remove the hard core from the tomatoes. Put them into a deep bowl and cover them with boiling water. Count to 10 and then pour off the water immediately; peel off the skins, slice and add to the onions. Season with salt, freshly ground pepper and sugar and add a generous sprinkling of chopped herbs: mint or basil are my favourites. Cook for just 5 or 10 minutes more, or until the tomato softens.

NOTE: This may be served not only as a vegetable but also as a sauce, a filling or a topping for pizza; reduce a little more for a pizza, or it may be too sloppy.

EASY TOMATO CHUTNEY

This is a fast recipe for ripe tomato chutney which may be made in 20–25 minutes approx. It keeps for one month or more.

8 oz/225 g very ripe tomatoes, peeled
$2^1/_2$ oz/70 g/$^1/_3$ cup sugar
2 oz/55 g/$^1/_2$ cup chopped onion
$^1/_2$ teaspoon salt

a pinch of white pepper
$^1/_4$ teaspoon Dijon mustard
a pinch of pimento *or* allspice
$^1/_4$ pint/150 ml/generous $^1/_2$ cup wine vinegar

PUT all the ingredients into a blender and reduce to a purée. Transfer the mixture to a stainless steel or enamelled saucepan. Cook and reduce over a low heat for approximately 20 minutes, until it becomes very thick ($^1/_2$–$^1/_3$ of its original volume). Pour into sterilised jars.

TOMATO SALAD

Serves 6

6 very ripe tomatoes
French dressing (see below)

2–3 teaspoons chopped fresh
basil *or* mint

salt, freshly ground pepper and sugar

SLICE each tomato into 3 or 4 rounds or into quarters. Arrange in a single layer on a flat plate. Sprinkle with salt, sugar and several grinds of black pepper. Toss immediately in *just enough* French dressing to coat the tomatoes and sprinkle with chopped mint or basil. Taste for seasoning. Tomatoes must be dressed as soon as they are cut to seal in their flavour.

FRENCH DRESSING

2 fl oz/55 ml/$\frac{1}{4}$ cup wine
vinegar
6 fl oz/175 ml/$\frac{3}{4}$ cup olive oil *or*
a mixture of olive and other oils,
e.g. sunflower and arachide
1 level teaspoon mustard (Dijon
or English)

1 large clove garlic
1 small spring onion (scallion)
sprig of parsley
sprig of watercress, optional
1 level teaspoon salt
few grinds of pepper

PUT all the ingredients into a blender and run at medium speed for about 1 minute, or mix oil and vinegar in a bowl, add mustard, salt, freshly ground pepper and mashed garlic. Chop the parsley, spring onion and watercress finely and add in. Whisk before serving.

PIPERONATA

Serves 8–10

This Italian vegetable stew reheats perfectly and is a valuable stand-by to have in your fridge.

1 onion

2 red peppers

2 green peppers

6 large tomatoes (dark red and very ripe)

2–2½ tablespoons olive oil

1 clove garlic

a few leaves of fresh basil

salt, freshly ground pepper and sugar

PEEL the garlic and make into a paste. Peel and slice the onion. Heat the olive oil in a casserole, add the garlic and cook for a few seconds; then add the sliced onion, toss in the oil and allow to soften over a gentle heat in a covered casserole while the peppers are being prepared. Halve the peppers, remove the seeds carefully, cut into quarters and then into strips, across rather than length-ways. Add to the onion and toss in the oil; replace the lid and continue to cook.

Meanwhile peel the tomatoes (scald in boiling water for 10 seconds, pour off the water and peel immediately). Slice the tomatoes and add to the casserole, season with salt, freshly ground pepper, sugar and a few leaves of fresh basil if available. Cook until the vegetables are just soft, for about 30 minutes. Serve with bacon, ham, beef, monkfish, lamb, etc., or as a filling for ome-lettes. Piperonata will keep in the fridge for 4 or 5 days.

Suggestions for Other Uses

1. A filling for omelettes, stuffed pancakes or vol-au-vents.
2. Vegetarian Lasagne (see page 184).
3. A sauce for pasta.

BUTTERED CABBAGE

Serves 6–8

The flavour of cabbage cooked in this quick way is often a revelation to people when they taste it.

1 lb/450 g fresh Savoy cabbage

1–2 oz/30–55 g/3–4 tablespoons butter

salt and freshly ground pepper

a knob of butter

REMOVE the tough outer leaves from the cabbage. Divide into four, cut out the stalks and then cut into fine shreds across the grain. Put 2 or 3 tablespoons of water into a wide saucepan with the butter and a pinch of salt. Bring to the boil, add the cabbage and toss constantly over a high heat; cover for a few minutes. Toss again and add some salt, freshly ground pepper and the knob of butter. Serve immediately.

BUTTERED COURGETTES

Serves 4

1 lb/450 g courgettes, no larger than 5 in/13 cm in length	a dash of olive oil
1 oz/30 g/2 tablespoons butter	salt and freshly ground pepper
	freshly chopped parsley

TOP and tail the courgettes and cut them into $1/4$ in/7 mm slices. Melt the butter and add a dash of olive oil, toss in the courgettes and coat in the butter and oil. Cook until tender, for about 4–5 minutes. Season with salt and freshly ground pepper. Turn into a hot serving dish, sprinkle with chopped parsley and serve immediately.

BUTTERED LEEKS

Serves 4–6

Many people dislike leeks, I think possibly because they have only had them boiled. Try them this way – they are meltingly tender and mild in flavour.

4 medium-sized leeks	1 tablespoon water if necessary
$1^{1}/_{2}$ oz/45 g/3 tablespoons butter	salt and freshly ground pepper
	chopped parsley *or* chervil

CUT off the dark green leaves from the top of the leeks (wash and add to the stock pot or use for making green leek soup). Slit the leeks about half way down the centre and wash well under cold running water. Slice into ¹/₄ in/7 mm in rounds. Melt the butter in a heavy saucepan; when it foams, add the sliced leeks and toss gently to coat with butter. Season with salt and freshly ground pepper and add the water if necessary. Cover with a paper lid and a close-fitting saucepan lid. Reduce the heat and cook very gently for about 20–30 minutes, or until soft and moist. Check and stir every now and then. Serve on a warm dish sprinkled with chopped parsley or chervil.

NOTE: The pot of leeks may be cooked in the oven if that is more convenient, 160°C/325°F/gas 3.

LEEKS MORNAY

Serves 8

8 medium-sized leeks
1 pint/600 ml/2¹/₂ cups milk
a few slices of carrot and onion
3 or 4 peppercorns
a sprig of thyme or parsley
roux (see glossary)
¹/₄ teaspoon mustard, preferably Dijon

5–6 oz/140–170 g/1¹/₂ –2 cups grated Cheddar cheese or 3 oz/85 g/³/₄ cup grated Parmesan cheese
buttered crumbs
(optional, see page 103)
salt and freshly ground pepper

TRIM most of the green part off the leeks (use in the stock pot). Leave the white parts whole, slit the top and wash well under cold running water. Cook in a little boiling salted water in a covered saucepan until just tender, approximately 15 minutes.

Meanwhile put the cold milk into a saucepan with the carrot and onion, peppercorns and thyme or parsley. Bring to the boil, simmer for 5 minutes, remove from heat and leave to infuse for 10 minutes. Strain out the vegetables, bring the milk back to the boil and thicken with roux to a light coating consistency. Add the mustard and two-thirds of the grated cheese, but keep the remainder of the cheese for sprinkling over the top. Season with salt and freshly ground pepper, taste and correct the seasoning if necessary.

Drain the leeks well, arrange in a serving dish, coat with the sauce and sprinkle with grated cheese mixed with a few buttered crumbs (if you have them to hand). Reheat in a moderate oven, 180°C/350°F/gas 4, until golden and bubbly.

CUCUMBER AND FENNEL

Serves 4–6

Many people love cucumber raw, but few think of cooking it as a vegetable. It is quite delicious prepared in this way and particularly good with fish.

1 cucumber, peeled	¹/₂ teaspoon snipped fresh fennel
1 oz/30 g/2 tablespoons butter	salt and freshly ground pepper

DICE the cucumber into ¹/₂ in/1 cm pieces. Melt the butter in a heavy saucepan or casserole, toss in the cucumber and season with salt and freshly ground pepper. Cover and sweat over a *low* heat until just soft, approximately 20 minutes. Stir occasionally. Add some snipped fresh fennel. Taste and correct the seasoning if necessary. (Cucumber may be cut into dice, rounds or turned in barrel shapes.)

MUSHROOM À LA CRÈME

Serves 4

¹/₂–1 oz/15–30 g/1–2 tablespoons butter	¹/₂ tablespoon chopped chives (optional)
3 oz/85 g/³/₄ cup finely chopped onion	4 fl oz/130 ml/¹/₂ cup cream
8 oz/225 g/2¹/₂ cups sliced mushrooms	a squeeze of lemon juice
	salt and freshly ground pepper
	chopped parsley

MELT the butter in a heavy saucepan until it foams. Add the chopped onion, cover and sweat on a gentle heat for 5–10 minutes or until quite soft but not coloured; remove the onions to a bowl. Increase the heat and cook the sliced mushrooms, in batches if necessary. Season each batch with salt, freshly ground pepper and a tiny squeeze of lemon juice. Add the onions and chives to the mushrooms in the saucepan, then add the cream and allow to bubble for a few minutes; taste and correct the seasoning. Sprinkle with chopped parsley.

NOTE: This may be served as a vegetable, or as a filling for vol-au-vents, bouchées or pancakes. It may also be used as an enrichment for casseroles and stews or, by adding a little more cream or stock, may be served as a sauce with beef, lamb, chicken or veal. A crushed clove of garlic may also be added when the onions are sweating.

COLCANNON

Serves 8

This traditional Irish potato recipe is comfort food at its very best.

2¹/₂–3 lb/1–1.35 kg 'old', 'floury' potatoes	2 oz/55g/4 tablespoons approx. butter
1 Savoy *or* spring cabbage	salt and freshly ground pepper
8 fl oz/250 ml/1 cup approx. boiling milk	

SCRUB the potatoes and cook them in their jackets. Put them in a saucepan of cold water, add a good pinch of salt and bring to the boil. When the potatoes are about half cooked, approximately 15 minutes for 'old' potatoes, strain off two-thirds of the water, replace the lid on the saucepan, put on to a gentle heat and allow the potatoes to steam until they are cooked.

Remove the dark outer leaves from the cabbage. Wash and cut into quarters, remove the core and cut finely across the grain. Boil in a little salted water or bacon-cooking water until soft. Drain, season with salt, freshly ground pepper and the butter. When the potatoes are just cooked, put on the milk and bring to the boil. Pull the peel off the potatoes, mash quickly while they are still warm and beat in enough boiling milk to make a fluffy purée. (If you have a large quantity, put the potatoes in the bowl of a food mixer and beat with the spade.) Then stir in the cooked cabbage and taste for seasoning.

Colcannon may be prepared ahead up to this point and reheated later in a moderate oven, 180°C/350°F/gas 4, for approximately 20–25 minutes. Cover with tinfoil while reheating so it doesn't get crusty on top.

Serve in a hot dish or with a lump of butter melting in the centre.

ULSTER CHAMP

Serves 8

I am indebted to Deborah Shorley for this recipe, which she calls Claragh Champ; we call it Ulster Champ down here and I prefer to cook the potatoes in their jackets rather than peeling them first.

4 lb/1.8 kg 'old', 'floury' potatoes	1 lb/450 g/4 cups young peas, shelled weight
2–4 oz/55–110 g/1/4–1/2 cup butter	8 tablespoons/1 cup chopped parsley
1 pint/600 ml/2 1/2 cups milk	salt and freshly ground pepper

COOK the potatoes in boiling salted water until tender; drain well, dry over the heat in the pan for a few minutes, peel and mash with most of the butter while hot. Meanwhile bring the milk to the boil and simmer the peas until just cooked, approximately 8–10 minutes. Add the parsley for the final 2 minutes of the cooking. Add the hot milk mixture to the potatoes. Season well, beat until creamy and smooth and serve piping hot with a lump of butter melting in the centre.

DUCHESSE POTATO

Serves 4

2 lb/900 g unpeeled 'old',
'floury' potatoes

1/2 pint/300 ml/1 1/4 cups creamy
milk

1–2 egg yolks *or*

1 whole egg and 1 egg yolk,
preferably free-range

1–2 oz/30–55 g/2–4 tablespoons
butter

salt and freshly ground pepper

SCRUB the potatoes well. Put them into a saucepan of water, add a good pinch of salt and bring to the boil. When the potatoes are about half cooked, about 15 minutes for 'old' potatoes, strain off two-thirds of the water, replace the lid on the saucepan, put on to a gentle heat and allow the potatoes to steam until they are cooked.

Peel immediately by just pulling off the skins, so you have as little waste as possible; mash while hot (see note below). (If you have a large quantity, put the potatoes into the bowl of a food mixer and beat with the spade.)

While the potatoes are being peeled, bring the milk to the boil. Beat the eggs into the hot mashed potatoes, and add enough boiling creamy milk to mix to a soft light consistency suitable for piping; then beat in the butter, the amount depending on how rich you like your potatoes. Taste and season with salt and freshly ground pepper.

NOTE: If the potatoes are not peeled and mashed while hot and if the boiling milk is not added immediately, the result will be lumpy and gluey.

If you have only egg whites they will be fine and, what's more, will make a delicious light mashed potato.

ROAST POTATOES

Everybody loves roast potatoes, yet people ask me over and over again for the secret of golden crispy roast potatoes.

1. First and foremost buy good quality 'old' potatoes. New potatoes are not suitable for roasting.
2. Peel them just before roasting.
3. Do not leave them soaking in water or they will be soggy inside because of the water they absorb. This always applies, no matter how you cook potatoes. Unfortunately, many people have got into the habit of peeling and soaking potatoes even if they are just going to mash them.
4. Dry potatoes carefully, otherwise they will stick to the tin, and when you turn them over you will lose the crispy bit underneath.
5. If you have a fan oven it is necessary to blanch and refresh the potatoes first, then proceed as below.
6. Heat the olive oil or fat in the roasting pan and toss the potatoes to make sure they are well coated.
7. Roast in a hot oven, basting occasionally, for 30–60 minutes depending on size.
8. For perfection, potatoes should be similar in size and shape.

PIPED POTATO SALAD

1 lb/450 g mashed *or* Duchesse potato (see page 197)
2–2¹/₂ tablespoons French dressing (see page 190)
2–2¹/₂ tablespoons mayonnaise (see page 23)

2–2¹/₂ tablespoons finely chopped parsley
2–2¹/₂ tablespoons finely chopped chives
salt and freshly ground pepper

ADD French dressing, mayonnaise, finely chopped parsley and chives to the stiff Duchesse potato. It should be of piping consistency. Taste and correct seasoning. Pipe on to individual leaves of lettuce or use to garnish a starter salad or hors d'oeuvre.

PLAIN BOILED RICE

Serves 8

I find this way of cooking in what we call 'unlimited water' to be very satisfactory for plain boiled rice, even, dare I say, foolproof. The grains stay separate and it will keep happily covered in the oven for up to half an hour.

14 oz/400 g/2 cups good-quality
    long-grain rice, e.g. Basmati
    1 1/2–2 teaspoons salt

a large pot of cold water
a few little knobs of butter
    (optional)

BRING a large saucepan of water to a fast boil, add salt, sprinkle in the rice and stir at once to make sure the grains don't stick. Boil rapidly, uncovered. After 4 or 5 minutes (depending on the type of rice) test by biting a few grains between your teeth – it should still have a slightly resistant core. If it overcooks at this stage the grains will stick together later.

Strain well through a sieve or fine strainer. Put into a warm serving dish, dot with a few knobs of butter, cover with tinfoil or a lid and leave in a low oven, 140°C/275°F/gas 1, for a minimum of 15 minutes. Remove the lid, fluff up with a fork and serve.

PUDDINGS

People spend a great deal of time and energy talking in total seriousness about diets and healthy food, calories and so on. But just watch the reaction when a sweet trolley comes round to the table in a restaurant! Caution is thrown to the wind as they cajole the 'trolley dolly' to pile their plates high with scrumptious 'puds'. The great Saturday night trick in Ballymaloe with a party of six or more is to start to eat your pud as fast as you can the minute it's served, so that by the time the last person at the table has got theirs you're ready to start all over again.

On the sweet trolley in Ballymaloe we always have a Meringue Gâteau and a Home-made Ice-cream. We use the egg yolks to make the delicious rich ice-creams and the egg whites to make the meringues, so there is no waste. At home if you decide to make ice-cream, make meringues also in the same session; you will then have two delicious puddings that will keep for ages, and don't forget to make an ice bowl to serve the ice-cream in so you can dazzle the guests! It's also a great idea to make at least twice, or better still four times, the ice-cream recipe and the same of meringues, so you will have enough for several meals. Ice-cream of course freezes for months (don't forget to cover it even in the freezer or it will get what I call a 'fridgie' taste).

Meringues also keep for ages in an airtight tin; if they do get a bit soft just pop them back into a low oven and then they will dry out and crisp again. They are one of the very best stand-bys – if you can manage to hide them away! The meringue recipe I use is virtually foolproof and works even for people who are quite determined they can't make meringues. They are cooked at a higher temperature than usual so even if your oven is not accurate at very low temperatures, and many aren't, it should be all right at 150°C/300°F/gas 2. The meringue mixture can be baked in any shape or size you fancy and you could even produce a heart-shaped one for Valentine's Day or to bring on a proposal! I've included recipes for Meringue Gâteau with Kiwi Fruit, Chocolate Meringue Gâteau and Meringue Nests.

Many people seem to have a mental block about using gelatine, but, again, I have a foolproof method for dealing with it, and include here several recipes for gelatine-based desserts. It may seem odd that some are termed mousses and others soufflés; the difference is often simply one of aesthetics: in a cold soufflé, a band of paper is tied around the dish and the mousse mixture poured in above the level of the rim to give the appearance of a risen soufflé.

Caramel is another very useful technique that causes quite unnecessary anxiety. Once you master it, it can be used in a mousse, an ice-cream or a Crème Caramel, or as a sauce.

Fruit puddings are always popular for their lightness. Room can usually be found for something fruity and delicious after even the most gargantuan repast. My husband is a fruit grower, so I couldn't resist including some desserts made from fresh summer fruit. The Summer Fruit Salad with Sweet Geranium Leaves, Summer Pudding and Black Currant Fool are three of his favourite recipes. His crowning glory is Summer Pudding but he asks me to remind you not to forget to weight it down and to resist turning it out until the next day. (He couldn't and we had much merriment as a result.)

Three of the other fruit-based recipes I've chosen use limes which add an exotic touch without being impossibly difficult to track down. In each case, they make a marvellously sophisticated and clean-tasting dessert. But you mustn't be tempted to serve whipped cream with any of them. It simply doesn't go well with the zingy, palate-cleansing quality limes bring to these puddings.

Whipped cream addicts need not fear, however: cream is a must with the two old-fashioned puddings here, Country Rhubarb Cake and Peter Lamb's Apple Charlotte – and don't forget to sprinkle them with a little soft brown sugar (my favourite). The Chocolate Meringue Gâteau is a totally decadent and absolutely scrumptious sandwich filled with rich rum and chocolate-flavoured cream. I can't think of a better thing to finish with. This is the sort of pudding everybody will greedily devour while they moan about their waistlines. Then they'll ask for more – and not regret a single crumb!

The Almond Tart recipe is another of my favourites and is really a treasure – so quick and easy to make, it really is a prime example of what this whole book is about: food that is 'Simply Delicious'.

BALLYMALOE
VANILLA ICE-CREAM
SERVED IN AN ICE BOWL

Serves 6–8

The Ballymaloe ice-creams are both very rich and very delicious, and are made with an egg mousse base to which softly whipped cream and flavouring are added. Ice-creams made in this way have a smooth texture and do not need further whisking during the freezing period. They should not be served frozen hard. Remove from the freezer at least 10 minutes before serving.

2 oz/55 g/^{1}/$_4$ cup sugar

4 fl oz/130 ml/^{1}/$_2$ cup water

2 egg yolks, preferably free-range

^{1}/$_2$ teaspoon pure vanilla essence

^{1}/$_2$ pint/300 ml/1^1/$_4$ cups cream, whipped

PUT the egg yolks into a bowl and whisk until light and fluffy (keep the whites for meringues). Combine the sugar and water in a small heavy-bottomed saucepan, stir over a low heat until the sugar is completely dissolved, then remove the spoon and boil the syrup until it reaches the 'thread' stage, 106°–113°C/223°–236°F. It will look thick and syrupy; when a metal spoon is dipped in, the last drops of syrup will form thin threads. Pour every drop of this boiling syrup in a steady stream on to the egg yolks, whisking all the time (be careful to use every drop of syrup). Add vanilla essence and continue to whisk until it becomes a thick creamy white mousse. Softly whip the cream – it should just hold the print of the whisk. Measure and make sure you have 1 pint/600 ml of whipped cream. Fold the softly whipped cream into the mousse, pour into a bowl, cover and freeze.

BALLYMALOE ICE BOWL

This ice bowl was Myrtle Allen's brilliant solution to the problem of keeping the ice-cream cold during the evening on the sweet trolley in the restaurant. I quote from *The Ballymaloe Cookbook*.

'It took me twelve years to find the solution to keeping ice-cream cold on the sweet trolley in my restaurant. At first we used to unmould and decorate our ices on to a plate. This was all right on a busy night when they got eaten before melting. On quieter occasions the waitresses performed relay races from the dining-room to the deep freeze. I dreamed about 19th-century ice boxes filled from ice houses, to my husband's increasing scorn, and then I thought I had a solution. A young Irish glass blower produced beautiful hand-blown glass cylinders which I filled with ice-cream and fitted into beautiful tulip shaped glass bowls. These I filled with ice cubes. Six months later, however, due to either the stress of the ice or the stress of the waitresses, my bowls were gone and so was my money.

In desperation I produced an ice bowl. It turned out to be a stunning and practical presentation for a restaurant trolley or a party buffet.'

To make a Ballymaloe ice bowl, take two bowls, one about double the capacity of the other. Half fill the big bowl with cold water. Float the second bowl inside the first. Weight it down with water or ice cubes until the rims are level. Place a square of fabric on top and secure it with a strong rubber band or string under the rim of the lower bowl, as one would tie on a jam pot cover.

Adjust the small bowl to a central position. The cloth holds it in place. Put the bowls on to a Swiss roll tin and place in a deep freeze, if necessary re-adjusting the position of the small bowl as you put it in. After 24 hours or more take it out of the deep freeze.

Remove the cloth and leave for 15–20 minutes, by which time the small bowl should lift out easily. Then try to lift out the ice bowl. It should be starting to melt slightly from the outside bowl, in which case it will slip out easily. If it isn't, then just leave for 5 or 10 minutes more: don't attempt to run it under the hot or even the cold tap, or it may crack. If you are in a great rush, the best solution is to wring out a tea-towel in hot water and wrap that around the large bowl for a few minutes. Altogether, the best course of action is to perform this operation early in the day and then fill the ice bowl with scoops of ice-cream, so that all you have to do when it comes to serving the ice-cream is to pick up the ice bowl from the freezer and place it on the serving dish. Put a folded serviette underneath the ice bowl on the serving dish to catch any drips.

At Ballymaloe, Myrtle Allen surrounds the ice bowl with vine leaves in summer, scarlet Virginia creeper leaves in autumn and red-berried holly at Christmas. However, I'm a bit less restrained and I can't resist surrounding it with flowers! However you present it, ice-cream served in a bowl of ice like this usually draws gasps of admiration when you bring it to the table.

In the restaurant we make a new ice bowl every night, but at home when the dessert would be on the table for barely half an hour, it should be possible to use the ice bowl several times. As soon as you have finished serving, give the bowl a quick wash under the cold tap and get it back into the freezer again. This way you can often get 2 or 3 turns from a single ice bowl. One more point: don't leave a serving spoon resting against the side of the bowl or it will melt a notch in the rim.

Nowadays, when we want to do something extra special, we freeze flowers, leaves or fresh herbs into the ice bowl and we've also done really pretty ones with berried holly for Christmas. Make sure nobody nibbles at the berries as it melts – they may well be poisonous!

PRALINE ICE-CREAM

Serves 6–8

Possibly the most delicious of all our ice-creams.

Vanilla Ice Cream (made according to the recipe on page 202)

PRALINE

4 oz/110 g/1 cup unskinned almonds
4 oz/110 g/¾ cup sugar

MAKE the vanilla ice-cream and put into the freezer for approximately 1–1½ hours or until semi-frozen.

Meanwhile, make the praline. Put the unskinned almonds together with the sugar into a heavy-bottomed saucepan over a low heat until the sugar gradually melts and turns a rich caramel colour. *Do Not Stir*. When this stage is reached, and not before, carefully rotate the pan until the nuts are completely covered with caramel. When the nuts go 'pop', pour the mixture on to a lightly oiled Swiss roll tin or marble slab. Allow to get cold. When the praline is quite hard, crush in a food processor or with a rolling pin. The texture should be quite coarse and gritty.

When the ice-cream has almost set, fold in 4 tablespoons of praline powder and freeze again (if you fold in the praline powder too early it will sink to the bottom of the ice cream.)

TO SERVE: Scoop into balls with an ice-cream scoop, serve in an ice bowl, and sprinkle with the remaining praline powder.

BALLYMALOE
COFFEE ICE-CREAM
WITH IRISH COFFEE SAUCE

Serves 6–8

2 oz/55 g/¹/₄ cup sugar

4 fl oz/120 ml/¹/₂ cup water

2 egg yolks,
preferably free-range

¹/₂ teaspoon vanilla essence

¹/₂ pint/300 ml/1¹/₄ cups cream,
whipped

3 teaspoons instant coffee grains

¹/₂ teaspoon boiling water

PUT the egg yolks into a bowl and whisk until light and fluffy (keep the whites for meringues). Put the sugar and water into a small heavy-bottomed saucepan on a low heat. Stir until all the sugar is dissolved and then remove the spoon and boil until the syrup reaches the 'thread' stage, 106°–113°C/223°–236°F. It will look thick and syrupy; when a metal spoon is dipped in the last drops of syrup will form thin threads. Pour every drop of this boiling syrup in a steady stream on to the egg yolks, whisking all the time. Add vanilla essence and continue to whisk until it fluffs up to a light mousse which will hold a figure of 8. Mix the instant coffee powder with just ¹/₂ teaspoon of boiling water. Add some mousse to the coffee paste and then fold the two mixtures together. Softly whip the cream – it should just hold the point of the whisk. Carefully fold the softly whipped cream into the mousse. Pour into a stainless steel or plastic bowl, cover and freeze.

Irish Coffee Sauce

8 oz/225 g/1 cup sugar

3 fl oz/75 ml/¹/₃ cup water

8 fl oz/250 ml/1 cup coffee

1 tablespoon Irish whiskey

PUT the sugar and water in a heavy-bottomed saucepan; stir until the sugar dissolves and the water comes to the boil. Remove the spoon and do not stir again until the syrup turns a pale golden caramel. Then add the coffee and put back on the heat to dissolve. Allow to cool and add the whiskey.

TO SERVE: Scoop the ice-cream into a serving bowl or ice bowl (see page 203). Serve the sauce separately.

CARAMEL ICE-CREAM WITH BUTTERSCOTCH SAUCE AND BANANAS

Serves 6–8

2 oz/55 g/¹/₄ cup sugar
4 fl oz/130 ml/¹/₂ cup cold water
4 fl oz/130 ml/¹/₂ cup hot water
2 egg yolks, preferably free-range
¹/₂ teaspoon pure vanilla essence
¹/₂ pint/300 ml/1¹/₄ cups cream, softly whipped

PUT the egg yolks into a bowl and whisk until light and fluffy (keep the whites for meringues). Combine the sugar and *cold* water in a small heavy-bottomed saucepan. Stir over a gentle heat until the sugar is completely dissolved, then remove the spoon and boil until the syrup caramelises to a chestnut-brown. Quickly pour on the *hot* water. Do not stir. Boil gently until it again becomes a smooth, thick syrup and reaches the 'thread' stage, 106°–113°C/223°–236°F. It will look thick and syrupy when a spoon is dipped in. Pour this boiling syrup on to the egg yolks in a steady stream whisking all the time. Add the vanilla essence and continue to whisk until it becomes a thick, creamy mousse. Softly whip the cream – it should just hold the print of the whisk. Measure and make sure you have 1 pint/600 ml of whipped cream. Fold the softly whipped cream into the mousse, pour into a bowl, cover and freeze.

BUTTERSCOTCH SAUCE

Serves approximately 12

This delicious sauce can be served with any ice-cream.

4 oz/110 g/½ cup butter
6 oz/170 g/¾ cup dark soft
brown, Barbados sugar
10 oz/300 g/¾ cup golden syrup

4 oz/110 g/generous ½ cup
granulated sugar
8 fl oz/250 ml/1 cup cream
½ teaspoon pure vanilla essence

3 bananas

PUT the butter, sugars and golden syrup into a heavy-bottomed saucepan and melt gently on a low heat. Simmer for about 5 minutes, remove from the heat and gradually stir in the cream and the vanilla essence. Put back on the heat and stir for 2 or 3 minutes until the sauce is absolutely smooth.

TO SERVE: Scoop the ice-cream into a chilled bowl or ice bowl (see page 203). Slice the bananas at an angle and add to the sauce. Spoon over the ice-cream or serve separately.

NOTE: Butterscotch sauce keeps for weeks in a glass jar in the fridge or cold place. It can be served hot or cold.

MERINGUE GÂTEAU
WITH KIWI FRUIT

Serves 6–8

Lots of people are apprehensive about making meringues, but this recipe makes it easy. It needs practically no skill to make, because you just add the icing sugar in with the egg whites at the beginning, so you don't have to worry about your 'folding in' technique. This meringue cooks faster and is baked at a higher temperature than ordinary Swiss meringue. It is also tremendously versatile because it can be piped or spread into any shape you like: heart shapes, rectangles, squares, numbers e.g. 21, or letters, not to speak of various kinds of rosettes and twirls.

2 egg whites
4½ oz/125 g/generous 1 cup icing sugar

FILLING

¼ pint/150 ml/¾ cup cream, whipped
4–6 kiwi fruit peeled and sliced

GARNISH
sprigs of fresh mint *or* lemon balm

PREHEAT the oven to 150°C/300°F/gas 2. Cover a baking sheet with silicone paper (see *Note* below), or grease and flour the sheet very carefully. Draw out 2 × 7½ in/19 cm circles on the paper or mark them with the tip of a knife on the flour.

Put the egg whites and all the icing sugar into a spotlessly clean and dry bowl and whisk until the mixture forms stiff peaks; this can take 8–10 minutes in an electric mixer. You can whisk it by hand but it takes quite a long time; even a hand-held mixer will speed up the operation. Divide the mixture between the 2 circles and spread evenly with a palette knife, making sure it's not too thin at the edges.

Bake in the preheated oven for 45 minutes or until the meringues will lift easily off the paper. Turn off the oven and allow them to cool in the oven – with the door slightly ajar – for about 20–30 minutes. (If you take the meringues out of the hot oven and put them down on a cold worktop they may crack.)

TO ASSEMBLE: Put one of the meringue discs on to a serving plate. Pipe on the whipped cream (keep a little to decorate the top), cover with slices of kiwi fruit and put the second disc on top. Pipe 5 rosettes of cream on the top, put a little piece of kiwi fruit on each and decorate with sprigs of fresh mint or lemon balm.

NOTE: Nuts are also delicious added to this recipe. Fold in 1½ oz/45 g/¼ cup finely chopped almonds just before you spread the meringue on to the silicone paper.

This gâteau is also delicious filled with fresh strawberries, raspberries, loganberries, peaches or nectarines.

Silicone paper is sold under the brand name Bakewell and is
available in many supermarkets and newsagents. It is invaluable
for cooking meringue because it is non-stick and the meringue can
therefore be peeled off easily. The paper can be re-used several
times.

CHOCOLATE MERINGUE
GÂTEAU

Serves 6

4¹/₂ oz/125 g/generous 1 cup icing sugar	2 rounded teaspoons cocoa powder
2 egg whites	

CHOCOLATE AND RUM CREAM

1 oz/30 g best quality dark chocolate	1 tablespoon Jamaican rum
	1 tablespoon cream
¹/₂ oz/15 g unsweetened chocolate	¹/₄ pint/150 ml/³/₄ cup cream, softly whipped

PREHEAT the oven to 150°C/300°F/gas 2.

Cover a baking sheet with silicone paper (see *Note* on pages
209–10), or grease and flour the sheet very carefully. Draw out 2
× 7¹/₂ in/19 cm circles on the paper or mark them with the tip of a
knife on the flour.

Put the egg whites into a spotlessly clean and dry bowl and add
all but ¹/₂ oz/15 g icing sugar all at once; whisk until the mixture
forms stiff, dry peaks, about 10 minutes in an electric mixer. You
can whisk it by hand but it takes quite a long time; even a hand-
held mixer will speed up matters a lot.

Sieve together the cocoa and the remaining icing sugar and fold
in very gently. Spread evenly with a palette knife into two circles
and bake immediately in the preheated oven for 45 minutes or
until the meringues will lift easily off the paper. Turn off the oven

and allow them to cool in the oven – with the door slightly ajar – for about 20–30 minutes.

Meanwhile, very gently melt the chocolate with the rum and 1 tablespoon of cream in the cooling oven, or in a bowl over simmering water. Cool and then fold the mixture into the softly whipped cream; don't stir too much or it may curdle.

Sandwich the two meringue discs together with the chocolate and rum cream and decorate with chocolate wafers (see page 216).

MERINGUE NESTS WITH STRAWBERRIES AND CREAM

Serves 6

2 egg whites
4^1/$_2$ oz/125 g/generous 1 cup icing sugar

FILLING

8 oz/225 g/1 cup strawberries
4 fl oz/120 ml/^{1}/$_2$ cup cream, whipped

GARNISH
fresh mint *or* lemon balm leaves

PREHEAT the oven to 150°C/300°F/gas 2. Cover a baking sheet with silicone paper (see *Note* on pages 209–10), or grease and flour the sheet very carefully. Draw out 4 × 3^1/$_2$ in/9 cm circles on the paper or mark them with the tip of a knife on the flour.

Put the egg whites and all the icing sugar into a spotlessly clean and dry bowl and whisk until the mixture forms stiff peaks. This can take 8–10 minutes in an electric mixer. You can whisk it by hand but it takes quite a long time; even a hand-held mixer will speed up matters a lot.

Put the meringue mixture into a piping bag with a number 5 rosette nozzle. Pipe a few blobs on to each circle and spread thinly with a palette knife. The meringue should not be more than

¹/₄in/¹/₂ cm thick. Then carefully pipe a wall of meringue rosettes around the edge of each circle.

Bake in the preheated oven for 45 minutes or until the meringue nests will lift easily off the paper. Turn off the oven and allow them to cool in the oven – with the door slightly ajar – for 20–30 minutes.

To ASSEMBLE: Remove the stalks from the strawberries and cut them into slices lengthways. Pipe some whipped cream into each nest and arrange the slices of strawberries on top. Decorate with tiny rosettes of cream and garnish with fresh mint or lemon balm leaves.

ALMOND TART OR TARTLETS WITH RASPBERRIES

Serves 12, makes 24 tartlets or 2 × 7 in/17.5 cm tarts

4 oz/110 g/¹/₂ cup butter
4 oz/110 g/¹/₂ cup caster sugar

4 oz/110 g/1 cup ground almonds

FILLING

fresh raspberries
poached rhubarb *or* sliced fresh peaches *or* nectarines *or*
loganberries, peeled and pipped grapes *or* kiwi fruit
¹/₄ pint/150 ml/³/₄ cup cream, whipped

GARNISH

lemon balm *or* sweet geranium leaves

CREAM butter, sugar and ground almonds together. Put a teaspoon of the mixture into 24 shallow patty tins or 2 × 7 in/17.5 cm sandwich tins. Bake at 180°C/350°F/gas 4 for about 20–30 minutes, or until golden brown. The tart or tartlets are too soft to turn out immediately, so cool in tins for about 5 minutes, but do not allow to set hard or the butter will solidify and they will stick to the tins. If this happens pop the tins back into the oven for a few minutes so the butter melts and then they will come out easily. Allow to cool on a wire rack.

Just before serving, arrange whole raspberries, slices of peeled peaches or nectarines, or any chosen fruit on the base. Glaze with redcurrant jelly (red fruit) or apricot glaze (green or yellow fruit). Decorate with rosettes of whipped cream and garnish with lemon balm or sweet geranium leaves.

NOTE: Use shallow tartlet tins and best-quality ground almonds.

Redcurrant Glaze

12 oz/350 g redcurrant jelly   1 tablespoon water approx.
(see page 241)

IN a small stainless steel saucepan melt the redcurrant jelly with the water. Stir gently, but do not whisk or it will become cloudy. Cook it for just 1–2 minutes longer or the jelly will darken. Store any left-over glaze in a sterilised airtight jar and reheat gently to melt it before use. The quantities given make a generous $^1/_2$ pint/300 ml of glaze.

Apricot Glaze

12 oz/350 g apricot jam   1–2 tablespoons water
juice of $^1/_4$ lemon

IN a small stainless steel saucepan, melt the apricot jam with the lemon juice and water, enough to make a glaze that can be poured. Push the hot jam through a nylon sieve and store in a sterilised airtight jar. Reheat the glaze to melt it before using. The quantities given make a generous $^1/_2$ pint/300 ml glaze.

CRÈME CARAMEL

Serves 6

CARAMEL

8 oz/225 g/1 cup sugar
$^1/_4$ pint/150 ml/generous $^1/_2$ cup water

CARAMEL SAUCE

2$^1/_2$ fl oz/60 ml/generous $^1/_4$ cup water

CUSTARD

1 pint/600 ml/2$^1/_2$ cups milk *or*
$^1/_2$ pint/300 ml/1$^1/_4$ cups milk
and $^1/_2$ pint/300 ml/1$^1/_4$ cups
cream

4 eggs, preferably free-range
2 oz/55 g/$^1/_4$ cup caster sugar
vanilla pod *or* $^1/_2$ teaspoon pure
vanilla essence (optional)

1 × 5 in/13 cm charlotte mould *or*
6 × 3 in/7.5 cm soufflé dishes

FIRST make the caramel. Put the sugar and water into a heavy-bottomed saucepan and stir over a gentle heat until the sugar is fully dissolved. Bring to the boil, remove the spoon and cook until the caramel becomes golden brown or what we call chestnut colour. Do not stir and do not shake the pan. If sugar crystals form around the side of the pan, brush them down with cold water. When the caramel is ready for lining the moulds, it must be used immediately or it will become hard and cold.

Coat the bottom of the charlotte mould or soufflé dishes with the hot caramel. Dilute the remainder of the caramel with 2$^1/_2$ fl oz/60 ml water to make the sauce: return to the heat to dissolve and keep aside to serve around the caramel custard.

Next make the custard. Whisk the eggs, caster sugar and vanilla essence (if used) until thoroughly mixed but not too fluffy. (Alternatively, infuse the vanilla pod in the milk and cream.) Bring the milk and cream to just under boiling point and pour on to the egg mixture, whisking gently as you pour. Strain and pour into the prepared moulds, filling them to the top. Place the moulds in a bain-marie of simmering water, cover with a paper lid and bake in a moderate oven, 180°C/350°F/gas 4, about 35 minutes for individual dishes and about 1 hour for a charlotte mould. Test the custards by putting a skewer in the centre; it will come out clean when the custards are fully cooked.

Cool and turn out on to a round, flat dish or individual plates. Pour the remaining caramel around. Serve with a little softly whipped cream.

CARAMEL MOUSSE WITH PRALINE

Serves 6

8 oz/225 g/1 cup caster sugar
4 fl oz/120 ml/½ cup cold water
¼ pint/150 ml/generous ½ cup hot water
4 egg yolks, preferably free-range

2 level teaspoons gelatine
2 tablespoons water
½ pint/300 ml/1¼ cups whipped cream

PRALINE DECORATION

1 oz/30 g whole almonds, unskinned
1 oz/30 g sugar

PUT the caster sugar and *cold* water into a heavy-bottomed saucepan and stir over a gentle heat until the sugar is dissolved and the water comes to the boil. Continue to boil until it turns a nice chestnut-brown colour. Remove from the heat and immediately add the *hot* water. Return to a low heat and cook until the caramel thickens to a thick, syrupy texture, approximately 3 or 4 minutes.

Meanwhile, whisk the egg yolks until fluffy, then pour the boiling caramel on to the egg yolks, whisking all the time until the mixture reaches the ribbon stage or will hold a figure of 8. 'Sponge' (see glossary) the gelatine in the 2 tablespoons of water in a small bowl, then put the bowl into a saucepan of simmering water until the gelatine has completely dissolved. Stir a few spoonfuls of the mousse into the gelatine, then carefully add the mixture to the rest of the mousse. Fold in the cream gently and pour into a serving dish. Chill until set.

To make praline: Put the almonds and sugar into a small heavy-bottomed saucepan on a low heat. Do not stir. Gradually the sugar will melt and turn to caramel. When this happens, and not before, rotate the saucepan so that the caramel coats the almonds. By now the almonds should be popping. Turn on to a lightly oiled tin, allow to get cold and then crush to a rough powder.

Decorate the mousse with rosettes of cream and crushed praline.

Note: If you would like to make this into a caramel soufflé, fold in the stiffly beaten whites of 2 eggs after the cream. Chill until set and decorate as before.

Orange Mousse with Chocolate Wafers

Serves 6–8

2 oranges (1 ½ if very large)
4 eggs, preferably free-range
2½ oz/70 g/generous ¼ cup
caster sugar
½ oz/15 g/level tablespoon gelatine

3 tablespoons water
1 lemon
4 fl oz/120 ml/½ cup cream,
whipped

CHOCOLATE WAFERS

2 oz/55g best-quality dark chocolate

DECORATION

2 oranges
4 fl oz/120 ml/½ cup cream, whipped
a pinch of caster sugar

WASH and dry the oranges; grate the rind on the finest part of a stainless steel grater. Put into a bowl with 2 eggs, 2 egg yolks (keep the whites) and the caster sugar. Whisk to a thick mousse, preferably with an electric mixer. Put 3 tablespoons of water in a little bowl, measure the gelatine carefully and sprinkle over the water. Leave to 'sponge' (see glossary) for a few minutes until the gelatine has soaked up the water and feels spongy to the touch. Put the bowl into a saucepan of simmering water and allow the gelatine to dissolve completely. All the granules should be dissolved and it should look perfectly clear.

Meanwhile, squeeze the juice from the oranges and the lemon, measure and if necessary bring up to $\frac{1}{2}$ pint/300 ml/$1\frac{1}{4}$ cups with water. Stir a little of the juice into the gelatine and then mix well with the remainder of the juice. Gently stir this into the mousse; cool in the fridge, *stirring regularly*. When the mousse is just beginning to set around the edges, fold in the softly whipped cream. Whisk the 2 egg whites stiffly and fold in gently. Pour into a glass bowl or into individual bowls. Allow to set for 3–4 hours in the fridge.

Meanwhile make the chocolate wafers. Melt the chocolate in a bowl over barely simmering water. Stir until quite smooth. Spread on a flat piece of heavy, white notepaper or light card. Put into a cold place until stiff enough to cut in square or diamond shapes.

While the chocolate is setting, make the orange-flavoured cream. Grate half the rind from one orange, add to the cream with a pinch of caster sugar to taste. Peel and segment the oranges. Decorate the top of the mousse with orange segments and pipe on some rosettes of orange-flavoured cream. Peel the chocolate wafers off the card and use them to decorate the edges of the mousse.

LEMON SOUFFLÉ

Serves 6–8

3 large eggs,
preferably free-range
8 oz/225 g/1 cup caster sugar
2½ lemons
½ pint/300 ml/1¼ cups cream

½ oz/15 g/3 rounded teaspoons
gelatine
2½ fl oz/60 ml/generous ¼ cup
water
oil

DECORATION

5 fl oz/150 ml/generous ½ cup
whipped cream
tiny sprigs of lemon balm *or*
sweet geranium leaves
2 tablespoons toasted chopped almonds

1 × 6 in/15 cm soufflé dish

BRUSH a collar of greaseproof paper lightly with a tasteless oil; tie it around the soufflé dish. Grate the rind of the lemons and squeeze and strain the juice; separate the eggs and put the yolks, caster sugar, grated lemon rind and strained lemon juice into a bowl. Place the bowl in a saucepan of barely simmering water, then whisk the mixture until quite thick and mousse-like. Remove from the heat and continue whisking until the bowl is cold. If you are using an electric food mixer, whisk the egg yolks, caster sugar and lemon rind until thick. Heat the lemon juice, add and continue to whisk until the mousse reaches the 'ribbon' stage, approximately 15 minutes.

Whip the cream softly and fold into the mixture. 'Sponge' (see glossary) the gelatine with the water in a small bowl. Put the bowl into a saucepan of simmering water until the gelatine has dissolved completely. Add some of the lemon mixture to the gelatine and then carefully fold both mixtures together. Whisk the egg whites until they form a stiff peak. Set the soufflé mixture on ice; just as the mixture begins to thicken, fold in the egg whites. Pour into the prepared soufflé dish and put in a cool place to set for several hours.

When the soufflé is set, peel off the paper. Press the toasted nuts gently round the sides. Decorate the top with rosettes of cream and tiny sprigs of lemon balm or sweet geranium leaves.

LIME SOUFFLÉ

Serves 6–8

FOLLOW the above recipe but use 3 limes. Decorate with very fine slices of lime which have been simmered in a sugar syrup until they are translucent.

HOT LEMON SOUFFLÉ

Serves 4–6

This is not a real soufflé in the generally accepted sense but an old-fashioned family pudding which separates into two quite distinct layers when it cooks: it has a fluffy top and a creamy lemon base.

1 oz/30 g/2 tablespoons butter
6 oz/170 g/3/4 cup caster sugar
1 lemon

2 eggs, preferably free-range
2 oz/55 g/1/2 cup flour
8 fl oz/250 ml/1 cup milk

DECORATION

icing sugar

1 x 2 pint/1.1 l capacity pie dish

CREAM the butter well. Add the caster sugar and beat well. Grate the rind of the lemon and squeeze and strain its juice. Separate the egg yolks and add one by one, then stir in the flour and gradually add the finely grated rind and juice of the lemon (see below). Lastly add the milk. Whisk the egg whites stiffly in a bowl and fold gently into the lemon mixture. Pour into a pie dish and bake in a moderate oven, 180°C/350°F/gas 4, for about 40 minutes. Dredge with icing sugar.

Serve immediately with softly whipped cream.

NOTE: If the lemons are very pale, use the zest of 1½ or 2 to give a sharper lemon flavour.

MANGOES IN LIME SYRUP

Serves 2

This simple recipe must be made with a perfectly ripe mango; if the fruit you buy is under-ripe, wrap it in newspaper and keep it in your kitchen for a few days.

1 ripe mango	4 fl oz/120 ml/½ cup water
4 oz/110 g/½ cup sugar	1 lime

PUT the sugar and water into a saucepan, stir over a gentle heat until the sugar dissolves, bring to the boil and simmer for 2 minutes; allow to cool.

Peel the mango and slice quite thinly down to the stone. Put the slices into a bowl and cover with the cold syrup.

Meanwhile remove the zest from the lime either with a zester or a fine stainless steel grater and add to the syrup with the juice of the lime. Leave to macerate for at least 1 hour. Serve chilled.

NOTE: Papayas are also delicious served in exactly the same way.

BANANAS WITH LIME AND ORANGE ZEST

Serves 4

4 bananas

4 oz/110 g/½ cup sugar

1 lime

1 orange

7 fl oz/200 ml/scant 1 cup water

MAKE a syrup by dissolving the sugar in the water over a medium heat, then simmer for 2–3 minutes and allow to cool. Pare the zests from the lime and orange with a swivel-top peeler; cut them into the finest julienne strips. Put the strips into a saucepan of cold water, bring to the boil and simmer for 4–5 minutes. Drain and refresh with cold water and drain again.

Squeeze the juice from the lime and orange. Slice the bananas at an angle or into rounds. Add the bananas with the fruit juices and zests to the cold syrup, reserving a little zest for decoration. Pour into a pretty dish. Sprinkle the reserved zests on top and leave the fruit to macerate in a cool place for at least 2 hours. Serve chilled.

A FRUIT SALAD OF PINK GRAPEFRUIT, MELON, KIWI FRUIT AND LIME JUICE

Serves 4

This is a very refreshing fruit salad, perfect to clear the palette after a rich meal. It should be fresh tasting but not so bitter as to make you gasp!

1 pink grapefruit

½ a ripe Ogen *or* Gallia melon

1–2 kiwi fruits

1 lime

1–2 tablespoons caster sugar

(taste and use more if necessary)

CAREFULLY segment the grapefruit into a white bowl. Scoop the melon into balls with a melon-baller and add into the bowl. Peel the kiwi fruit thinly and cut into $^1/_4$ in/7 mm slices. Juice the lime and pour it over the fruit. Add caster sugar to taste. Allow to macerate for at least 1 hour before serving.

SUMMER FRUIT SALAD WITH SWEET GERANIUM LEAVES

Serves 8–10

Quite the most delicious summer fruit recipe, made in minutes.

4 oz/110 g/1 cup raspberries

4 oz/110 g/1 cup loganberries

4 oz/110 g/1 cup red currants

2 oz/55 g/$^1/_2$ cup black currants

2 oz/55 g/$^1/_2$ cup blackberries

2 oz/55 g/$^1/_2$ cup blueberries (optional)

2$^1/_2$ oz/70 g/$^1/_2$ cup *fraises du bois* (optional)

SYRUP

14 oz/400 g/2 cups sugar

$^3/_4$ pint/450 ml/scant 2 cups water

2 large *or* 6–8 medium-sized sweet geranium leaves (see *Note*, below)

PUT all the fruit into a white china or glass bowl. Put the sugar, cold water and sweet geranium leaves into a saucepan and bring slowly to the boil, stirring until the sugar dissolves. Boil for 2 minutes. Pour the *boiling* syrup over the fruit and allow to macerate for several hours. Remove geranium leaves. Serve chilled, accompanied by shortbread biscuits (page 237), softly whipped cream or Ballymaloe Vanilla Ice-cream (page 202). Garnish with a few fresh sweet geranium leaves.

NOTE: The geranium we use in cookery and for garnishing is the lemon-scented *Pelargonium graveolens*. It has pretty pale purple flowers in summer.

Cultivated blueberries have been appearing in our shops from the end of July to the end of September for the last few years. They are quite delicious, so if you can find them, use them in this fruit salad.

Fraises du bois or Alpine strawberries are much more difficult to come by, unless you grow them in your garden; in this case you'll have lots, because after a few years they spread into every nook and cranny. They look so pretty, and the good varieties have an intense flavour and a long fruiting season.

APPLE AND SWEET GERANIUM COMPOTE

Serves 6

Use the scented geranium, *Pelargonium graveolens*, to flavour this delicious apple compote – just a few leaves give it a haunting lemon flavour.

8 medium-sized eating apples, e.g. Golden Delicious	juice of 1 1/2 lemons
6 oz/170 g/3/4 cup sugar	2–3 strips of lemon rind
	4 large, sweet geranium leaves

PEEL, quarter, core and slice the apples into 1/4 in/7 mm segments. Put them into a stainless steel or enamel saucepan. Add the sugar, lemon rind and juice and sweet geranium leaves. Cover with a greaseproof paper lid and the lid of the saucepan; cook on a gentle heat until the apples are soft but not broken. They may be cooked in a moderate oven, 180°C/350°F/gas 4, if that is more convenient.

Serve warm or cold with softly whipped cream.

Green Gooseberry and Elderflower Compote

Serves 6–8

When I'm driving through country lanes in late May or early June and I spy the elderflower coming into blossom, I know it's time to go and search on gooseberry bushes for the hard, green fruit, far too under-ripe at that stage to eat raw, but wonderful cooked in tarts or fools or in this delicious compote. Elderflowers have an extraordinary affinity with green gooseberries and by a happy arrangement of nature they are both in season at the same time.

2 lb/900 g green gooseberries

1 lb/450 g/2 cups sugar

2 *or* 3 elderflower heads

1 pint/600 ml/2½ cups cold water

GARNISH

fresh elderflowers

First top and tail the gooseberries. Tie the elderflower heads in a little square of muslin, put in a stainless steel or enamelled saucepan, add the sugar and cold water. Bring slowly to the boil and continue to boil for 2 minutes. Add the gooseberries and simmer just until the fruit bursts. Allow to get cold. Serve in a pretty bowl and decorate with fresh elderflowers.

Blackcurrant Fool

Serves 10–12

Fools can be made from many different kinds of fruit. We are particularly fond of blackcurrant, gooseberry and rhubarb, but strawberry, raspberry, blackberry and fraughans (wild blueberries) are all wonderful too.

8 oz/225 g/1 cup sugar
1/2 pint/300 ml/1 1/4 cups water
softly whipped cream

12 oz/340 g/3 cups
blackcurrants

DISSOLVE the sugar in the water. String the blackcurrants and cover them with syrup. Bring them to the boil and cook until soft, about 4–5 minutes. Liquidise or purée the fruit and press through a nylon sieve, measure. When the purée is quite cold, add up to an equal quantity of softly whipped cream, according to taste.

NOTE: A little stiffly beaten egg white may be added to lighten the fool. The fool should not be very stiff, more like the texture of softly whipped cream; if it is stiff, whisk in some milk. Serve with Jane's Biscuits (page 237).

COUNTRY RHUBARB CAKE

Serves 8

This delicious rhubarb cake made from an enriched bread dough used to be made all over Ireland. Originally it would have been baked in a bastible or baker beside an open fire. My mother, who taught me this recipe, used to vary the filling with the seasons – from rhubarb to gooseberries, to damsons, blackberries and apples.

12 oz/340 g/3 cups flour
2 oz/55 g/1/4 cup caster sugar
a pinch of salt
1/2 teaspoon bread soda
3 oz/85 g/6 tablespoons butter
1 egg, preferably free-range
6 fl oz/175 ml/3/4 cup buttermilk
or sour milk

egg wash (see glossary)
1 1/2 lb/675 g rhubarb, finely
chopped
6–8 oz/170–225 g/3/4–1 cup
granulated sugar
caster sugar for sprinkling

1 × 10 in/25 cm Pyrex *or* enamel plate

PREHEAT the oven to 180°C/350°F/gas 4.

Sieve into a bowl the flour, caster sugar, salt and bread soda; rub in the butter. Whisk the egg and mix with the buttermilk. Make a well in the centre of the dry ingredients. Pour in most of the liquid and mix to a soft but not sticky dough; add the remainder of the liquid if necessary.

Sprinkle a little flour on the work surface, turn out the dough and pat gently into a round. Divide into two pieces: one should be slightly larger than the other; keep the larger one for the lid. Meanwhile dip your fingers in flour. Spread the smaller piece on to the plate. Scatter the finely chopped rhubarb all over the base, egg-wash the edges and sprinkle the rhubarb with sugar. Roll out the other piece of dough until it is exactly the size to cover the plate, lift it on and press gently to seal the edges. Make a hole in the centre for the steam to escape, egg-wash and sprinkle with a very small amount of sugar.

Bake in the preheated oven for 45 minutes to 1 hour or until the rhubarb is soft and the crust is golden. Leave it to sit for 15–20 minutes so that the juice can soak into the crust. Sprinkle with caster sugar. Serve still warm with a bowl of softly whipped cream and some moist, brown sugar.

SUMMER PUDDING

Serves 8

Everyone seems to become wistful when you mention summer pudding. Bursting with soft fruit and served with lots of softly whipped cream, it's one of the very best puddings of summer. We make ours with cake but many people line the bowl with slices of bread instead. I've used a mixture of fruit here, but it is also delicious made with blackcurrants alone. Summer Fruit Salad with Sweet Geranium Leaves (see page 222) also makes a successful filling, but you need to cook the blackcurrants and redcurrants until they burst and then add the soft fruit. Remember to pour the fruit and syrup *boiling* into the sponge-lined bowl, otherwise the syrup won't soak through the sponge properly.

8 oz/225g/2 cups blackcurrants	1¼ lb/560 g/2½ cups granulated
8 oz/225 g/2 cups redcurrants	sugar
1 lb/450 g/4 cups raspberries *or* 8	1¼ pints/700 ml/3 cups water
oz/225 g/2 cups raspberries and	8–10 sweet geranium leaves,
8 oz/225 g/2 cups strawberries	optional

FOR the sponge, see Great Grandmother's Cake on page 234. Cut each sponge round in half, horizontally. Keep one layer of sponge for the top. Line a 3 pint/1.7 l bowl with the rest of the cake, crusty-side inwards. It doesn't matter if it looks quite patched, it will blend later.

Dissolve the sugar in the water, add the sweet geranium leaves if using, and boil for 2 minutes, add the blackcurrants and red-currants and cook until the fruit bursts – about 3 or 4 minutes – then add the raspberries (and strawberries). Taste. Immediately, ladle some of the hot liquid and fruit into the sponge-lined bowl. When about half full, if you have scraps of cake put them in the centre. Then fill to the top with fruit. Cover with a layer of sponge. Put a plate on top and press down with a heavy weight. Allow to get cold. Store in the refrigerator for a minimum of 24 hours before serving, but it will keep for 4 or 5 days.

TO SERVE: Unmould on to a deep serving dish and serve with any left-over fruit and syrup around it, and lots of softly whipped cream.

PETER LAMB'S
APPLE CHARLOTTE

Serves 6–8

This is the scrummiest, most wickedly rich apple pudding ever. A friend, Peter Lamb, makes it as a special treat for me every now and then.

1 1/2 lb/675 g apples (Cox's
Orange Pippin are best but
Bramley Seedling can be very
good also)
1/2 oz/15 g/1 tablespoon butter
1 tablespoon water
6 oz/170 g/3/4 cup butter

2 egg yolks,
preferably free-range
1 oz/30 g/1/8 cup caster sugar
1 small loaf of good-quality
white bread
1 egg white, lightly beaten
softly whipped cream to serve

1 × 2 pint/1.1 l capacity loaf tin

PEEL and core the apples and cut into slices. Melt the small
quantity of butter in a stainless steel saucepan with the water. Toss
in the apples and the sugar, cover and cook over a gentle heat until
soft. Remove the lid if they are getting too juicy – you'll need a
dry purée. Stir well, taste and add a little more sugar if necessary.
Allow to cool for a few minutes and then beat in the egg yolks.

Meanwhile clarify the butter (see page 46).

Preheat the oven to 200°C/400°F/gas 6.

Cut the crusts off the loaf and carefully cut the bread into thin
slices, about 1/4 in/7 mm thick. Brush the tin with some butter and
sprinkle with the caster sugar. Take 2 large pieces of bread, one to
line the base of the tin and one for the top of the tin. Dip both sides
of the bread into the melted butter. Line the base first. Cut the last
of the bread into manageable-sized pieces, about 1 1/2 in/3.5 cm
wide, and line the sides with the buttery bread, making sure there
are no gaps. Seal all the joins with lightly beaten egg white. Fill the
centre with the sweetened apple purée and put the lid of buttery
bread on top. Bake in the preheated oven for about 20 minutes and
then reduce the heat to 190°C/375°F/gas 5 for a further 40 minutes
or so, or until the bread is crisp and golden brown. Leave to settle
for 10 minutes or so before turning it out of the tin.

Serve warm with a bowl of softly whipped cream – heavenly!

BREADS, BISCUITS AND JAMS

One of my very favourite things in the world is teaching people how to make bread. For some reason baking bread seems to provide enormous satisfaction – it doesn't matter how long you've been doing it. I've been cooking most of my adult life, yet I still get a thrill every time I take a nice crusty loaf out of the oven. But I get even more satisfaction when I see the look of delight on my students' faces when they bake their first really good loaf. And it's a funny thing, but if you make a loaf of lovely fresh soda bread for a dinner party, it doesn't matter what other star turn you produce, everyone will remark on the bread – which may only have taken you five minutes to make.

I feel passionately that *everyone* should have good bread *every* day. I would just love *everyone* in the whole country to be able to bake delicious home-made bread: it's so quick and easy. Irish soda breads are particularly fast to make and I've included here Brown and White Soda Bread and Sweet White Scones, all of which are made by a similar method. None of them takes more than five minutes to mix. (Don't forget to cut a deep cross into the dough before baking it to let the fairies out! Let the cuts go over the sides of the bread to make sure of this.)

We all know quite well that good wholesome fresh food is vital for our own health and that of our families, so let's start by making Brown Soda Bread, and when you've mastered that, let's move on to Yeast Bread. Many people have a hang-up about using yeast and the general feeling is that it's frightfully difficult and time-consuming. Fear not! Ballymaloe Brown Yeast Bread is just the recipe for beginners. All you have to do is mix everything together. There's no kneading involved, and only one rising, and even though it's made from 100 per cent stone-ground wholemeal flour, it's light and has a wonderful rich and nutty flavour. Yeast differs from bread soda or baking powder in that it's a living organism, so you've got to be careful to treat it right. If you kill it, it won't rise your bread. Cold doesn't kill yeast but a temperature over 43°C/110°F does. Yeast likes a lukewarm temperature and if possible something sweet to feed on. It feeds on sugar, and gives off bubbles of carbon dioxide which, of course, will rise your bread for you. I have easy access to fresh yeast and I prefer to work with it, but dried yeast makes a perfectly delicious loaf too (use half the quantity). You could use any sugar in this bread, e.g. brown sugar, golden syrup, honey or molasses, but it's treacle that gives Ballymaloe Brown Yeast Bread its particular flavour.

Whereas soda breads are best eaten on the day they are made, Ballymaloe Brown Yeast Bread keeps perfectly for three or four days. Once they are mixed, soda breads should be put into a fully preheated oven right away, otherwise they will not rise properly. The same applies to risen yeast bread.

The dough for Ballymaloe Cheese Biscuits is quick to make but it must be rolled quite thinly and then pricked with a fork. The biscuits keep for ages in an airtight tin and are good not only with cheese but also with pâtés and are perfect for snacks. Great Grandmother's Cake is perfect of its type; both it and the scones are irresistible filled with home-made raspberry jam and cream.

Many people feel that there is some great mystery to jam making; not so if you follow a few basic rules. For really good jam you *must* have really good fruit. The other great secret in my opinion is to make your jam in small quantities and to cook it for the minimum amount of time, then every pot will have perfect flavour and colour. If the fruit is as it should be, there is absolutely no need for artificial pectin or special sugar. A common belief is that if fruit is not good enough for anything else, it's all right for jam. Wrong! If the fruit is not perfect, cut your losses and dump it; don't throw good money after bad by making it into jam which will taste indifferent and soon go mouldy.

Nowadays many people have freezers, so the best thing is to buy your fruit in peak condition in season, when its flavour is best and the price is lowest; then freeze it immediately so you can make your jam in small quantities during the year, as you need it. Jam made from frozen fruit tastes much fresher and more delicious than jam kept on your storeroom shelf for five or six months.

BROWN SODA BREAD

BICARBONATE of soda (or bread soda) is the raising agent used in all soda breads. It is an alkali, and even though it is one of the ingredients used in baking powder, it can be used on its own to react with an acid, e.g. sour milk, or buttermilk. This produces bubbles of carbonic acid which fill up with air and rise the bread. So the main thing to remember is to use bicarbonate of soda (bread soda) with buttermilk or sour milk, and baking powder – which is a mixture of acid and alkali substances – with ordinary milk.

1 1/2 lb/675 g/4 1/2 cups brown wholemeal flour, preferably stone-ground
1 lb/450 g/3 1/4 cups white flour
1 oz/30 g/1/4 cup fine oatmeal
2 rounded teaspoons/10 g salt
1 egg (optional)

2 rounded teaspoons/10 g bread soda, sieved
1 oz/30 g/2 tablespoons butter (optional)
1 1/4–1 1/2 pints/700–850 ml/3–3 3/4 cups sour milk *or* buttermilk

FIRST preheat the oven to 230°C/450°F/gas 8.

Mix the dry ingredients well together. Rub in the butter. Make a well in the centre and add the beaten egg, then immediately add most of the sour milk or buttermilk. Working from the centre, mix with your hand and add more milk if necessary. The dough should be soft but not sticky. Turn out on to a floured board and knead lightly, just enough to shape into a round. Flatten slightly to about 2 in/5 cm. Put on to a baking sheet. Mark with a deep cross and bake in a hot oven 230°C/450°F/gas 8 for 15–20 minutes, then reduce the heat to 200°C/400°F/gas 6 for around 20–25 minutes, or until the bread is cooked and sounds hollow when tapped.

BROWN SODA SCONES

MAKE the dough as above. Form it into a round and flatten to approximately 1 in/2.5 cm thick. Stamp out into scones with a cutter, or cut with a knife. Bake for about 30 minutes in a hot oven (see above).

NOTE: Bread should always be cooked in a fully preheated oven, but ovens vary enormously so it is necessary to adjust the temperature accordingly.

WHITE SODA BREAD

1 lb/450 g/3¼ cups flour
1 teaspoon/2.5 g sugar
1 teaspoon/2.5 g salt

1 teaspoon/2.5 g bread soda
sour milk *or* buttermilk to mix –
12–15 fl oz/350–425 ml/1½–
scant 2 cups approx.

FIRST preheat the oven to 230°C/450°F/gas 8.

Sieve the dry ingredients together. Make a well in the centre. Pour most of the milk in at once. Using one hand, mix in the flour from the sides of the bowl, adding more milk if necessary. The dough should be soft but not sticky. When it all comes together, turn it out on to a floured board. Knead lightly for a few seconds, just enough to tidy it up. Pat the dough into a round about 1½ in/4 cm deep and cut a deep cross in it. Bake in a hot oven, 230°C/450°F/gas 8 for 15 minutes, then reduce the heat to 200°C/400°F/gas 6 for 30 minutes or until the bread is cooked and sounds hollow when tapped.

WHITE SODA SCONES

MAKE the dough as above. Form it into a round and flatten to approximately 1 in/2.5 cm. Cut into scones. Bake for about 20 minutes in a hot oven (see above).

MUMMY'S SWEET WHITE SCONES

MAKES 18–20 scones using a 3 in/7.5 cm cutter

This recipe has taken Ireland by storm. I have had grateful letters from all over the country from people who felt they could never make good scones before but have had success with this recipe – thanks, Mum!

2 lb/900 g/6½ cups flour
2 oz/55 g/¼ cup caster sugar
½ oz/15 g/3 heaped teaspoons
baking powder

6 oz/170 g/¾ cup butter
3 eggs, preferably free-range
¾ pint/450 ml/scant 2 cups milk
to mix

pinch of salt

FOR GLAZE
egg wash (see glossary)
granulated sugar for sprinkling on top of the scones

FIRST preheat the oven to 250°C/475°F/gas 9.

Sieve all the dry ingredients together. Rub in the butter. Make a well in the centre. Whisk the eggs with the milk, add to the dry ingredients and mix to a soft dough. Turn out on to a floured board. Knead lightly, just enough to shape into a round. Roll out to about 1 in/2.5 cm thick and stamp into scones. Put on to a baking sheet. Brush with egg wash and sprinkle with granulated sugar.

Bake in the hot oven for 10–15 minutes until golden brown on top. Cool on a wire rack.

Serve split in half with home-made raspberry jam and a blob of whipped cream.

FRUIT SCONES

ADD 4 oz/110 g plump sultanas to the above mixture when the butter has been rubbed in. Continue as above.

GREAT GRANDMOTHER'S CAKE

4¹/₂ oz/125 g/generous ¹/₂ cup butter

6 oz/170 g/³/₄ cup caster sugar

3 eggs, preferably free-range

6 oz/170 g/1¹/₄ cups flour

1 rounded teaspoon/5 g baking powder

1 tablespoon milk

FILLING

8 oz/225 g/³/₄ cup home-made raspberry jam (see page 238)

¹/₂ pint/300 ml/1¹/₄ cups whipped cream

caster sugar to sprinkle

2 x 7 in/18 cm sponge cake tins

PREHEAT the oven to 190°C/375°F/gas 5.

Grease and flour the tins and line the base of each with a round of greaseproof paper. Cream the butter and gradually add the caster sugar; beat until soft and light and quite pale in colour. Add the eggs one at a time and beat well between each addition. (If the butter and sugar are not creamed properly and if you add the eggs too fast, the mixture will curdle, resulting in a cake with a heavier texture.) Sieve the flour and baking powder and *stir* in gradually. Mix all together lightly and add 1 tablespoon of milk to moisten.

Divide the mixture evenly between the 2 tins, hollowing it slightly in the centre. Bake for 20–25 minutes or until cooked. Turn out on to a wire tray and allow to cool.

Sandwich together with home-made raspberry jam and whipped cream. Sprinkle with sieved caster sugar. Serve on an old-fashioned plate with a doily.

BALLYMALOE BROWN YEAST BREAD

Yeast is a living fungus and to grow it requires warmth, moisture and nourishment. It feeds on sugar and produces carbon dioxide which makes the bread rise. Hot water above 110°F will kill yeast; have the ingredients and equipment at blood heat. The yeast will rise on sugar or treacle. At Ballymaloe we use treacle. The dough rises more rapidly with 4 oz/110 g yeast than with only 2 oz/55 g yeast.

The flour we use is stone-ground wholemeal. Different flours produce breads of different textures. The amount of natural moisture in flour varies according to atmospheric conditions. The quantity of water should be altered accordingly. The dough should be just too wet to knead – in fact it does not require kneading. The main ingredients – wholemeal flour, treacle and yeast – are highly nutritious.

FOR 4 LOAVES

3¹/₂ lb/1.6 kg/11¹/₄ cups wholemeal flour

2¹/₂ pints/1.4 l/6¹/₄ cups water at blood heat (mix yeast with ¹/₂ pint/300 ml/1¹/₄ cups lukewarm water approx.)

1–1¹/₂ tablespoons/20 g salt

1–2 well rounded teaspoons black treacle

2–4 oz/55–110 g/¹/₂–1 cup fresh (baker's) yeast

sesame seeds (optional)

4 × loaf tins, 5 × 8 in/13 × 20 cm approx.

FOR 1 LOAF

1 lb/450 g/scant 3 cups wholemeal flour

1 rounded teaspoon/5 g salt

1 teaspoon black treacle

1 oz/30 g/¹/₄ cup fresh (baker's) yeast

12–15 fl oz/350–450 ml/1¹/₂–scant 2 cups water at blood heat (mix yeast with ¹/₄ pint/150 ml/generous ¹/₂ cup lukewarm water approx.)sesame seeds (optional)

1 × loaf tin, 5 × 8 in/13 × 20 cm approx.

PREHEAT the oven to 230°C/450°F/gas 8.

Mix the flour with the salt and warm it very slightly (in the cool oven of an Aga or Esse, or in a gas or electric oven when starting to heat). In a small bowl, mix the treacle with some of the water (as indicated in ingredients list) and crumble in the yeast. Put the bowl in a warm position such as the back of the cooker. Grease bread tins and put them to warm; also warm a clean tea-towel. Look to see if the yeast is rising. It will take about 5 minutes to do so and will have a creamy and slightly frothy appearance on top.

When ready, stir it well and pour it, with most of the remaining water, into the flour to make a wettish dough. The mixture should be too wet to knead. Put the mixture into the greased, warmed tins and sprinkle with sesame seeds if you like. Put the tins back in the same position as used previously to raise the yeast. Put the tea-towel over the tins. In about 20 minutes the loaves will have risen by twice their original size. Remove the tea-towel and bake the loaves in a hot oven, 230°C/450°F/gas 8 for 45–50 minutes, or until they look nicely browned and sound hollow when tapped.

We usually remove the loaves from the tins about 10 minutes before the end of cooking and put them back into the oven to crisp all round, but if you like a softer crust there's no need to do this.

NOTE: Dried yeast may be used instead of baker's yeast. Follow the same method but use only half the weight as given for fresh yeast. Allow longer to rise.

BALLYMALOE CHEESE BISCUITS

Makes 25–30 biscuits

We serve these biscuits with our Irish farmhouse cheese trolley in the Ballymaloe restaurant. Although we make them fresh every day, they do keep for several weeks in an airtight tin and also freeze well.

4 oz/110 g/1 cup brown flour	1 oz/30 g/2 tablespoons butter
4 oz/110 g/1 cup white flour	1 tablespoon cream
1/2 teaspoon salt	water as needed, 5 tablespoons
1/2 teaspoon baking powder	approx.

MIX the brown and white flour together and add the salt and baking powder. Rub in the butter and moisten with cream and enough water to make a firm dough.

Roll out to approximately 1/8 in/3 mm thick. Prick with a fork. Cut into rounds with a 2 1/2 in/6.5 cm round cutter. Bake on an ungreased baking sheet at 150°C/300°F/gas 2 for about 45 minutes or until lightly browned.

JANE'S BISCUITS

Makes approximately 25 biscuits

These delicious little shortbread biscuits are easy to make and we serve them with fruit fools, compotes or just with a cup of tea.

6 oz/170 g/1 1/4 cups flour	4 oz/110 g/1/2 cup butter
2 oz/55 g/1/4 cup caster sugar	

SIEVE the flour and sugar into a bowl and rub in the butter with the fingertips. Within a few minutes the mixture will start to come together, so gather it up and knead it lightly in the bowl. (This is a shortbread so do not use any liquid.)

Roll out to 1/4 in/7 mm thickness on a lightly floured board. Cut into 2 1/2 in/6.5 cm rounds or into heart shapes. Bake in a moderate oven, 180°C/350°F/gas 4, for about 15 minutes, until pale brown. Remove and cool on a rack. Dredge lightly with icing or caster sugar.

RASPBERRY JAM

Makes 3 × 1 lb/450 g pots

Raspberry jam is the easiest and quickest of all jams to make, and one of the most delicious.

2 lb/900 g/8 cups fresh raspberries	2 lb/900 g/4 cups white sugar (use a little less if raspberries are very sweet)

WASH, dry and sterilise the jars in a moderate oven, 180°C/350°F/ gas 4, for 15 minutes. Heat the sugar in a moderate oven for 5–10 minutes.

Put the raspberries into a wide stainless steel saucepan and cook for 3–4 minutes until the juice begins to run, then add the hot sugar and stir over a gentle heat until fully dissolved. Increase the heat and boil steadily for about 5 minutes, stirring frequently.

Test for a set by putting about a teaspoon of jam on a cold plate and leaving it for a few minutes in a cool place. It should wrinkle when pressed with a finger. Remove from the heat immediately. Skim and pour into sterilised jam jars. Cover immediately.

Hide the jam in a cool dry place or else put it on a shelf in your kitchen so you can feel great every time you look at it! Anyway, it will be so delicious it won't last long.

LOGANBERRY JAM

Makes 5 × 1 lb/450 g pots approx.

Loganberries rarely appear for sale in the shops, so if you have a little space in your garden it would be well worth putting in a couple of canes, particularly of the new thornless varieties.

3 lb/1.35 kg/12 cups loganberries	3 lb/1.35 kg/6 cups white sugar

WASH, dry and sterilise the jars in a moderate oven, 180°C/350°F/

gas 4, for 15 minutes. Heat the sugar in a moderate oven for 5–10 minutes.

Put the loganberries into a wide stainless steel saucepan and cook for 5–6 minutes until the juice begins to run, then add the hot sugar and stir over a gentle heat until fully dissolved. Increase the heat and boil steadily for about 5 minutes, stirring frequently.

Test for a set by putting about a teaspoon of jam on a cold plate and leaving it for a few minutes in a cool place. It should wrinkle when pressed with a finger. Remove from the heat immediately. Skim and pour into sterilised jam jars. Cover immediately.

NOTE: If you are short of loganberries you could use half raspberries and half loganberries, and that will also make a delicious jam.

BLACKBERRY AND APPLE JAM

Makes 9–10 × 1 lb/450 g pots

All over the countryside every year, blackberries rot on the hedgerows. Think of all the wonderful jam that could be made – so full of vitamin C! This year organise a blackberry picking expedition and take a picnic. You'll find it's the greatest fun, and when you come home one person could make a few scones while someone else is making the jam. The children could be kept out of mischief and gainfully employed drawing and painting home-made jam labels, with personal messages like 'Lydia's Jam – keep off!', or 'Grandma's Raspberry Jam'. Then you can enjoy the results of your labours with a well-earned cup of tea.

Blackberries are a bit low in pectin, so the apples help to set it as well as adding extra flavour.

5 lb/2.3 kg/20 cups blackberries   4 lb/1.8 kg/9 cups sugar
2 lb/900 g cooking apples (Bramley, or Grenadier in season)

WASH, peel and core and slice the apples. Stew them until soft with 1/2 pint/300 ml of water in a stainless steel saucepan; beat to a pulp. Heat the sugar in a moderate oven for 5–10 minutes.

Pick over the blackberries. Cook until soft, adding about ¼ pint/145 ml of water if the berries are dry. If you like, push them through a coarse sieve to remove seeds. Put the blackberries into a wide stainless steel saucepan or preserving pan with the apple pulp and the heated sugar, and stir over a gentle heat until the sugar is dissolved.

Boil steadily for about 15 minutes. Skim the jam, test it for a set (see page 239) and pot in warm sterilised jars.

DAMSON JAM

Makes 9–10 × 1 lb/450 g pots

Damson jam was always a great favourite of mine as a child. My school friends and I used to collect damsons every year in a field near the old castle in Cullohill. First we ate so many we almost burst – the rest we brought home for Mummy to make into jam.

6 lb/2.7 kg damsons 1½ pints/850 ml/3¾ cups water
6 lb/2.7 kg/12 cups sugar

PICK over the fruit carefully, wash and drain well and discard any damaged ones. Put the damsons and water into a greased stainless steel preserving pan and stew them gently until the skin breaks. Heat the sugar in a moderate oven (160°C/325°F/gas 3), add it to the fruit and stir over a gentle heat until the sugar is dissolved. Increase the heat and boil steadily, stirring frequently. Skim off the stones and scum as they rise to the top. Test for a set after 15 minutes boiling (see page 239). Pour into warm sterilised jars and cover. Store in a cool dry place.

NOTE: The preserving pan is greased to prevent the fruit from sticking to the bottom.

REDCURRANT JELLY

Makes 3 × 1 lb/450 g pots

Redcurrant jelly is a very delicious and versatile product to have in your larder because it has so many uses. It can be used like a jam on bread or scones, or served as an accompaniment to roast lamb, bacon or ham. It is also good with some rough pâtés and game, and is invaluable as a glaze for fruit tarts, e.g. the Almond Tart with Raspberries (see page 212).

This recipe is a particular favourite of mine, not only because it's fast to make and results in a delicious intense flavoured jelly, but because you can use the left-over pulp to make a fruit tart, so you get double value from your redcurrants.

Redcurrants are in season in August, but they are by no means as common as raspberries and strawberries, so if you can find them be sure to buy some and freeze a few pounds to use for jelly and sauces during the winter. They freeze perfectly even with the strings on.

2 lb/900 g red currants
2 lb/900 g/4½ cups granulated sugar

REMOVE the strings from the redcurrants either by hand or with a fork. Put the redcurrants and sugar into a wide stainless steel saucepan and stir continuously until they come to the boil. Boil for exactly 8 minutes, stirring only if they appear to be sticking to the bottom. Skim carefully.

Turn into a nylon sieve and allow to drip through; do not push the pulp through or the jelly will be cloudy. You can stir it gently once or twice just to free the bottom of the sieve of pulp.

Pour the jelly into sterilised pots immediately. Redcurrants are very high in pectin so the jelly will begin to set just as soon as it begins to cool.

NOTE: Unlike most other fruit jellies, no water is needed in this recipe.

STRAWBERRY AND REDCURRANT JAM

Makes 7 × 1 lb/450 g pots

4 lb/1.8 kg strawberries
4¼ lb/1.9 kg/8½ cups sugar
¼ pint/150 ml/generous ½ cup redcurrant juice (see below)
or if unavailable the juice of 2 lemons

FIRST prepare the fruit juice using about 1 lb/450 g fruit to obtain ¼ pint/150 ml of juice. Put the strawberries into a wide stainless steel saucepan, use a potato masher to crush about three-quarters of the berries, leave the rest intact in the juice. Bring to the boil and cook the crushed strawberries in the juice for about 2–3 minutes. Heat the sugar in a moderate oven (160°C/325°F/gas 3) and add to the fruit; stir over a gentle heat until the sugar is completely dissolved. Increase the heat and boil for about 10–15 minutes, stirring frequently, until it reaches a set, skim. Pot immediately into hot sterilised jars, cover and store in a cool dry cupboard.

Redcurrant Juice

PICK over the fruit carefully, no need to remove the strings. For every 1 lb/450 g of redcurrants use 6 fl oz/175 ml of water. Put into a large saucepan and boil to a pulp for about 20 minutes. Strain through a fine sieve or jelly bag. The pulp can be frozen and used at some later stage to make a fruit tart.

GREEN GOOSEBERRY AND ELDERFLOWER JAM

Makes 6 × 1 lb/450 g pots

3 lb/1.35 kg hard tart green
gooseberries
5–6 elderflower heads

2 pints/1.1 l/5 cups water
3½ lb/1.6 kg/7 cups sugar

WASH the gooseberries if necessary, top and tail and put them into a wide stainless steel preserving pan with the water. Tie the elderflowers in a little muslin bag and also add to the pan. Simmer until the gooseberries are soft and the contents of the pan are reduced by one third – approximately 30 minutes. Heat the sugar in a moderate oven (160°C/325°F/gas 3). Remove the elderflowers and add the warm sugar, stirring until it has completely dissolved. Boil rapidly for about 10 minutes until setting point is reached (220°F on a jam thermometer). Pour into hot clean sterilised jars, cover immediately and store in a dry airy cupboard.

This jam should be a nice fresh green colour, so be careful not to overcook it.

SUGGESTED MENUS

SPRING

A Warm Salad of Goat's Cheese with Walnut Oil Dressing
Lamb Roast with Rosemary and Garlic
Hot Lemon Soufflé

Chinese Fish Soup with Spring Onions
Poached Salmon with Hollandaise Sauce
Chocolate Meringue Gâteau

Spring Cabbage Soup
Casserole Roast Chicken with Leeks and Bacon
Country Rhubarb Cake

Watercress Soup
Sauté of Calf's Liver with Whiskey and Tarragon
Caramel Ice-cream with Butterscotch Sauce and Bananas

SUMMER

Fish Mousse with Courgette Flowers
Spiced Lamb with Aubergines
Summer Pudding

Old-fashioned Salad with Lynda's Dressing
Sea Trout with Cream and Fresh Herbs
Green Gooseberry and Elderflower Compote

Lettuce, Cucumber and Mint Soup
Filipino Pork with Peppers and Fresh Ginger
Mangoes in Lime Syrup

Tomatoes stuffed with Crab Mayonnaise
Poached Monkfish with Red Pepper Sauce
Almond Tart with Raspberries

AUTUMN

Hot Buttered Oysters
Baked Plaice with Chanterelles
Peter Lamb's Apple Charlotte

Celery and Lovage Soup
Ballymaloe Irish Stew
Ballymaloe Coffee Ice-cream with Irish Coffee Sauce

Wild Mushroom Soup
Carpaccio with Mustard and Horseradish Sauce
Crème Caramel

Salade Tiède with Avocado, Bacon and Walnut Oil Dressing
Skate with Black Butter
Orange Mousse with Chocolate Wafers

WINTER

Crudités with Garlic Mayonnaise
Cod Baked with Cream and Bay Leaves, with Duchesse Potato
A Fruit Salad of Pink Grapefruit, Melon, Kiwi Fruit and Lime Juice

Mussel Salad with a Julienne of Vegetables
Boeuf Bourguignon
Ballymaloe Vanilla Ice-cream

Pink Grapefruit Sorbet
Pheasant with Apples and Calvados
Meringue Gâteau with Kiwi Fruit

A Warm Winter Salad with Duck Livers and Hazelnut Oil Dressing
Fillet of Beef with Black, White and Pink Peppercorns
Lemon Soufflé

GLOSSARY

ARACHIDE OIL: Peanut or groundnut oil.

BAIN-MARIE (or water bath): Can be any deep container, half-filled with hot water, in which delicate foods, e.g. custards or fish mousses, are cooked in their moulds or terrines. The bain-marie is put into a low or moderate oven and the food is protected from direct heat by the gentle, steamy atmosphere, without risk of curdling. The term bain-marie is also used for a similar container which will hold several pans to keep soups, vegetables or stews warm during restaurant service.

BALSAMIC VINEGAR: A special old vinegar made in Modena in north-east Italy, aged slowly in oak casks so that it gradually becomes more concentrated. It must be at least 10 years old before it is sold, and is now beginning to appear in our shops. It is rare and expensive – well worth searching for.

BLANCH: This cooking term can be confusing because it's used in many different senses. Usually it means to immerse food in water and to bring to the boil, parcook and extract salt or loosen skins as in the case of almonds.

BOUQUET GARNI: A small bunch of fresh herbs used to flavour stews, casseroles, stocks or soups, usually consisting of parsley stalks, a sprig of thyme, perhaps a bay leaf and an outside stalk of celery. Remove before serving.

CLINGFILM (or 'Saran Wrap' as it is called in the United States): Used for sealing food from the air. Use 'pure' clingfilm or 'Glad Wrap'. Clingfilm containing PVC is considered harmful in contact with food.

COLLOP: A word sometimes used to describe pieces of monkfish or lobster tail, round in shape and about $^1/_4$ in/7 mm thick unless otherwise stated.

CONCASSÉ: Concassé means roughly chopped, usually applied to tomatoes. Pour boiling water over very firm, ripe tomatoes, leave for 10 seconds, then pour off the water. Peel off the skin, cut in half, remove the seeds with a teaspoon or melon-baller, cut in quarters and chop into $^1/_4$ in/7 mm or $^1/_8$ in/3 mm dice. Concassé may be added to a sauce or used as a garnish.

DE-GLAZE: After meat has been sautéed or roasted, the pan or roasting dish is de-greased and then a liquid is poured into the pan to dissolve the coagulated and caramelised pan juices. This is the basis of many sauces and gravies. The liquid could be water, stock or alcohol, e.g. wine or brandy.

DE-GREASE: To remove surplus fat from a liquid or a pan, either by pouring off or by skimming with a spoon.

EGG WASH: A raw egg beaten with a pinch of salt; it is brushed on raw tarts, pies, buns and biscuits to give them a shiny, golden glaze when cooked.

GRILL PAN: A heavy cast-iron pan, with a ridged bottom, either rounded or rectangular. The ridges mark the food attractively while keeping the meat or fish from direct contact with the fat. A heavy pan gives a good even heat.

LARDONS: A French term for narrow strips of streaky bacon.

MACERATE: To soak fruit in syrup or other liquid so that it will absorb the flavour and in some cases become more tender.

PALETTE KNIFE: A useful but not essential piece of kitchen equipment, it is a blunt knife with a rounded tip, and a flexible blade useful for spreading meringue etc.

PAPER LID: When we are sweating vegetables for the base of a soup or stew, we quite often cover them with a butter wrapper or lid made from greaseproof paper which fits the saucepan exactly. This keeps in the steam and helps to sweat the vegetables.

QUENELLE: Usually refers to an exquisitely light fish dumpling shaped with spoons into three-sided ovals.

RAMEKINS: Little dishes, usually made of pottery or china, approximately 3 in/7.5 cm in diameter and 2 in/5 cm deep.

REDUCE: To boil down a liquid in an uncovered saucepan to concentrate the flavour. This is a very important technique in sauce-making.

ROUX: Many of the sauces in this book call for roux. Roux is a basic liaison of butter and flour which is used as a thickening agent. Use equal quantities. Melt the butter and stir in the flour. Cook on a low heat for 2 minutes, stirring occasionally.

SEASONED FLOUR: Plain white flour which has been seasoned with salt and freshly ground pepper. Fish for frying is usually coated in seasoned flour.

SHERRY VINEGAR: A rich dark vinegar made from sherry and fermented in oak casks.

SILICONE PAPER: A non-stick parchment paper that is widely used for lining baking trays, cake tins etc. It may be used several times over and is particularly useful when making meringues or chocolates, because they simply peel off the paper. 'Bakewell' is the brand name; it is available in most supermarkets and newsagents.

(TO) SPONGE: A term used when working with powdered gelatine. The gelatine is sprinkled over a specified amount of liquid and left to sit for 4–5 minutes. During this period, the gelatine soaks up the water and becomes 'spongy' in texture – hence the name. Gelatine is easier to dissolve if it is sponged before melting.

SWEAT: To cook vegetables in a little fat or oil over a gentle heat in a covered saucepan, until they are almost soft but not coloured.

INDEX

almond tart, 202, 212–13:
  with raspberries, rhubarb, peaches,
    nectarines, loganberries, grapes or
    kiwi fruit, 212–13
apple(s)
  and blackberry jam, 239–40
  and calvados, pheasant with, 133–4
  and carrot salad with honey and
    vinegar dressing, 52, 56
  and sweet geranium compôte, 223
  charlotte, Peter Lamb's, 201, 227–8
  sauce, 164, 170–1
apricot glaze, 213
Arnold Bennett omelette, 109
artichokes, globe, 188
aubergines, spiced lamb with, 142,
  160–1
avocado
  and toasted pine kernels, warm salad
    of scallops with, 65–6
  bacon and walnut oil dressing, salade
    tiède with, 63–4
  mousse with tomato and basil salad,
    60–1

bacon, 163
  and leeks, casserole roast chicken
    with, 122, 124–5
  avocado and walnut oil dressing,
    salade tiède with, 63–4
  chicken livers and croûtons, salade
    tiède with, 53, 62–3
  chop, Ballymaloe, 163, 165
  glazed loin of, 163, 164–5
  smoky, and potato soup, 2, 5
baked cod with cream and bay leaves,
  71, 95–6
baked eggs, 174, 185, 187
  with cheese, 186
  with fresh herbs and Dijon mustard,
    186
  with piperonata, 186
  with tomato fondue, 186

baked plaice
  or sole with herb butter, 71, 89–90
  with chanterelles, 92–3
  Ballycotton fish pie, 119–20
Ballymaloe
  bacon chop, 163, 165
  brown yeast bread, 229–30, 235–6
  cheese biscuits, 230, 236–7
  cheese fondue, 174, 180
  chicken liver pâté, 121, 135–6
  coffee ice-cream with Irish coffee
    sauce, 206–7
  fish terrine with tomato coulis, 34–6
  hot buttered lobster, 115
  ice bowl, 203–4
  Irish stew, 142, 159–60
  vanilla ice-cream served in an ice
    bowl, 202
banana(s)
  and butterscotch sauce, 208
  fried, 163
  with lime and orange zest, 221
basil
  and prawn pâté, 46
  and tomato salad, avocado mousse
    with, 60–1
bass, 71, 72
bay leaves and cream, baked cod with,
  71, 95–6
bean(s)
  and green lentil salad, 173, 176–7
  haricot, and tomato, lamb with,
    161–2
  stew, Provençale, 173, 175–6
Béarnaise sauce and pommes
    allumettes, pan-grilled steak with,
    140, 147–9
Béchamel sauce, 71, 91–2, 101
beef
  fillet of, with black, white and pink
    peppercorns, 139, 144–5
  fillet of, with mushrooms and thyme
    leaves, 139, 143–4